DEBRETT'S
GUIDE TO ENTERTAINING

Also by Charles Mosley

Lichfield in Retrospect
American Presidential Families
Debrett's Handbook: 1981 Edition (editor)
Burke's Peerage and Baronetage: 1996 (editor)

DEBRETT'S GUIDE TO ENTERTAINING

The Complete Book of Modern Entertaining

Charles Mosley

HEADLINE

First published in 1994
by HEADLINE BOOK PUBLISHING

Reprinted in this edition in 1994
by HEADLINE BOOK PUBLISHING

10 9 8 7 6 5 4 3 2 1

British Library Cataloguing in Publication Data

Mosley, Charles
    Debrett's Guide to Entertaining: Complete
    Guide to Modern Entertaining. – New ed
    I. Title
    395.3

    ISBN 0 7472 1104 3

Typeset by
Letterpart Limited, Reigate, Surrey

Printed and bound in Great Britain by
Mackays of Chatham PLC, Chatham, Kent

HEADLINE BOOK PUBLISHING
A division of Hodder Headline PLC
338 Euston Road
London NW1 3BH

To Grace, most memorable of hostesses

Contents

Acknowledgements

A book such as this is not just the product of many months' feverish research in the Reading Room of the British Museum or the rabbit warren of shelves that is the London Library, glad though I was to have the services of both institutions. It is primarily the result of mature cogitation following a lifetime's social activity, sometimes intense, sometimes relaxed and intermittent, both in the UK and abroad. Some of the lessons I have learnt were imbibed many years ago, perhaps without their knowing it at the time, from hosts or hostesses long dead, or scattered long since to the four corners of the earth. Perhaps they may have forgotten I ever attended their party, luncheon, dinner, weekend or drinks session. It has not slipped my mind, however. More often I would like to think that, if alive, they retain some memory, however blurred, of at least one of the guests who have swum through their drawing rooms.

Then again, some of the people mentioned below have given me just as valuable a lesson on how to entertain by being my guests rather than the other way round. Not that the label 'host' or 'guest' limits the person concerned to that role in the eyes of the author; but it is in the capacity stated that he or she has proved most useful when it came to writing this book. I have also consulted various institutions for information on how best to entertain people from a very different religious or cultural background to those common among the British generally. Accordingly, I would like to acknowledge the help and advice, sometimes solicited, sometimes unsolicited, sometimes conscious, sometimes unconscious, of the following:

Mr Samuel and the Hon. Mrs Abel-Smith, of Rutland and Spain; Mr and Mrs John Allen, of Co. Tipperary; Digby Anderson, eating guru, of the Social Affairs Unit, London; Lady Arnott, hostess, of Dublin.

Ms Mary Banks, formerly of the International Coffee Organisation, Berners Street, London, now a freelance coffee consultant;

Mimi Bashford, opera singer and hostess, of Paris and Montevideo; Patrick Bashford, guitarist and man-about-town, of London; Mr and Mrs Nicholas Beale, assiduous party-givers, of London; Peter Beauclerk-Dewar, genealogical and heraldic expert, of London; the Hon. Eleanor Berry, writer, hostess and weekend guest, of London; Anthony Blond, publisher, writer and host, of London and France; the late Lady Bonham-Carter, party-giver, of Hampshire; Mr and Mrs David Bowen-Jones, of London and Tuscany; the British Tourist Authority, of London, in particular its helpful functionary Mr Andrew Macnair; Mr and Mrs Eric Butterfield, formerly of Hertfordshire, now of Knightsbridge and Co. Wexford; John Button, host, of Gloucestershire; Hugh Bygott-Webb, host and television producer, of London, the Bahamas and the Channel Islands; Mr and Mrs Justin Bygott-Webb, host and hostess, of Montgomeryshire and London.

Mlle Christine Caceras, hostess and cookery expert, of Provence and London; Mr and Mrs David Campbell, formerly of Paris, now of London; Miss Miriam Campion, of Durrow, Co. Laois; Mr and Mrs Taidhg Campion, munificent host and hostess, of Birr, Co. Offaly; Mrs Marilyn Caron de Lion, hostess, late of Paris, now of Kensington, London; Mr and Mrs Pat Cash, party-givers, of Co. Laois; Ms Mary-Gaye Caven, of Dallas, Texas; Mr and Mrs Walter Caven, host and hostess, of Austin, Texas, and Johnson City, Texas; the late Mrs June Churchill, of Cornwall Gardens, South Kensington, and Lanzarote; Maria Clark, late of Madrid, now of Cheyne Walk, Chelsea; Alfred Cochrane, designer and host, of Dublin and Bray, Co. Wicklow; John Colclough, of Abbeyleix, Co. Laois; the Commission for Racial Equality; Signorina Caterina Corbaz, of Rome; Signora Margot Corbaz, hostess, of Rome and Geneva; Janet Coveney, of Co. Galway; the late Professor and Mrs Maurice Cranston, of Regent's Park, London; Lady Cusack-Smith, indefatigable hostess, of Co. Galway.

George De Peers, cookery expert and exemplary house guest, late of Somerset, now of Dublin; Dicky De Stacpoole, host, late of Shropshire, now once more of Connemara, also of Co. Tipperary; Tom Dobson, host, of Co. Laois; Ms Mary Dockwrey, house-guest tolerator and cocktail party-giver, of Hampstead and Nova Scotia; Mr and Mrs Robert Dupuy, party-givers and house-guest pamperers, formerly of Austin, Texas, now of Dallas; Miss Philippa Durnford, hostess, late of Menton, Alpes Maritimes, currently of London, to whom I am particularly indebted for guidance through the jungle of business entertaining; Ms Regina Dwyer, hostess, late of Co. Laois, now of Dublin.

Carolyn Eadie, hostess, of Westminster and Buckinghamshire; Stephen Erskine-Hill, host, formerly of Co. Kilkenny and Co. Wicklow, now of London; Mr and Mrs David Evers, host and hostess, of London and Oxfordshire; Miss Alexandra Eversole, hostess, of London.

John Farrington, host, of Co. Laois; Micky Feld, fellow house guest, of Chelsea; Lino Ferrari, guest, of London and Berkshire; Olivier Ferrer, host, of Campden Hill, London; Marlain Fielding, hostess, of St James's, London; Mr and Mrs Alec Finn, assiduous party-givers, of Oranmore Castle, Co. Galway; Adrian FitzGerald, fellow guest, of Kensington and Co. Kerry; Desmond Fitz-Gerald, the Knight of Glin, host and guest, of Glin Castle, Co. Limerick; Flora Fraser, hostess, of London.

Scott Gibson, formerly of London, now of Rome; John Gilmartin and Madam Gilmartin, host and hostess, of Dublin; Miss Colette Gleeson, as charming a guest as she is a hostess, of Knightsbridge; Mr and Mrs Dermot Gleeson, host and hostess, of Co. Clare; Mr and Mrs Dermot Gleeson (a different lot of Gleesons), host and hostess, formerly of Fulham, now of Guildford; Mr and Mrs David Gomme, host and hostess, of Buckinghamshire; Mr and Mrs Geoffrey Gomme, most generous and long-suffering of hosts, of Terrick, Buckinghamshire; Archie Gorst-Williams, munificent host, cookery expert and doyen of charity ball organisers, formerly of Kent, now of Kensington, London; Mr and Mrs George Gossip, host and hostess, of Co. Offaly; Mr and Mrs Richard Graham, host and hostess, of Co. Tipperary; David Gransby, as generous a guest as he is a host, late of Tyburnia, London, now of Thailand; Mr and Mrs Bertie Grattan-Bellew, host and hostess, of Suffolk and Co. Galway; Mr and Mrs Godfrey Green, host and hostess, of Co. Kildare; Mr and Mrs Robin Green, host and hostess, also of Co. Kildare; Ms Jawj Greenwald, hostess, formerly of Buckinghamshire and Sussex, now of San Francisco; Mr and Mrs Robert Gregson, host and hostess, also guests, formerly of London, now of Bath; the Hon.

Desmond Guinness, host and guest, of Leixlip Castle, Co. Dublin.

Mr and Mrs Roger Hall, host and hostess, of Narrow Water Castle, Co. Down; Mrs Nathalie Hambro, hostess, of London; Count and Countess Axel Hamilton, host and hostess, of Sweden and Co. Offaly; Mr and Mrs Hubert Hamilton, host and hostess, of Co. Laois; the Hon. Julia Hamilton, hostess, of London; Ms Mary Harney, TD, guest and hostess, of Dublin; David Hart, best of country weekend hosts, also most munificent of party-throwers in London, of St James's and Suffolk; Mr and Mrs Reginald Hastings, best of hosts and guests, and people to spend 'a night on the town' with, formerly of Dublin and Spain, now again of Spain, also of Co. Clare; Lady Selina Hastings, hostess and guest, of London; Mr Robin and Lady Olga Hay, host and hostess, of London and Norfolk; Mrs Shauna Heneage, hostess, of London and Co. Galway; Ms Renagh Holohan, hostess and guest, of Dublin; Toby Horton, host, of Kensington and Yorkshire; Roger Houghton, so munificent a host towards me in that specialised form of entertaining, the business lunch, that I really don't know why he didn't write that particular section of the book himself instead of commissioning me to do it; Mr and Mrs Andrew Howard, of Henley-on-Thames, Oxon; Mr and Mrs Nicholas Huskinson, host and hostess, of Wiltshire and Chelsea; the late John B. Hyde and Mrs John B. Hyde, host and hostess, of Marshall, Texas; Mrs Alice Hyde-Smith, hostess, of London.

David Johnson, of Dublin; Mr and Mrs Andrew Jolliffe, of Kensington; Mrs Jerene Jones, of Texas and London; Michael Jones, of Hampstead.

Captain and Mrs Mark Keogh, host and hostess, of Galway City; Mr and Mrs Nicholas Kindersley, of Co. Longford; Mr and Mrs Jonathan King, house-guest putter-uppers, of London; Rory Knight-Bruce, of London and Shropshire; Mr and Mrs Peter Kuntz, host and hostess, of Co. Tipperary.

Count Christopher Lackner, formerly of Styria, Austria, latterly of New Zealand and the Royal Opera House, Covent Garden; Mr Charles and Lady Elizabeth Lambton, host and hostess, of Wiltshire; Mr and Mrs William Lambton, host and hostess, sometime of Co. Galway, also of Co. Offaly; Dr Jean Le Brocquy, hostess, formerly of Dublin, now of Cape of Good Hope, South Africa; Mr and Mrs Jeffrey Lefroy, of Carrigglas Manor, Co. Longford;

Stephen Lenhoff, guest, of Holland Park, London; Desmond Leslie, of Castle Leslie, Co. Monaghan, and the South of France; Dr Julian Lewis, club-man host, of Golders Green and Swansea; Sir Gilbert Longden, host and guest, of South Kensington; Ms Catriona Lorimer, hostess, of London; Charles Lysaght, host, of Dublin.

The late George Macbeth and Mrs George Macbeth, hosts and guests, of Moyne Park, Co. Galway; Miss Catherine MacClancy, hostess and expert on game bird shooting parties, polo and charity fund-raising entertainments, of Belgravia, London; Mr and Mrs David McCormick, host and hostess, of Kensington and Spain; Hamish McFall, guest, of London; Mr and Mrs Humphrey McFall, host and hostess, formerly of Lincolnshire, now of Oxford; Michael McFall, of Lancashire and London, for information on hosting game bird shoots; the McGillicuddy of the Reeks, formerly of Co. Kerry, then of France; Ms Bridget McLaughlin, of Dublin; Ms Dee McQuillen, guest and hostess, of London; Mr and Mrs Tin McSwiney, of Edinburgh; Mr and Mrs Lindsay Masters, formerly of Holland Park, subsequently of Knightsbridge; Miss Victoria Mather, guest and hostess, of London; Mrs Peter Maxwell-Stuart, fellow guest, and Miss Catherine Maxwell-Stuart, hostess of Traquair House, Innerleithen, Peeblesshire, Scotland; Paul Mercer, fellow guest, of Leicestershire; Mr and Mrs Nigel May, host and hostess, of London; the Hon. Christopher Monckton, host, fellow guest and guest, formerly of London, now of Perthshire, Scotland; Major Nigel Morgan, late the Irish Guards, host, of Herefordshire; the Hon. John and Mrs Morris, of Dublin; Frances Mosley, hostess, of Gloucestershire; Stephen Mudge, host, of Campden Hill, London; Mr and Mrs John Mulcahy, host and hostess, also guests, of Dublin; Miss Fidelma Murphy, hostess, of Dublin; the late Mr Derek Mynott and Mrs Derek Mynott, host and hostess, of London; Lawrence Mynott, host and guest, formerly of London, now of Tangier, Morocco.

The late Mr Peter Newington and Mrs Peter Newington, fellow guests, of London; David Nicholson, MP, host, of London; Lady Celestria Noel, fellow guest, of London; the Hon. Richard Norton, fellow guest, of London.

Ms Bawn O'Beirne-Ranelagh, most long-suffering of hostesses, also most helpful of house guests, of London and Languedoc-Roussillon; Mr and Mrs John O'Beirne-Ranelagh, host and hostess, of Cambridge; Patrick O'Callaghan, host, of London and Lincolnshire; Miss Mary-Geraldine O'Donnell, best of hostesses, of London; Mr and Mrs David O'Leary, host and hostess, also guests, of Oxfordshire and London; Miss Hazel O'Leary, best of country house hostesses, also superb London hostess, formerly of Suffolk, now of St James's; Helen O'Neill, of Dublin; Mr and Mrs John O'Reilly, of Dublin; William O'Reilly, of Dublin; Dawn O'Sullivan, of Co. Tipperary; Michael O'Sullivan, most practised of guests, of Dublin.

Mr John and the Hon. Mrs Paxman, of Co. Tipperary; Noel Persse, guest, of Dublin; Sven Persson, guest, of Sweden, London and Co. Offaly; Hugh Peskett, genealogist and guest, of Winchester; Harry Phibbs, host and guest, of London; Mr and Mrs Jeremy Pilcher (the latter a.k.a. Meredith Etherington-Smith), host and hostess, of Chelsea; Wendy Plummer, of the Alternative Shooting Company, Burford, Oxfordshire; Claude Pope-Lane, host and guest, of Texas; Michael Portillo, MP, host and guest, of London; Homan Potterton, fellow guest, formerly of Dublin, now of New York; Mr and Mrs Paul Power, host and hostess, also guests, of Co. Cork; Paul Proud, guest, of Dublin and Banagher, Co. Offaly; Mrs Grace Pym, hostess, of Ballaghmore Castle, Co. Laois, and Co. Galway.

Mr and Mrs Stephen Raleigh, host and hostess, of London; Brian Rathbone, of London; Timothy Rearden, guest, of the Isle of Man and Co. Wexford; Richard Ritchie, of London; Mr and Mrs Sam Rosen, guests, of London; The Earl and Countess of Rosse, best of hosts, of Birr Castle, Co. Offaly; Mr and Mrs Alan Rubin, host and hostess, of London; the Hon. Lisa Runciman, guest, of London; Mr and Mrs Patrick Ryall, host and hostess, of Co. Kildare; Mr and Mrs Sean Ryan, best of hosts, of Leap Castle, Co. Tipperary; Tony Ryan, of Dolla, Co. Tipperary.

Richard Salmon, host, of Kensington; Stefan Sanchez, guest and professional mounter of party entertainments, of London and Mexico; M. Philippe Sartori, party-giver, of Lyon and London; Roger Scruton, party-giver, of London and Boston; Stephen Sherbourne, party-giver, of London; Miss Josephine Sheridan, hostess and guest, of South Africa and London; Mr and Mrs Patrick Sim, host and hostess, of Wiltshire; Miss Anne Skelly, hostess, of London; Miss Susan Slade, guest and portrait painter, of Chelsea; Luke Smallpiece-Whitington, guest, of Sydney, Australia, Tuscany and Dublin; Lt-Col Sir Blair Stewart-Wilson, late Deputy Master of the Household and Equerry to Her Majesty The Queen; Barry Stonehill, host, of Chelsea, the Bahamas and Mayfair; Mrs Martin Stopford, hostess, of Hampstead; Mrs Caroline Stroud, hostess, of London; Miss Margaret Sutton, hostess, formerly of Chicago, now of Vancouver, British Columbia; Miss Monica Symes, hostess and guest, of Lyme Regis.

Mr and Mrs Brian Thompson, host and hostess, of Cloghan Castle and Emmel Castle, Co. Tipperary; David Thomson, guest, of Wolverhampton; Pauline Tierney, guest, of Dublin; Count Nikolai Tolstoy, charity ball patron and sometime fellow guest, of Berkshire; Peter Townend, socialite, of Chelsea; Mr and Mrs Trevor Trevor, host and hostess, of Trawscoed Hall, Shropshire; Mr and Mrs Geoffrey Tucker, political host and hostess, of London and Tuscany.

Hans Van Bemmeln, host and guest, sometime Counsellor at the Royal Netherlands Embassy, Dublin; Richard Vaughan-Rowlands, guest, of Anglesey and Vienna; the Hon. Elizabeth Vereker-Marshall, hostess and cookery and catering expert, of Abbeyleix, Co. Laois, and the Isle of Man.

The Hon. Lady Waley-Cohen, hostess, of Somerset; Eli Wallitt, host, of Brooklyn and London; Mr and Mrs Des Walsh, host and hostess, of Co. Tipperary; Brigadier and Mrs Michael Webb, host and hostess, of Paddington, Dorset; Christopher Wesolowski, host and guest, formerly of Norfolk, Cornwall and South Kensington, subsequently of Berkshire; Charles Wheeldon, guest, of London; John Whittingdale, MP, host, of London; Jeremy Williams, socialite, promoter of conviviality and guest, of Dublin and Co. Kilkenny; Alex Woodcock-Clarke, munificent host, of London; Mrs Sylvia Woodcock-Clarke, hostess and guest, of Larnaca, Cyprus.

Introduction

Entertaining is as old as civilisation. One could discuss endlessly its historic rituals and how they have evolved through aeons. But this is a book concerned with modern usage. I therefore propose when launching on an historical overview to serve up only gobbets, and even these are of use principally insofar as they help us understand the present. First, although it is modern developments – advances in catering, the hectic pace of life, the extinction of the domestic servant and the proliferation of cramped accommodation due to overpopulation, to say nothing of a revolution in manners – which justify the writing of a book like this in the first place, certain basic aspects of entertaining are very old indeed. Chief of them is the notion that hospitality is sacred. In its extreme form this notion holds that the guest can do no wrong, while the host must be prepared to put himself to infinite trouble. Such an attitude can be ferociously expensive. Some guests will regard themselves as so privileged that they make off not just with the teaspoons but with something as hefty as a piece of lead garden statuary (I myself was victim of larceny on this sort of scale by an overnight guest only last year), or seduce their host's wife/hostess's husband – even, these days, both. Conversely, some hosts have bankrupted themselves in an effort to treat their guests in proper fashion: President Thomas Jefferson of the United States, for instance, or the Second Duke of Buckingham and Chandos in England. Those examples are relatively recent, which shows how much staying-power the doctrine of the Divine Right of Guests possesses. Certainly the conviction that hospitality is bound up with the sacred remains strongest in traditional societies, so one can reasonably assume it is as old as hospitality itself.

But how old is hospitality? It might be pushing things a bit far to maintain that our forefathers vied with the cave-dwellers next door to win kudos by entertaining each other, for we simply don't know how keen their social instincts were. And to argue that the cave paintings at Lascaux and Altamira are mute survivors of the

1

ultimate art gallery exclusive private view would be downright precious. But most of the best-known biblical incidents involve hospitality: the serpent tempts Eve by offering food, even if it isn't his to offer; Jacob cheats his brother Esau of the latter's birthright by playing the bountiful host to a hunting man weary after a day spent in the chase; the highlight of the Babylonian captivity is cast in terms of Belshazzar's Feast, the ultimate flop in parties, one feels, for all its Jean-Michel Jarre-style special effects. The New Testament is just as hospitality-conscious. Jesus's mission starts with a boost to a lacklustre wedding party in turning water to wine at Cana and finishes with the Last Supper.

Nor is the pagan world any different. The Trojan War, if one is to believe the *Iliad*, starts because a foreigner, Paris, abuses a Greek king's hospitality by seducing and abducting the king's wife. The *Odyssey* supplies a series of object lessons in how to escape over-pressing hosts and hostesses. And it culminates in a drastic example of how to get rid of unwanted guests when Odysseus shoots down his wife's suitors like partridges at an Edwardian battue. So much for Homeric Greece. A few centuries later the Athenians of Classical times were so taken up with entertaining that Plato conveyed his philosophy through the medium of the boozing session. The Romans are popularly supposed to have become so enslaved by entertaining that they neglected their empire and poisoned themselves gourmandising out of lead pots. And the most memorable episode of the most memorable work of prose fiction to emerge from Roman civilisation is Trimalchio's Feast in the *Satyricon*. (Trimalchio, the *parvenu* host impressing guests by conspicuous, not to say ostentatious, consumption, is with us yet.)

Many a notable event in British history and legend involves entertaining. The case of King Alfred's cakes illustrates the folly (and impoliteness) of asking guests to 'help with the washing up', or whatever the chore may be. It is true that not every guest is a statesman preoccupied with some knotty problem of governance, as King Alfred was, but the principle is a good one. (If they volunteer that is another matter.) Macbeth's usurpation of Duncan's throne when playing host to His Majesty is considered particularly horrible because it offends against the laws of hospitality. Even Lady Macbeth affects to feel this, for on pretending to hear for the first time the shocking news of the king's murder she exclaims 'Not in my house!' whereupon Banquo makes the very reasonable point that what matters more is the regicide itself. The Macbeth incident is one reason why it is better for royalty to entertain than be entertained – or so it must have seemed in tenth-century Scotland. But by the sixteenth century things had moved on. Royal progresses round England, notably by Elizabeth I, had become a recognised method of reducing court expenditure. At the same time they had the advantage of impoverishing One's hosts, drawn from One's richer subjects, to the point where they were in little danger of becoming over-mighty.

Nor has English history been insular where entertaining is concerned, even though socialising with Continentals has often had the most profound consequences. William the Conqueror obtained the reversion of the English throne from Edward the Confessor when he was the latter's house guest in England. (Even today a house party can involve sizeable real estate transfers: a friend of mine once spent a weekend playing poker and won a tropical island. On the Monday of his departure he gave it to his hostess as a thank-you present.) Some years after his coup while a guest of the Confessor's, William got Harold to confirm the deal when he was Harold's host in Normandy.

Even those Continentals who, unlike the Normans, avoided foreign conquests elevated entertaining to a branch of statecraft. During the Renaissance the Borgias considered dinner parties a series of career moves just as much as does any corporate wife today. Their ambition in that line provoked Max Beerbohm to remark that 'An invitation to dine at the Palazzo Borghese was accounted the highest social honour . . . But . . . though you would often in the fifteenth century have heard the snobbish Roman say, in a would-be off-hand tone, "I am dining with the Borgias tonight," no Roman ever was able to say "I dined last night with the Borgias." '

Anybody writing on a subject like entertaining is going to have read a good many books on etiquette, correct form, precedence and so on for background information. I was no exception. What struck me was the arbitrariness of many of the authors. Sheltering in a book of 1926 behind the anonymous label 'A Member of the

Aristocracy', one author I came across would say things like: 'The coffee cups containing coffee should be brought on a silver salver,' as if not having a salver of silver nine years after the Bolshevik Revolution and in the year of the General Strike precluded giving dinner parties altogether. 'A Member' (as for brevity's sake I shall henceforth call him, or perhaps it was a her) also comes up with the following: 'A foreign prince bearing the title of Serene Highness should be addressed as "Prince", and not as "Sir", by the aristocracy and gentry, and as "Your Serene Highness" by all other classes.' 'A Member' follows this immediately with: 'A foreign princess, also bearing the title of Serene Highness, should be styled "Princess" when addressed colloquially by the upper classes, but not as "Ma'am"; and as "Your Serene Highness" by all other classes.'

This gives rise to a good many more queries than it answers. For instance, what of foreign prince(sse)s entitled to be styled as His/Her Highness (HSH and HH – which are strictly speaking styles of address and not titles at all – are used of different ranks of Continental, mostly Germanic, nobles and minor royalty)? Then again, how do the aristocracy and gentry mentioned in the first passage differ from the upper classes of the second (does the latter category include the upper middle class, for instance)? Or again, why should advice on addressing the princess be given for a colloquial context but not as regards addressing the prince?

'A Member' could be even more muddling, not to say muddled. In his (or her) Table of General Precedence he (or she) mentions the Lord Chancellor of Ireland, although by 1926 the Irish Free State had been in existence for four years.

Another writer on the subject, in a book also first published in 1926 but reprinted as recently as 1987, has an obsession about providing whisky and soda along with wine at dinner and lunch parties. In the most generous interpretation this amounts to no more than the reflection of the author's personal taste for the stuff. Elsewhere she contradicts herself on two successive pages. To be fair, the writers I have mentioned also offer much sensible and useful information, and even where the rules and *obiter dicta* which were the last word in correct form for, say, 1926 have become obsolete since, they retain a certain period charm for the antiquarian. But it is a cruel practical joke for a publishing house

4

to bring out new printings of such works in the 1980s, for impressionable readers may be grossly misled.

Citing the aforementioned examples may be thought unfair since surely, you will say, not all books of advice on correct form and etiquette are so out of date. Not all, perhaps, but a good few. In any case I have a more fundamental criticism to make. In nearly all past writing on the subject of entertaining no distinction tends to be made between (a) a course of behaviour that is compulsory inasmuch as to depart from it is a grave social error and (b) a course of behaviour that is not so much compulsory as advisable, since to behave otherwise is not quite fashionable, or (c) a course of action that is recommended because it is plain expedient.

Accordingly I have tried to present each section of this book in something of a dual form. In one part of each section there will tend to be a practical guide to entertaining, giving advice but not laying down the law, if only because circumstances alter cases, and although I have tried to anticipate every situation in which you may find yourself there are an infinite variety of unusual ones I haven't the space to cover, even if I were clairvoyant. Another part will deal with each form of entertaining as it should ideally be conducted if the hostess operates according to the full rigour of convention as it still exists today. The argument for this second approach, something that may as well be called one of extreme formality, was, and remains, that it saves one having to think. Provided it is flexible enough to fit today's heterogeneous society that may still be a recommendation. Lots of people dislike thinking, particularly busy hosts. But since entertaining well should be fun, even creative, many readers may be of the opinion that a set of rules which makes thinking unnecessary is rather tame and boring. On the whole I am of that opinion myself.

Another reason for placing the more pragmatic, less formal approach in front of the rigid, etiquette-bound one is that entertaining is very nearly a universal human activity. Even Bohemians, hippies, squatters and students entertain their friends at some point. Even the least sociable of people tend to organise an occasional lunch, if only for relatives at, say, Christmas. Nobody apart from the genuine 100 per cent recluse fails to go out *somewhere* – and the genuine 100 per cent recluse is more a character from fiction than from real life.

Accordingly any problems in modern entertaining are not likely to be psychological, though having said that I would observe that parties can change character very rapidly once even a single new guest of powerful personality enters the room. More of this later. Nor, despite the recession of the last few years, need there be any particular financial constraints on one's entertaining. This book is aimed at all types of readers: if you are one of those lucky people with an infinitely elastic budget for entertaining, you will find just as much instruction and advice here as will those who are obliged to economise. The worldly means of a host have very little to do with successful entertaining. The most generous hosts are very often people of slender resources, while everybody has his own memory of some appalling piece of meanness on the part of a rich host. No, the problems to do with entertaining today are first logistical and secondly behavioural/cultural. Let us take logistics first.

LOGISTICAL CONSTRAINTS ON ENTERTAINING

First there is the pace of life problem. Work takes up so much of one's time; so does shopping; so does preparing a dinner party, cocktail party, bridge evening, dance or whatever, to say nothing of clearing up afterwards. Couples, either married or living together, fare better than single people because they have double the time and double the energy, but even that is not sufficient if both are in full-time employment. And a single person who entertains has either a well-paid job, a badly paid one or no job at all. The first kind of job usually involves long working hours. And even at weekends one is often too exhausted to do much anyway. The badly paid person is likely to have to work as little as eight hours a day, but of course has more time to plan the entertainment of his friends. Students and the unemployed, unless they are of that dwindling band of people on fat unearned incomes, have to entertain with the cheapest of ingredients. From the point of view of pure hospitality, the badly paid person is best placed in that he has the optimum combination of leisure and means with which to entertain. Even so, the hell of shopping at a time when everyone else does it – late-night opening in supermarkets towards the end of the week, Saturday mornings – diminishes the pleasure of preparation a good deal. And the pleasures of entertaining are confined to the preparation and performance. Nobody I've ever heard of gets a kick out of clearing up afterwards. Unfortunately, on a small income it is seldom feasible to pay another person to do it.

A related problem is that of the time one's guests have at their disposal. Oddly enough, since domestic servants all but disappeared dinner parties have tended to go on much longer. One of the etiquette books I mentioned earlier says a smart, formal London dinner party should start about 8.30 p.m. and the guests should begin to leave between 10.30 and 11. And don't forget there were more courses served in those days. Nowadays anybody in London who gives a dinner party starting at 8 p.m. should reckon on it lasting until past midnight at the earliest. Not that all the guests will stay till then: the well-paid employed are likely to want to leave a dinner early – the Frankfurt Bourse starts trading at the British equivalent of 8 a.m. next morning, they are prosecuting in a fraud case up in Birmingham the following day, their views on Maastricht are being sought live on tomorrow's *Today* programme and so on. The badly paid employed can stay on a bit, but if they are ambitious they need to get to the office reasonably on time and with reasonably clear heads together with unimpaired digestions. They want promotion, after all, so as to make it to well-paid employed grade. Only incurable topers, those in peak physical condition and students will stay on to hear the dawn chorus and if there is not unlimited wine to hand you can safely eliminate the topers anyway. Rather a pity. There's nothing more enjoyable in the conviviality line – and no surer sign of a successful dinner party – than an immensely prolonged, civilised chat over civilised food and drink.

Secondly there is what I referred to earlier as the extinction of the domestic servant. Perhaps 'extinction' overstated matters: cleaning women still exist; hired waiters can still be had – at a price. Without babysitters social life outside the house for those with small children would cease entirely – and even if parents always play host instead of going out to other people's houses as guests, the strain of superintending children while entertaining friends can be unbearable. Certainly the reliable domestic who knows where to put back the silver, who can fix the dishwasher when it plays up and who is prepared to tackle the first-rate mess that a first-rate dinner party invariably generates is a very rare beast indeed. For most people, then, entertaining at home means superintending preparations at the very least, plus serving and clearing up afterwards.

Then there is what I referred to earlier as cramped accommodation. Most Britons are city-dwellers. Most city-dwellers, if living in houses, have small ones. Flat-dwellers may have bigger individual rooms than those in town houses but fewer of them. In any case most flat-dwellers cannot take advantage of a garden in summer, which is much the best season for entertaining, even indoor entertaining.

So far I have discussed the difficulties, particularly the lack-of-time-for-preparation problem, almost entirely as if the host is a single person. Obviously that is not the case, even nowadays, when so much of the paraphernalia of the conventional family is breaking down. Single-person households, although on the increase, are still not the norm. At the same time the old orthodoxy of breadwinner father, housewife mother and the statistically correct two children, Janet and John – the very stuff of a fifties advertisement for Ovaltine – has taken a terrible beating. Increasingly wives or cohabiting partners (henceforward CPs) as well as husbands (or cohabiting male partners) go out to work, or feel they ought to. Sometimes it is the wife/CP who is the breadwinner.

Even a partner who stays at home doesn't want to be thought of as just a housewife (presumably still less, if male, as a 'non-working' house-husband). Rather, she is increasingly being persuaded to cultivate additional interests. This has meant that the wife/CP who devotes her entire life to entertaining her husband's business colleagues is more a *beau idéal* than a hard fact of everyday life, for such geisha-like self-effacement is rare at the best of times and women now rightly want more from their existence than just that. But any sensible wife whose husband earns more than she does (I do not say such a state of affairs is right, merely that it is how things usually are) presumably wishes him to do as well as possible, certainly to retain his job while all about him may be losing theirs. By hosting enjoyable entertainments with sparkle and efficiency she is probably doing as much to boost his career as he is himself by clocking on for thirteen hours a day at the office. Clearly a book like this that helps the wife/CP advance her husband's career, hence her own and the children's well-being, is a must.

BEHAVIOURAL/CULTURAL CONSTRAINTS ON ENTERTAINING

A fancy phrase perhaps, but what it boils down to is problems arising from the very fluid sort of society we live in these days, and the wide variety of manners people exhibit. Both phenomena make entertaining much more complicated than formerly. For instance, at any given party one's guests may easily include old-fashioned types from the few remaining rural backwaters and citified post-moderns, vegetarians and carnivores, foreigners and xenophobes, recent immigrants and those who are so anxious to play down their immigrant parents' background that they act super-British, adherents of any or all religions and those who have none, not to mention members of any race, or a mixture of races. Someone you knew as super-rich until last year might have become suddenly poor because of over-exposure to Lloyd's. Someone you knew as super-poor till last year might have inherited a fortune, sold out what used until a few months ago to be a struggling electronics company to a conglomerate for several millions or won the Booker Prize. Someone you knew as a boring, safely married solicitor might have come out of the closet. Someone you knew as a swinger might have settled down to domestic vegetation on getting married.

Entertaining can be difficult enough if all guests are from the same background – it is coteries that tend to wage the bitterest feuds, after all – and although a party sometimes goes very well with a wide mix of guests one can't count on it. As Lady Clarinda Bossnowl remarks in Thomas Love Peacock's novel *Crotchet Castle* 'It was rather ill judged in Mr Crotchet to invite him [a ferocious game-preserving squire] today. But the art of assorting company is above these *parvenus*. They invite a certain number of persons without considering how they harmonise with each other.' Nor are fundamental differences of outlook merely a matter of which generation you belong to. Superannuated hippy survivors of the sixties can be just as conventionally unconventional as young fogies, a quarter of a century their juniors (sometimes indeed their own children), are unconventionally conventional.

Laying down the law as to a precise code of dress, comportment, form of address and so on is pretty futile if half the people one encounters socially have never heard of such things, let alone obeyed them. That does not eliminate the need for a book like this, one which instructs readers not just in what is good form, but also in what are good tactics. At the same time this book is a guide, not Holy Writ. It points the way, makes suggestions, discusses what I hope will convince you on its merits is the most sensible course of action in a set of given circumstances. The fatuity of the old etiquette books was that they said 'Such-and-such is not done,' or 'Calling so-and-so a thingummy is incorrect,' like a nanny ticking off a naughty child. One was never told *why* whatever it was was not done or incorrect. Sometimes there were good anthropological reasons, such as that a particular form of behaviour would once have been thought inconsiderate or discourteous to the aged, who at remote times had been revered more than was the case by the time the etiquette book was written. But often what was operating was sheer blind prejudice. Not surprisingly, the most recent generation or two, less prone to take on trust the lessons taught them by their elders, have tended to reject conventional etiquette. The trouble is that they have thrown the baby of basic consideration for others, everyday politeness towards the fellow human beings with whom we are obliged to share this planet, out along with the bathwater of musty *idées reçues* inherited from a pre-industrial, deferential society.

Good form, like the Ovaltine ad family, may have taken a terrible beating but it is still out there somewhere, surviving shyly in a few sheltered corners like Jacobites after Culloden. If you want to, you can learn all about it here, too. Who to send into dinner with whom; how to extend invitations to formal dinners or dances; what to wear as a host and what to stipulate as wear by your guests; when to sit down to dinner and when to get up from it again; which fork to hold in which hand; which wine to serve with which course – the whole canon of rules and laws, diktats and ukases, prohibitions and regulations, taboos and *sine qua nons* that made up Western civilisation, assured in its correctness of outlook until only half a generation ago, and which still does in exalted or remote circles. But from vast swathes of modern social life it has been almost expunged. So when good form is widely flouted by others, you the host must not get too downhearted. Besides, there are various counter-measures to the barbarian in the drawing room, of which more later.

Another constraint is the puritanism of the times. We live under the shadow of a collective neurosis about too much cholesterol, alcohol, refined sugars and gluten in the diet. And neurosis is affecting executive government. Modern policemen wield breathalysers rather than truncheons, and are readier to collect urine samples from a professional man at a checkpoint than fingerprints from a criminal suspect lurking near the scene of a felony. In addition the state, not wanting to seem soft when confronted by increasingly barbaric behaviour, makes a nuisance of itself, not to the barbarians themselves, but to the solid citizens who are the easier targets for bureaucratic bossiness. And legislators, who as MPs and peers are the only occupational group in the country with their own in-house bar free from the obligation to acquire a liquor licence, have the impertinence to hector us to drink less.

Now the good news. In some ways entertaining has never been easier. There have never been so many different kinds of food, never so many delicatessens and really first-rate supermarkets to buy them in, never so many fridges or freezers to store them in, nor so many receptacles, from blenders through microwaves to woks, to prepare them in, nor so many delicious wines to sluice them down with, nor so many pretty decors on which to feast the eye while pampering the stomach. Instant communications such as phone or fax make impromptu entertaining easy, or contingency plans against non-appearing guests instantly executable. Food is not just infinite in its variety but available all year round. British catering is at last shedding the terrible reputation it (and we) suffered under for the best part of a century. The takeaway has not perhaps quite come of age so that one can employ it for a dinner party rather than a snack in front of the television wherever in Britain one lives. And even in London neither Claridge's, the Connaught, the Berkeley, nor the Savoy will bring a ready-cooked meal round to your house, no matter how near you live, though they confess that if you have an HRH (His/Her Royal Highness) in front of your name the position is altered. Wilton's in St James's will provide hampers of smoked salmon and oysters, but such

11

things are only acceptable as picnic food or a first course.

Nevertheless, the advances outweigh the deterioration. So cheer up. It is no good lamenting the dutiful and underpaid servants, structured society, punctilio in answering invitations and writing thank-you letters afterwards of times past – all the aids to entertaining we have lost. Better to make the most of what we have gained, then build on it. And with a little ingenuity one can always recreate past glories if one wants to. Emulating the Second Duke of Buckingham and Chandos is not a bad way to bow out.

Please note: Throughout this book 'host' applies to both host and hostess. Likewise the reader should assume that rules and advice are valid for men and women alike unless specified otherwise. But to avoid the clumsiness of recurrent he/shes and his/hers, I have alternated the sexes, sometimes more or less with each paragraph, according to whether it is more usual for the task in question to be performed by a man or a woman. Thus if I am talking about decanting wine I use 'he' and 'his'; if about writing the letter of invitation to a dinner party 'she' and 'her'. This is not to say that decanting wine is exclusively a man's job and writing invitations to dinner parties exclusively a woman's, and certainly not that there ought to be a hard and fast demarcation rule about such activities, merely that this is how it usually is.

PART 1

Meals

CHAPTER 1
Dinner Parties

The dinner party remains the supreme form of entertaining. It is possible to spend more – much more – on a wedding; you can get drunker at a wake. There will probably be a greater quantity of delicious food at the *kiddush* held after a Barmitzvah. The women are usually more beautiful and the men more handsome at a film première, the wit is more honed in a salon, the silver and jewels more sparkling at Buckingham Palace banquets for visiting heads of state. But for the combination of all these desirable qualities in a single place and for a single period of a few hours a good private dinner party is unbeatable.

How Many Guests?
First you need to choose the guests, Some authorities suggest eight is the optimum number for a dinner party, but that is a wildly arbitrary rule since it depends on the size of your dining room, the size of your dining table and perhaps most importantly the size of your acquaintance. By the last I mean the number of friends you have who are of more or less equal social accomplishments. Gross imbalance in the latter between one guest and another can be fatal where such relatively small numbers are concerned. Here we are speaking of dinner parties only: large-scale stand-up parties are an entirely different matter. Many hosts who have given lots of them reckon that the more you mix people the better. Jeffrey Archer is among their number and, reluctant though I am to salute his judgement in most matters, I believe he is right here.

Eight can in fact be rather an unsuitable number. There is a slight tendency for the guests to separate into two quartets. Or, with a long, relatively narrow table, there is a risk that people will shout at each other along a diagonal from one corner to the other, especially if the intermediate diners aren't up to coping with a compulsive talker.

The Dining Room

Before decreeing numbers let us examine the size of the dining room, or more accurately its shape. If it is square and not more than 12ft by 12ft you will have either a square table or a round one. Round ones are better, of course. Sometimes, indeed, they are *de rigueur*. When Charles X of France was deposed in 1830 he proceeded with dignity towards the frontier preparatory to going into exile. On the way he stopped at an obscure manor house and the loyal squire put him up for the night. Although by now an ex-monarch he was treated as if still a reigning one. Tradition decreed that the King of France could not eat at a square table so the only dining table in the house had its corners sawn off.

If you have a round table you start with an advantage over and above the ability to entertain kings of France. With narrow chairs and slim guests you could at a pinch seat eight even in the broom-cupboard proportions typical of a modish artisan's cottage, the sort that so painfully sets its purchaser back many hundreds of thousands of pounds when in Chelsea. If in a small dining room you have a square table it would be best to confine sit-down dinner parties to four people. Four people can make for a very enjoyable evening and there is the advantage that the host, if without help (as will presumably be the case in such a small house), doesn't have to spend more than a relatively short amount of time carving in the kitchen, fetching more wine, getting others their second helpings and so on. If you feel embarrassed about not being able to accommodate more than four people simultaneously you can take up bridge, which gives the perfect excuse for *parties carrées*. Alternatively, you can invite many more than four and throw a buffet supper instead. (We will come to buffets, and bridge, too, later.)

What if you have no dining room at all? Flat-dwellers are often in that unhappy plight. Indeed, the kitchen which changes halfway along its walls from utilitarian, steam-resistant, washable surfaces to chic or would-be chic accent-on-living tones, described by the naffer estate agents as the 'dinette', more prosaically the dining area, has in the last few years probably become a rule rather than the exception. If you simply have no choice about such matters there is an end of it. However, there are certain tactics which are advisable in such circumstances. Do not plan a menu which entails pungent smells, for these will waft their way to the dining area and linger throughout subsequent courses. Do not plan a menu involving clouds of steam, for the dining area will quickly come to resemble a laundry on a humid day coping with the local rugby team's kit after a particularly muddy match. Do try to discourage smoking at the table, even when it's time for the port and nuts to be circulated (you can take your guests to the drawing room for these), or the kitchen end will become contaminated. Oddly enough, eating in the kitchen – even entertaining there generally on an informal basis – works best in farmhouses or country houses, even though they tend to be the one sort of dwelling where it isn't really necessary because the place is big enough to have a dining room as well. Perhaps this has something to do with the kitchen's historic function as the venue for harvest suppers, tuck-ins after a day's rough shooting and other bucolic diversions.

An alternative to the dining room in a small flat is the hall, which features increasingly in estate agents' particulars as utilisable for just that function ('entrance hall/dining area 9ft × 7ft'). If you do use the hall make sure no draught from the front door sweeps it, and that the lavatory is situated in another part of the flat, not just off the hall. Lavatorial sounds which are only too audible in the dining area are distinctly off-putting.

Sometimes you just have no choice. In cities like New York, where accommodation is even more cramped than in London, quite well-off people often live in studio apartments and entertain their friends exclusively at restaurants, which tend to be cheaper than here. Use of restaurants is a subject which will be touched on later, but for the present I would only say that no dwelling, however small, is useless for entertaining in, provided you have ingenuity. I have been to a dinner party in a Paris garret given by an extraordinarily elegant and stunningly beautiful lesbian couple – at which a Duke was present, incidentally – where the superbly cooked meal had miraculously been contrived over spirit lamps in the same cramped room at one end of which the marital (if that's the right word) divan was installed and in the centre of which we dined, and where presumably the washing up was to be done afterwards – in the hand basin. Even if your furniture has been repossessed, you can seat your guests on the floor on cushions and declare that the dinner is to be *à la turc*. The poverty-stricken family in Dodie Smith's *I Capture the Castle* give a dinner party at which they serve their guests on a grand piano, the table having been either hocked at the pawnbroker's or chopped up for firewood some months previously. Do not feel that just because your flat is tiny you must give up entertaining at home and either hit your pocket hard by treating your friends in restaurants or live as a hermit. Confine your dinners to the summer, concentrate on presentation (though never, I hope, to the detriment of what is palatable), laying out the food on your guests' plates before they sit down – the apotheosis of the airline meal if you like, though of far superior quality – and you can still build a reputation as a prince or princess of entertaining.

Numbers Dining

If your dining room is large you can be more ambitious. Six, eight, ten, twelve – the sky's the limit, provided you have enough cutlery, wine glasses and plates to go round. I am speaking of even numbers, however, and although an even number will probably be your aim, it may happen that you end up with an odd number, because of a last-minute cancellation, say. This really need not be a disaster nowadays. But in the past people would go to almost any lengths to avoid it. If they were people of consequence living in the country they might send a note round to the vicar asking him to leave his wife behind, come up to the big house and dine *en garçon* so that the men and women should be balanced. In nineteenth-century Paris there were professional fourteenth men called *quatorzièmes* who could be hired at a few minutes' notice to make up the numbers when for one reason or another it looked as if the dinner party might have to sit down thirteen at table.

Unlucky Numbers

Whether you think thirteen is so fatally unlucky a number that you would actually pay someone money for you and your guests to avoid it is up to you. Only the very closest of friends can be asked at thirty minutes' notice to come round if you cannot hire anyone – and as far as I know the professional fourteenth man does not exist any longer. More practically, it is worth bearing in mind that in other countries and cultures some other numbers are regarded as unlucky. For the Japanese thirteen is a perfectly innocent number but 4, 44, 444 – in fact anything containing the digit 4 – suggest death. (Four is '*Shi*' in Japanese and the verb *Shinu* means to die.) The Chinese have a similar superstition about 4 and 14 and 24. If you had Italian guests coming to dinner, it would be as well to ensure that you did not sit down seventeen to dinner, as this is an unlucky number in Italy. This being the case it seems unlikely that thirteen is thought unlucky principally because there were thirteen at the Last Supper, though this explanation is often put forward. After all, the Last Supper in itself, as opposed to the events that succeeded it, is so far from being a disaster that it is actually commemorated (or partially re-enacted, according to your theology) every time a Christian takes communion. In any case, thirteen was regarded as unlucky in civilisations that existed long before Christianity. And in pagan Norse mythology Loki turns up to make the thirteenth guest at a banquet in Valhalla where Baldur is later killed.

Grace
If you and your guests find yourselves thirteen at table despite all your precautions, you are supposed to be able to prevent one of your number dying within a year – the standard fate in such circumstances – by all joining hands and standing up simultaneously. In addition, it probably wouldn't do any harm to say Grace. This has rather gone out of fashion unless a cleric is among those dining, although giving thanks to some deity or other before eating a meal is not exclusively Christian. It may be objected that many people these days are embarrassed about having anything to do with religion introduced into a dinner party atmosphere. You have a problem if you regard your guests' wishes as supreme, know a substantial number of them will squirm inwardly if Grace is said, yet have it said all the same. Leaving the purely moral pros and cons to one side – and only the individual host can resolve moral questions – I would recommend dividing your friends according to whether they are religiously minded or otherwise, and inviting the religious to one sort of dinner party, where Grace may be said, and the secular lot to profane dinner parties where the nearest anyone comes to expressing gratitude to the Divinity is to praise the hostess for her angels on horseback.

Large Numbers

Lady Troubridge (not the notorious Una, another one), writing on the etiquette of entertaining in 1926, talked of an average dinner being of twelve to eighteen people and implicitly in London, not the country when such numbers were involved. (Even nowadays one does tend to have more room if one lives in the country.) On the other hand she pointed out that dinner-giving was an expensive way of entertaining and that nobody expected people of small or moderate means to give dinner parties. Well, that was another era. Tea parties, the badly off person's dinner party substitute in Lady Troubridge's day, have become as outmoded as whist drives. The dinner party has taken over as the natural form of entertaining. Everyone gives an occasional one nowadays.

By all means follow Lady Troubridge's circle and entertain eighteen or more at a sit-down dinner. Only do bear in mind how much time you will have to spend working out the seating arrangement (rather an arduous exercise in sheer intellectual concentration and the higher diplomacy, I find). Worse, you will be obliged to expend your social energy in shepherding guests to their seats, urging on the progress of the sauce boat round the table (if it stops at the elbow of a compulsive talker nothing you can do will get him to notice it and speed it on its way), guiding the conversation, topping up your guests' glasses and so on. Put succinctly, Mosley's Law of Entertaining states that for every number of guests (x) by which a dinner party increases in numbers, the host's work in ergs is augmented by the square of that number (where x is greater than 1), for even if you have servants to do the menial tasks you will have to superintend them (and no mere servant can be expected to keep the conversation going, anyway). I rather stress this point about greater numbers demanding greater effort because although nobody should undertake entertaining unless they are prepared to work reasonably hard at it, enjoyment is essential to being a good host. True, in the real world people give dinner parties for all sorts of other reasons as well – showing off their house or cooking, sucking up to the boss, working off social obligations, giving the in-laws up from the country a glimpse of the big city – but if the person in charge is not getting some kind of kick out of the evening, however perverse, the fact will always be apparent and a sense of unease will gently percolate through the assembly like week-old stewed cabbage in a boarding house.

AWKWARD MOMENTS

One must confess that the sort of person whose delight at entertaining is of a perverse kind is better read about than experienced. I remember a dinner party at a castle in the west of Ireland where the châtelaine, who had ridden her favourite hunter into the hall when the local hunt ball was held there the previous week, kept on murmuring to herself that she wanted now to try to leap the dining-room table on the beast (it was a very large dining room). Her step-son, a model of calmness and reasonableness considering the circumstances, tried continuously to dissuade her. I privately decided that if she looked like carrying out her plan I would rise and lead such of my fellow guests as would follow me from the building. Riding your horse into the house is such a hackneyed way of showing off. Just because the Ascendancy used to do it throughout the nineteenth century there's no reason nowadays for blow-ins to risk their guests' lives just to prove they're equally daredevil. If the hostess had ridden a bear into the room, as Squire Mytton, of the celebrated Shropshire family, was said to have done in the nineteenth century, it would have been a different matter, though candidly I think I might still have left before the fun started. Later in the meal this same hostess rose and walked round to one of the guests and asked her in a stage whisper to talk more quietly. All in all, not one of the more comfortable evenings.

OSTENTATION

My pathetically neurotic hostess on the occasion I have just mentioned was really just trying to show off, which brings us to an appropriate juncture to discuss this aspect of entertaining. Don't let them browbeat you into believing that it is ostentatious to put your best silver and gold on the table, dress yourself and your guests up in best bib and tucker, light a thousand scented candles and feast on ortolans and larks. One man's ostentation is another's artistic display. What is the point of giving dinner parties at all if we can't make a bit of a show? Why own pretty silverware if you can't display it to your friends – and in a useful form such as a salt cellar rather than as a mere ornament behind a display cabinet's glass door with steel bars across it to deter burglars? Provided you don't let an obsession with ceremony and decor prevent people enjoying themselves, and the consensus is that the Victorians did tend to make this mistake, you should let your instincts rip. If jealous acquaintances or prying, guttersnipe gossip columnists cry extravagance, shrug your shoulders, issue a broadside of writs for slander or libel and see if the heavens fall. They won't.

But in an era when your friends may be subject to very sharp reverses of fortune it could be heartless to go in for too much display. It is all too easy for people to think they cannot match your level of hospitality if you do. True, some people can dine with a rich man one day in full splendour and invite him over to their tiny garret a week later, give him some spaghetti and be so insouciant about it that he goes away thinking it is he who has profited from the exchange. Perhaps he has, particularly if the company has been amusing whereas his own friends are a dull lot. But it depends too much on the rich man having the necessary vision to admit this to himself, and on the poor man having the necessary imagination, for – radical though it sounds to say so – poor people are not necessarily more interesting than rich ones.

BALANCING THE SEXES
In these enlightened times it is no longer as necessary to balance the sexes as formerly. Just as well, because even the most conventional list with the highest equilibrium factor, one pairing off men and women, marrieds and unmarrieds, divorcés and divorcées, singles still hoping to change their status and singles who'd die rather than do so – the best list, then – can be ruined by the last-minute defection of a vital personage on it, a victim of 'flu a delayed flight in from Bahrain, terrorist action in Threadneedle Street, a three-line whip: the whole gallimaufry of modern civilisation. If you are lucky the shortfall of one guest will be counterbalanced by another guest who asks if she can bring her latest lover along. Whether you succumb will depend on how well you know the guest, how much you rather fancied her yourself before she let drop this bombshell, and the sort of man you know by long acquaintance she is likely to go for. If there's a good chance he's presentable well and good. If she likes rough trade you may have to give a polite but firm no.

22

What may be far more crucial for the success or failure of your dinner party is to balance the ages. Even those spry old boys and girls who are famous for getting on with young men and women of an age to be their grandchildren may flag as the hour gets later and later. The jokes and allusions that entrance one generation will be lost on another, ditto reminiscences, levels of bawdiness, tolerance of alcohol. I think a stand-up party is a better venue for mixing the generations.

Some of your guests may bring their babies unannounced, either because the sitter let them down at the last moment or because they are so besotted with the little beasts themselves they don't think anybody else could possibly object. The only guest babies you should permit in the house at the same time as a dinner party are ones so small and sleepy that they can be relied on to spend the entire time unconscious, apart perhaps for the odd crying bout, but this shouldn't last more than a minute or two. Parents who make a habit of bringing any baby which is more trouble than that should be dropped.

MATCHMAKING DINNER PARTIES

It is interesting to note how frequently the famous couples who make up the regular population of the gossip columns are said to have met at a dinner party. Being the host at a dinner party where some serial divorcee tycoon meets the PR girl a third his age who subsequently becomes his fourth wife may seem a cause for congratulation. So it is for the time being. But introducing two people who subsequently marry or settle down to cohabit must be its own reward. If they later split up – and what is more likely in the case of our fictional tycoon and his youthful PR girl? – the person who introduced them will be resented, and probably by both parties. I know of too many hosts in such a situation who have ended up not being spoken to by either person in the couple, sometimes for ever after.

It may not be the fault of you, the host, that Tycoon and PR Girl subsequently wrangled about the size of his alimony settlement, any more than it was your fault that they took a shine to each other in the first place. But it was under your roof that they met, even if one of them was brought along at the last moment by a third party who didn't even have the politeness to ask you for permission beforehand. You must just accept it as among the fortunes of entertaining.

Seating Arrangements

Purists state that the host should have his most important, i.e., highest-ranking, lady guest on his right (*mutatis mutandis* the hostess and most important gentleman guest on her right), second most important on his/her left hand, and so on. Fine as far as it goes. There is such a thing as a table of precedence, as it happens (*see* Appendix), and in the formal surroundings of grand country houses, together with less grand country houses if situated in remote areas (Scotland, for instance), to say nothing of embassies and the more official entertainments in cities, this table becomes even more important than the one you and your guests are eating off. A friend of a friend of mine once found herself at a dinner party where every male was either a king or heir apparent to a throne – something of a poser precedence-wise.

In less exalted spheres it is often impossible to say who the most important guest is, particularly as a fair number of peers and baronets these days don't care to use their titles. Foreigners other than royalty, Ambassadors, High Commissioners and senior statesmen, however exalted professionally and however genuine their titles, if they are merely noble but not career-minded, don't count as regards precedence in either England and Wales or in Scotland (there are two main systems of precedence, one for each of the two historic kingdoms that make up Britain). Yet since people move about so much more these days and we become increasingly enmeshed in the EC, the problem can't just be ignored. There ought to be some sort of Europe-wide table of precedence. I would hope the Foreign Office is giving it some attention (though when I inquired I was given to understand that it isn't), for precedence is laid down by statute; it isn't just a whim of a few old sticklers for correct form. Accordingly, if we don't look out we could have Jacques Santer using one of his Euro-decrees to ram some ludicrous Euro-precedence down our throats, a system for example whereby EC commissioners and VAT inspectors of grades one to twenty-two go into dinner before Dukes of the Blood Royal unless said Ds of the B R are graduates of the Ecole d'Administration or Members of the European Parliament in good standing, when they would take precedence of all except members of the Conseil d'Etat of not less than four years' seniority.

Even if it is possible to identify the highest-ranking guest, a thoughtful host without a houseful of servants to help him should consider how much he as host may be bobbing up and down from his seat during the meal, moving about the room, opening bottles, trotting backwards and forwards from the kitchen and so forth, because in those circumstances it is important to give the seat on your right and left to people who can hold their own conversationally even though one of their neighbours – the host – is *hors de combat* for much of the time. Nothing is more forlorn than the shy guest who manages at last to get a dialogue going with the host, only for the pathetic little trickle of conversation to be dammed a few feet from its source because the host is springing to his feet every few seconds.

Even when precedence was king it was possible to depart from it a little if either of the two highest-ranking guests, male and female, were close relatives of the hosts or if strict adherence to the rules meant a husband and wife would have to sit together. Seating a married couple next to each other at a dinner party is still inadvisable, though it's noteworthy how many couples, particularly if still in love with each other, try to arrange to sit side by side. All the more reason to work out your seating beforehand and tolerate no insubordination when assigning your guests their places. This is best done orally if you wait till your guests have trooped into the dining room to seat them. I am fully aware that writing out place cards and distributing them round the table in holders of silver or other precious metal is hallowed by tradition, but it forces everybody to play hunt-the-slipper round a big table (and it's unnecessary anyway at a small one). The resulting traffic jam can make Hyde Park Corner at peak rush-hour seem spacious. Moreover the light is usually bad because candles are being employed and the short-sighted among us don't much want to advertise the fact by peering and squinting across acres of table.

An alternative is to display a plan of the seating arrangement in the hallway or drawing room. The objection to this is that it makes what should be a private house resemble an army staff college. As we know, many private country houses have done duty as army establishments in their time. But the result has usually been disastrous aesthetically and from the point of view of atmosphere. Now atmosphere is one of the most important aspects of private entertaining, and in general few things are as depressing as a mansion on which the dead hand of institutionalisation has been laid.

In circles where precedence is still taken seriously the conventional method of protesting at being seated in too lowly a position (nobody protests at being placed too high) is to turn one's plate upside down – before it's had any food put on it, naturally. Do not be crestfallen if it occurs. Such things bedevil even leading diplomatists in their professional lives. The Shell heiress Olga Deterding's father, who rather naughtily styled himself Sir Henri Deterding, and persuaded *Who's Who* so to style him, although as a subject of a foreign country his KBE was honorary, had this happen to him at a formal banquet. If a guest of yours turns her plate upside down it is advisable to confer (or have your most imposing servant confer) with her hurriedly and whisper a request to whichever guest she thinks has displaced her that they swap places. If more than one of your guests behaves in this way you could seat them at two different tables – round ones. Indeed, the original Round Table made by Merlin for Uther Pendragon was so designed to avoid problems of precedence. (It is said to have seated 150, ambitious hostesses please note.) Arranging dinner parties at two or more separate round tables – it has to be a big dining room, of course – is not a bad method of giving dinner parties generally. You can always swap guests round between tables as the evening wears on. But don't put all the lions on one table. Mix them with the riff-raff.

By all means alternate the sexes among your guests when seating them, i.e., man, woman, man, woman – but don't make a fetish of it. If any of your guests do not arrive – and the hazards of modern life which may lead to this and which we touched on previously are growing more common – you may easily end up with a majority of one sex or the other. The topics in which your individual guests are interested may be such that a little juggling with the conventional seating is better than having the conversation splutter and stall. It is in any case not a bad idea to rotate the guests halfway through the dinner if, say, the table is so large that not more than three or four guests can see and speak to each other

26

at any one time. The gentlemen can be shifted round two spaces to the right, three spaces to the left or whatever. It is better to be a bit dictatorial here rather than let people sit where they like, otherwise the pretty girl at the end of the table will be surrounded by admirers while her dowdier fellow women are left on their own.

My old friend the property millionaire David Hart, Downing Street blue eminence of the Thatcher years, adopts a typically incisive method when seating one of his luncheon or dinner parties. It illustrates the point I made earlier about the difficulty in less formal circumstances of one's being able to say outright just who the most important person is. A typical Hart Saturday-night dinner party list of guests might comprise a British cabinet minister, a US presidential adviser, a Nobel Prize-winner, a sprinkling of earls' daughters, a practitioner of the higher journalism (usually but not always of Conservative bent) and a pop star plus an assortment of ordinary folk, though none of them the less delightful company for being that. David's method is to assemble the guests at one end of his generously proportioned dining hall and with curt nods assign each person to his place at table, running his eye speculatively over them beforehand. He himself, like royalty, sits halfway down one side of the table rather than at its head. We are told that God is likely to seat a repentant thief by his side, whereas David Hart prefers the prettiest girl in the room, but otherwise I imagine the Last Judgement will operate along the same lines.

Where should you and your husband, as hostess and host, seat yourselves? The conventional positions are at the head (host) and foot (hostess) of the table. As with so many other conventions, rigid adherence to the rule may be inconvenient. If you have little or no help you may both wish to be near the door leading to the kitchen. If the host is concentrating on carving meat and pouring wine, it might be best for him to sit near the sideboard and cellaret, or wherever else the bottles of wine for the evening are kept. In such circumstances only the hostess would be near the kitchen door. If the table is round there is of course no such thing as a head or a foot. If it is narrow and long there may be a case for placing the host halfway down one side and his hostess halfway down the other side opposite him. But if this sort of table is very long neither host nor hostess will be able to see, let alone converse

27

with or attend to the comfort of, their remoter guests, those seated at the very ends of the table. I am inclined to recommend the practice of some titled friends of mine in the country (I only mention that they are titled to show that the practice has the very highest social sanction): the seating of husband-host, wife-hostess, eldest-son-subsidiary-host and daughter-subsidiary-hostess round their enormous table (it can seat forty easily) in what one might call 'spheres of influence'. In other words, each member of the family is surrounded by eight to ten guests in the immediate vicinity and can make sure that each member of their particular groupuscule is being adequately fed, wined, watered and conversed with.

ASSORTING GUESTS

At a dinner party, even the largest kind, your guests are going to be thrown together for longer and in more intimate circumstances than in any other social gathering except a house party (of which more later) or seance. And perhaps a seance is not strictly speaking a social gathering. Anyway, whereas at a large stand-up party with people moving from one room to another, drinking, dancing, conversing and so on, it matters relatively little if you have two or more people present who dislike each other, at a dinner party it is fatal. I have been at a dinner party where two of the female guests were deadly foes. One of them spiked the other's drink with meths halfway through the evening, as well as engineering a nuisance telephone call to her enemy's boyfriend half an hour later. And the dinner party was a relatively informal one where we were seated all over the room on cushions and sofas eating from plates held on our laps, and one could sit where one liked or deemed prudent. True, the enmity between these two women was exceptional in its virulence (the one who spiked the other's drink had set fire to her victim's hair at a cocktail party a year or two earlier), but even if the hostility is confined to speech rather than action it can ruin an evening.

A really efficient-minded host will keep a card file on all his acquaintances, noting which topics should be shunned when X is in the house, mention of which anecdote will launch Y on his interminable life-story, what dietary fads Z is martyr to, how much hard work it is to draw P out, or shut Q up. Most of us rely on our memories, however, and think vaguely that 'So-and-so is a karate black belt while such-and-such a person once took a course in self-defence, so they ought to get on well together – or at least have something to talk about.' In any case human beings are seldom quite so predictable as to be reducible to a few notes on a card file. The awful truth lies elsewhere. It is this, that even identity of interests, let alone vague affinity, does not necessarily produce soul-mates.

One could even make a case for turning conventional wisdom on its head and arguing that the more people have in common intellectually and culturally the less likely they are to agree. A Saki short story, 'The Oversight', describes a hostess around 1913, at a time when the Balkan Wars were raging. Lady Prowche is arranging a house party. She takes the greatest care over the two guests staying the longest. She sets in train the profoundest inquiries beforehand and discovers that they are both Liberal, Evangelical, mildly opposed to female suffrage; they even approve the stewards' decision about that year's Derby winner, Craganour. All seems set fair. Yet they quarrel violently, even coming to blows. As Lady Prowche puts it when discussing the affair afterwards with a friend: 'My dear, we were fools not to have thought of it. One of them was pro-Greek and the other pro-Bulgar.' Given our current Balkan troubles, the story is particularly apposite.

So unless you know your guests very well indeed, and preferably have seen the potential dining-table neighbours you have in mind in action together already, do not be too swayed by the thought that they have interests in common. Conversely the oddest combinations sometimes establish a rapport. Other than when monomaniacs are diametrically opposed in their obsessions to other monomaniacs and *their* obsessions, where clearly close proximity will give rise to altercation, even violence, one might almost as well shuffle the guests like a pack of cards as plan any seating strategy with more than hope of a 10 per cent success. The single exception to this is the case of gropers, who should not be placed next to comely individuals of the opposite (or in certain sophisticated circles the same) sex. Of course the hardened groper is likely to clutch at anything under the table, rather like drowning men at straws, so that there is probably nothing you can do about it however hard you try. Your only consolation in such cases is that the distinctly plain guests either side of him might be undergoing a rare treat.

A rather different problem is to decide what proportion of your guests can be 'duty invitees', people whom you ask back because they asked you to dinner once but whom you don't much like, or relatives with whom you have nothing in common but blood ties, or colleagues you see quite enough of in office hours but to whom you owe a favour. I would have thought never more than one couple out of a total of four ought to fall into this category. And I would recommend diluting the mix still further if you detest both your cousin and his wife, as opposed to just detesting your cousin and being indifferent to his wife. Tempting though it may be to work off all your social obligations in a single evening, so that your guests have no link other than that you wouldn't be having them there if you didn't feel you had to, it is a recipe for utter social disaster. Social disaster doesn't necessarily come in melodramatic form, such as the dinner catching fire or the cook going mad or someone's chair collapsing under him. Any of those can be quite funny, though perhaps all three together would be a bit over-whelming. No, real social disaster is a much more low-key affair – awkward silences, stifled yawns, brittle attempts to get conversation going, muttered excuses for leaving early followed by hang-dog departure of a guest.

Invitations

Having drawn up a list of potential guests, and having prepared a second, rather smaller, list from which to supplement the first if anybody on it can't come, you set the invitation machinery in motion. Most people distribute invitations by phone. There is no prohibition on it. Not that current practice is in itself any great recommendation: almost everybody neglects to send thank-you letters after a dinner or party, but I would be failing in my duty if I condoned this. There are several reasons why it is better to send an invitation to a dinner party by letter. First, telephoning people can catch them at inconvenient moments – and some telephoners have an awkward knack of ringing just when one has got into the bath or warm milk is about to boil. Here is a case where the disappear-ance of the domestic servant has paradoxically made the use of a modern invention less desirable, not more so, because in former times one's manservant could answer the telephone whereas nowadays one is probably going to have to do it oneself. The same goes for those potential guests you telephone.

Secondly, not every telephonee has her diary right by her to check then and there whether she is free on the night you suggest. It is just as much a bore and waste of time for her to scour the house for it as it is for you to be left hanging on the phone while she scours. Thirdly, if any of your acquaintances don't want to come they can, if written to, concoct a good excuse at their leisure rather than stammer out some unconvincing nonsense on the spot, which will only hurt your feelings and embarrass them. Fourthly – a still more terrible thing to have to say, but equally realistic – they are more likely to take the invitation seriously and, having accepted, turn up, rather than forget it, or 'honour' a subsequent and more attractive invitation for the same night. Fifthly, it is easier for practical jokers to extend invitations by telephone than by post. The racehorse trainer Henry Cecil tells in his autobiography how the Newmarket trainer Hugh Sidebottom once impersonated Lord Fairhaven's butler over the phone and invited numerous other trainers in the area to dinner at Anglesey Abbey (Lord Fairhaven's then residence, near Cambridge). On arriving at the Abbey, dolled-up and with wives in tow, they were informed by the real butler that Lord Fairhaven was in France.

If you must make the first approach by telephone rather than post, it's not a bad idea to send a postcard a few days later confirming the time, date and place of the function. I assume you will have telephoned at least a week before the function; certainly the said postcard should arrive about forty-eight hours before the great day. My old friend Archie Gorst-Williams, doyen of charity entertainment organisers, regularly follows this practice and there's not much a charity entertainment organiser doesn't know about getting people to turn up at the right place and at the right time and in the right dress and in the right mood. His bread and butter depend on it.

It is rather a pity that invitations to dinner parties are no longer usually written or engraved on cards. They were in 1926, when Lady Troubridge was pontificating. Would some leader of fashion revive the trend? Sending cards of invitation to dinner parties has

Mr and Mrs Clive Adams

Mrs Charles Mosley
at Home

to remind Thursday, 4th June

~~R.S.V.P.~~

Ballaghmore Castle,
Borris-in-Ossory,
Co. Laois

Dinner
8 for 8·30pm

'At Home' card used as a reminder

several advantages. It would give harmless pleasure to recipients of such invitations to be able to sport them over the fireplace. (The usual objection to this with party invitations, that it hurts the feelings of friends of both host and invitee who may happen to catch sight of it and have not been invited, doesn't hold good for dinners as opposed to big parties, because nobody is expected to invite all their acquaintance to a single dinner party.) A dinner-party invitation card propped against the carriage clock or Dresden china goddess would help remind the busy of their social calendar. It would save the letter-writer having to labour for literary effect to dress up her invitation when all that is really necessary is the summons, an indication of what kind of dress to wear, a date and a time. As it is, people who send letters of invitation do tend to try to make them a little less curt than a mere recital of time, place and dress, as if issuing orders for a military operation. With female guests it is wise to be fairly specific about the degree of dressiness you are aiming for at your dinner party – unless you aim to mortify them by misleading them into under- or over-dressing.

Until such time as the card idea catches on again generally, instead of leading a rarefied existence in certain pockets of high formality, you should write in the second person, and perhaps add a touch of spice to the letter by hinting at an exciting guest list, though the brandishing of the specific name of a lion is a mite vulgar unless your guest of honour is royal, when it is only fair to other guests to let them know to whom they are going to be presented. (And here you would be advised to use a card.) Any mention of the fact that dinner is a meal, with food being ingested, was once thought vulgar too, but it is now socially OK to be a foodie, hence the topic can be referred to in a letter of invitation.

The letter should be written by the wife, if the hosts are married. Even if they are not, it is highly probable that the partner who already deals with the social correspondence of the household is the woman. The letter should be addressed to the wife if a married couple is invited, or for that matter the female partner if the couple live together unmarried. If the couple are of the same sex, write to the more feminine of the two. I am assuming that both partners in a cohabiting couple of long standing should be invited, however unorthodox their sexual preferences, but you may have ideas of your own on that and it is not a subject on which one can lay down hard and fast rules. Indeed, since quite refined, civilised and educated male homosexuals often have a taste for dangerous rent boys of little honesty and less learning and who are half their age, there is clearly a case for showing (or affecting) a degree of stuffiness of outlook and inviting just the senior partner. Here is an example of a typical letter to a wife or female partner:

Dear Mary,

Can you and John come to dinner on Wednesday 13 October at 8? An old friend is over from America and he has heard so much about you he very much wants to meet. I have just discovered a delicious new recipe – we had a tasting session of our own before inflicting it on guests, so don't fear you're being used as a guinea pig – and I'm dying to see what you think of it. Old friends and new recipe: the best combination. Don't bother to dress. I'm only going to wear my old suede cat-suit. If you want to ring me back to let me know if you can come I'll be in on Tuesday morning.

Love, Jane

And another, to someone you know less well:

Dear Mrs Bultitude,

We are organising a dinner party for Wednesday 13 October and very much hope you and your husband can come. It is to be a black-tie affair. Not that we set great store by formal dress, you understand, but a relatively grand occasion spurs the Cordon Bleu girl we usually get in to 'do' for us to give of her very best. Come at eight. And please don't feel you must go to the trouble of writing a reply. A phone call to let us know one way or the other will do.

Yours sincerely,
Jane Richards

I had Jane Richards add the bit explaining why she and her husband were stipulating black tie because some guests get a sinking feeling on being asked to a black-tie dinner at a private house, suspecting it may be pretentious. Roddy Llewellyn hints as much in his advice on how to be a perfect guest (*Daily Mail*, 16 October 1993), and there are few people in the world who have moved in more exalted circles than he has, so one must assume he knows what he's talking about.

You will note that Mrs Richards invited both guests for 8 p.m. In the country it might be a little earlier, 7.45 or even 7.30. In London it has been getting later and later for some years now, so that 8.30 or even occasionally 9 are not unknown. As people's working hours have got later, so the hours for dining have followed suit. You are within your rights to expect your guests to arrive up to half an hour later than the time given, but not any earlier than the time given and seldom at the exact hour. The timing of invitations is an odd thing. Since telephone invitations came in, the one hour at which it is thought naive for one to arrive at one's host's is the very one specified.

If you want to impress on your guests a specific time for arriving and then going into dinner, you could write 8.15 for 8.30, or some variation thereof, on the invitation. (This constitutes yet another argument for sending written invitations.) Remember that for any guests who normally live abroad the time mentioned in the invitation may denote a completely different schedule from what it does in Britain. A friend of mine who studied in Paris for a year while at university was once asked to a dinner party and bidden to come at 7.30. Assuming this would mean 8 in practice she arrived at the latter hour, to find that the family she was dining with were still in the process of taking baths, getting dressed and so on. In those circles at that time 7.30 meant more like 9.

I have yet to hear of an invitation to a dinner party being sent by fax and suspect that reports of it are what they call an urban myth. Still, the idea might take off in a year or two, so what about it? First, the fax would have to be typed or printed out from one's word processor, otherwise the current poor reproduction of hand-written faxes would run the risk of it being illegible. Secondly, you don't know who's going to be the reader of a fax, whereas you do know who you should be speaking to with a phone call or, one hopes, who will be reading your letter. Thirdly, a fax can be just as intrusive at an awkward moment as a telephone call. Fourthly, there's no guarantee anyone will read it; it may spew out of the fax machine the other end when the entire household is away (this is

---

Colonel and Mrs John Mustard

Sir John and Lady Falstaff

request the pleasure of * *your company*
at Dinner
on Tuesday, 29th February
at 8 for 8.30 o'clock

R.S.V.P.
  2300 Cadogan Square,   *Black tie*
  SW1Z 4QS

---

* or 'honour of'

Invitation to a formal dinner party

the obverse of my second point, really). No, faxed invitations don't make sense.

Note that even if you send a letter of invitation, you imply by your request for a telephoned reply that the invitee would be over-punctilious to write back rather than give an immediate response. It might be argued that since you have started the correspondence she ought to continue it in the same form, but that overlooks the likelihood of postal delays holding up her reply. Of course, a postal delay may affect your original invitation too. But if you live in a district where the post is irregular you can allow for it by sending the invitation a day or two earlier. The invitee should realise that the fact you are putting yourself to the trouble of organising hospitality quite voluntarily demands as rapid a reply as possible. If your invitee doesn't phone back within a reasonable time after you have written – say three days maximum – you can then ring up and express anxiety lest the original letter has got lost in the post. This gently lets off the hook a sloppy invitee, one who has failed to answer your invitation promptly, and at the same time, if she has any conscience at all, piles a bit of pressure on her to accept it. There is no need to feel guilty about applying pressure. All invitations are in some sense applying social pressure and ones from royalty are in the nature of a command, which must be obeyed at the expense of pre-existing engagements.

If your invitee is not on the phone it may be because he is so poverty-stricken he should be entertained in special circumstances. For instance, you might send your car to pick him up before the dinner party and get it to take him back afterwards as well. Alternatively he may not be on the phone because he is so Bohemian he has forgotten to pay the bill and the phone has been cut off. In that case he may not be very good at turning up on the right day and at the right time and you must plan accordingly. Some semi-recluses and mechanophobes are not on the phone out of deliberate choice. I say semi-recluses rather than full recluses, because such people can sometimes be enticed out to dinner if you lay on their transport to the extent described above; my father was just such a one. Another type of semi-recluse can be induced to accept hospitality if the host comes to the semi-recluse's house laden with food and perhaps drink as well, prepares it in the semi-recluse's house, serves it up, washes up afterwards and then

36

goes away again. This type of semi-recluse is clearly so selfish he will only be tolerable company if preternaturally amusing. Oddly enough some semi-recluses are, at least for an hour or two.

If your invitee has gone abroad or into hospital or down to a country health farm to lose weight or something of that sort, the fact will become apparent when you try to make the follow-up phone call a day or two after sending your letter. Two weeks in advance is about the right length of time to send out dinner invitations, though I note with interest that Lady Troubridge recommends up to three weeks during 'the season'. Fair enough. And some diners out are so popular they inhabit a 'season' all of their own the whole year round, hence have to be invited weeks, perhaps months in advance. Henry James is said to have dined out nearly every night during his early winters in London. Some hostesses plan a good deal further ahead and give invitees a choice of dates, which puts a different kind of pressure on them. That may strike you as unfair, for if someone truly does not wish to turn an acquaintance with you into friendship they should be allowed, as it were, to slide out of any obligations before they are incurred.

There is, however, one very cogent objection to sending out written or printed invitations to dinner, even if you follow them up with a phone call a day or two later. It is that if the invitee was away when the invitation arrived and gets home only a day or two before your dinner party, he may be perfectly within his rights to accept the invitation even though from his point of view it is a last-minute one. Meanwhile you, of course, got no answer when you phoned him two days after sending out the invitation in the first place and have probably invited a substitute. I do not think this sort of awkwardness makes the sending out of invitations wholly impracticable, for in such circumstances you are probably having a large dinner party and you may well have to juggle with numbers towards the last moment anyway. (Clearly the more guests you invite the greater the likelihood of last-minute cancellations.) I have already pointed out that odd numbers and a preponderance of one sex over the other need not be regarded as ruination. Certainly a genuine late acceptance of the sort just indicated must be honoured by you as hostess.

RENEGING GUESTS

If hospitality is traditionally bound up with the sacred, then the obligation on a guest to attend a function to which he has accepted an invitation is absolute. The Duke of Dorset in *Zuleika Dobson* is obliged to leave Zuleika's side on his last night on earth (he has just postponed his imminent suicide, planned out of unrequited love for her, from that day to the morrow, with her sanction) because, though he loves her, he has a prior engagement. She is displeased that he can place his social duty above the pleasure of dining in her company. She asks him what he would have done about his prior engagement if she hadn't let him off his pledge to die for her that day. Is it not terribly incorrect to stand up his guests, she inquires? 'Death,' he retorts, 'cancels all engagements.'

I cannot wholly agree. Unpremeditated death may do so, but strictly speaking his original decision to kill himself in such a way, or rather on such a date, as to contravene the laws of hospitality was underbred. Of course in today's world there crop up many other reasons – some of them already noted – why your guest may not be able to attend. He should alert you as soon as possible, even if it's on the very night of the dinner party. Not everyone will, though. Some people will just not turn up on the night. If they are aboard a hijacked aeroplane they may be unable either to turn up or to telephone, but there are few other circumstances which justify non-notification, particularly as mobile phones are now so widespread. And I would just warn would-be backsliders who try the hijacked aeroplane excuse the following week, when they unexpectedly meet their would-have-been hostess in the Food Hall at Harrods, that skyjacking is now almost unknown. It never happened on El Al anyway, so don't claim you were skyjacked on your way to or from Tel Aviv.

If an absentee is proven to have let you down when he could have done otherwise, you must make up your mind whether you value his company so much that you will overlook the breach. If not you should consider dropping him, at any rate for a time. The social cut has gone out of fashion, but everything comes round again sooner or later. A few cuts shrewdly aimed by fashionable hostesses against those who really deserve it would go far towards restoring a more courteous society.

RENEGING HOSTS

What if you have to cancel your own dinner party? Or rather, in what circumstances are you justified in cancelling your own dinner party? It was one of the advantages of Victorian times that a death in the family – almost any death, of no matter how remote a relative – constituted good grounds for aborting social activity. In Ireland it still does, at least for business. The back page of *The Irish Times* is awash every day with announcements that such-and-such a drapery store or solicitor's office will be closed next Monday out of respect for the lately deceased mother of the junior partner. It may be because Mary Killen, the *Spectator*'s social arbiter, is Irish that she mischievously in the 24 July 1993 issue recommends that a hostess who can't face going ahead with her dinner party should pretend she's in mourning. But I think I should warn you that the 'Dear Mary' column purportedly written by Mary Killen often has its tongue so firmly in its cheek that it gets its pronouncements a bit twisted. For my part I can't countenance crying off from hosting a dinner party because you 'can't face it'. For the most part you must just grit your teeth and get on with it.

Agreed, there are certain cases where cancellation is in order. Funnily enough, the ones that most people would agree were permissible are domestic and rather utilitarian: the pipes bursting, the central-heating system breaking down, power failure. Some people would say the sudden death of a parent, your child, your spouse or your live-in lover is justification for cancelling.

The trouble is, there's a vocal faction which argues that it's better for one to be distracted from emotional trauma by activity, including social activity. In my own case I know I have never entertained on such a scale and so often as in the first few months after my father's suicide, and that this intense burst of social activity was a balm. The point is, you must judge what makes cancelling permissible, not just according to the old Victorian rules which invoked something as personally remote as the death of a second cousin once removed, but by the more self-centred considerations prevailing today, such as 'Will I feel better or worse if I throw my friends over?' Even for someone as self-centred as modern urban man it's not a question with an easy answer. The thought that you can't face going ahead with a dinner party, the bitter regret that you have invited a whole horde of guests round to invade your privacy in your own house, particularly as it is now revealed there's going to be a good movie on television that evening and you've never yet managed to learn to work the video recorder, occurs to all of us sooner or later. This brings us back to what I said earlier about entertaining generally. If you really and truly don't enjoy it, don't do it. But most people do enjoy it eventually, even if they sometimes have second thoughts soon after issuing invitations, usually when full realisation of the amount of effort involved hits them. Try to remember how you always snapped out of the momentary feeling of panic before.

Utilitarian domestic problems are easier to cope with than emotional traumas when deciding for or against going ahead. Some people revel in their ability to transcend a crisis such as the breakdown of the central-heating system. If you are a bad cook a power failure might even be the answer to your problems when giving dinner to friends: send out to Wilton's for smoked salmon and oysters, to a good Indian or Chinese restaurant for a takeaway hot course, ideally one that the restaurant will deliver, and get your friends to supply the wine on the grounds that the temperature control and ventilation system of your own cellar has gone to pot.

If you are well off, you should even regard it as being bound up with your social prestige to be able to rise above such domestic trivialities as a cut in the power supply. I once attended a luncheon party on one of the oldest plantations in Jamaica, a property that had been in the same hands since the English conquest in Cromwellian times, when the cook went mad, running amok with a cleaver just as we were arriving. I do not know whether she was a good cook or not but the meal was a write-off and it is possible that the lady of the house, like the Anglo-Indian memsahibs who came home to Tunbridge Wells from the Punjab after Independence in 1947, didn't herself know even how to boil an egg. Anyway, we guests were invited to splash around in the swimming pool – there must have been about eight of us – while the family sent in to Kingston for a new cook. Meanwhile, for three or four hours we were served Cuba Libres in silver goblets from the diving board by liveried black servants. Lunch, when it came, could not have been better.

Decamping from your own dinner party, even if it's already underway, is still worse than cancelling it because you 'can't face it'. This is so obviously one of the most heinous social offences that I would hardly bother to mention it if the specific case I have in mind didn't illustrate how fatally easy it is for a hostess to get a reputation for spending too much time in the kitchen. Anyway, one of my dearest friends did once behave in this very fashion. Her guests had all arrived. She had seated them. She had prepared the meal. Being methodical and efficient she had placed the first course on the table before seating her guests, while the second course was so planned that the guests could serve themselves. She is a superlative cook, and the guests knew it. They were in for a treat. They unfolded their napkins. Meanwhile their hostess suddenly recollected an invitation she had received some days before to an entirely different dinner party to be held the same evening. Plying her guests copiously with alcohol and telling them repeatedly that they were to treat the place as if it were their own, help themselves and so on, she hurried from the room, and indeed from the flat.

Thinking she was spending her time in the kitchen, the guests, who after all had been explicitly told to stay in the dining room (actually the living room as it's a small flat), didn't notice that she had entirely disappeared until about half an hour later. Even then they thought she had just popped out to get more coriander or another bottle of wine. By the time it became obvious she had left for the rest of the evening, the good food and wine had done most of their work and the episode seemed merely funny. So while I don't commend this sort of behaviour, I do point out that it is just about technically practicable. And of course the central dilemma of whether to attend a dinner party one has accepted an invitation for or go ahead with one's own dinner party arranged absentmindedly for the same evening is unresolvable in any other way. Certainly many resident hostesses spend so much time in the kitchen that they have almost no existence as denizens of the dining room. Do not become one of them.

Receiving Guests

Before you even seat your guests at table you will receive them. Unless you have servants to do this you should greet them at the front door, or even, if you live in a house with a cramped drive and little turning space and your guests are arriving by car, out of doors altogether. It is wise in such circumstances to plan where such-and-such a guest will park his car, taking into account the likely order of arrival and departure, size and manoeuvrability of cars and so on. In winter turn on any outside lights before guests arrive, sweep or get the gardener's boy to sweep any snow off the drive, salt it against skid-inducing ice and so on. If guests are coming to your house for the first time, send them beforehand a sketch map of the immediate environs, together with printed instructions. Now that word processors are so common you can easily have such details on file and run a print-out for every new guest. Once your guests are inside the house you should show them where they can leave their coats and where the lavatories are. The euphemism 'I'll show you where to wash your hands' is still the regular way of effecting this. 'Would you like to powder your nose?', said to women, is now so archaic as to sound facetious.

The next stage of the evening will take place in the sitting or drawing room. You should introduce each new guest to the assembled company as he arrives. Lady Troubridge deprecates this as swamping the newcomer with too many names to be taken in all at once. She has a point. With a large number of people to meet one cannot easily remember all the new names, and there is the difficulty of catching the names properly in the first place. Even guests with acute hearing frequently find it impossible when introduced in a crowded room with a babble of conversation drowning out all but the most clearly enunciated consonants. In Lady Troubridge's day it seems one was rather niggardly with introductions anyway. For instance, at her eighteen-guest dinner parties she introduced a guest only to two or three people. That strikes me as deplorable. It is certainly not the custom now, not for a number as small as eighteen at any rate. Clearly a banquet for fifty or more is a different matter, but these days such large numbers are likely to be dealt with at an official or corporate level, or if in a private house in the form of a buffet supper at a dance or similarly loose-structured function, when guests are to a large extent expected to make themselves known to each other.

The difficulty of a guest's remembering every fellow guest's name on first being introduced is not insuperable. If politicians, who are generally of low intelligence, and royalty can manage, the rest of us ought to be able to. It's just a question of practice. If one is going to be a frequent diner-out one must go into training. It is possible to build up your memory by practising on dummies, first getting a friend to introduce you to them while they have name tags attached. You then leave the room and re-enter a few minutes later when your friend has removed the name tags. Now see how many you can remember. Do this over and over again until word-perfect with up to forty or fifty people. If you are unable to procure dummies or unwilling to go to the expense, then dolls, cardboard cut-outs or even cushions will do, provided the cushions are differentiated from each other in pattern and size in roughly the way humans are in appearance.

A similar problem is that of the host who after a few drinks finds he cannot remember the names of all his guests, even though he has known every man jack of them since they were at university together thirty years before. If you as host find yourself in that position say vaguely, 'You know each other, don't you?' and then smite your forehead with your hand and exclaim 'God, I've left the grill on!' and rush from the room. Ten to one the guests will have introduced themselves to each other by the time you return five minutes later.

The rest of us just muddle along as best we can. Nobody can seriously mind being asked a few minutes after an introduction what their name is, whereas calling Sebastian Bulteel 'Septimus Bultitude' might cause deathless offence. On the other hand if you have a surname like Plunkett-Ernle-Erle-Drax you would be pretty curmudgeonly if you took umbrage every time a new acquaintance asked you for it over again. My old friend Christopher Wesolowski has got so tired of having to spell his name out to sub-literate morons every time he orders something over the phone that he calls himself Christopher West, and perhaps at very hectic social events one might follow the same procedure. But at a dinner party I think you must use the proper name of a guest when introducing him to the others. If he wanted to change it he would have done so years ago.

When introducing a guest you already know to your husband or wife or other member of your family for the first time it is only fair to spell out the relationship. With lovers it is more difficult, unless

43

you are one of those facetiously inclined people who can get away with saying 'This is my better half Bill/Rose.' From the point of view of the guest, who may be new to the house, 'better half' might mean current boy/girlfriend or spouse. A similar problem is when the host and most of her guests are old friends, each of them perhaps with a nickname. The guest who is new to the house keeps on wondering who this person Pixie is that they're all talking about – likewise who on earth is BoBo, Binghy (or was it Dinghy?), Trowser and Fluffles? – given that she herself has only been introduced to a Rosemary, a Margaret, a Sally and a Laura. Can it be a man? But then all the men were clearly spelled out as Rollo, Tom, James, Gregory and Hubert. A good hostess would turn to her new guest early in the evening and explain who the nicknames applied to.

The old rule of asking a woman whether you can introduce a man to her, rather than just treating two people who have not met before as being on an equal footing regardless of their sex, is now pretty well obsolete. But if one of your guests is immensely distinguished and fairly old it is best to lead other guests up to him and introduce them in the old conventional fashion.

In these democratic times one is often introduced to peers as if they were commoners, for example: 'This is John Loamshire,' for John Bohun, Earl of Loamshire. I confess I have handled an introduction this way myself on occasion, though my excuse is that it was in the Republic of Ireland, where the peerage has no constitutional or official standing. In any case the peer in question had always conducted himself in a friendly and unstandoffish fashion to all and sundry. Nevertheless I had got it wrong, for later in the evening (it was a party with numerous guests milling around promiscuously, not a dinner) I heard him introduce himself to another guest by his title only ('Loam-shire'). If the title is a sonorous one like 'Dunsandle and Clanconal', the person to whom the peer is making himself known can scarcely not be aware that he is meeting either a bishop or a peer. But if the title is monosyllabic and vaguely similar in sound to a forename (as in (Lord) Brent, for instance) there is a danger that the peer may be mistaken for one of those people who like to introduce themselves by their Christian names or forenames only.

44

The trouble is, you never know who is going to come over pompous on inheriting a title. A friend of mine had known someone – let us call him the Hon. Julian Chinless – for twenty years. One day he inherited his papa's barony of Theyne (not a very old one, a Ramsay MacDonald creation, in fact) and a few weeks later she introduced him at one of her regular parties as 'Julian Ch—, sorry, Theyne.' He leant forward to the person being introduced to him and said '*Lord* Theyne, actually.' The point is that in all the years she had known him hitherto he had been the epitome of urbanity, intelligence, charm, wit and gentle self-deprecatory humour. So you must sound out your noble acquaintances well before introducing people to them at dinners, drinks parties, balls and so on. The greater the self-regard of the person in question, the harder it is to broach the topic beforehand in a non-shy-making way. I can only suggest getting your peer in for a few drinks in advance of everyone else and then, when alcohol has softened him up, putting your pretty, rather goofy adolescent daughter up to asking him the $64,000 question of how he likes to be introduced.

PRE-DINNER DRINKS

You or your servant should offer drinks. The nature of pre-dinner drinks varies enormously. It is a mistake to ask guests what they would like if you do not have a great variety of drinks on hand. Instead say, 'Would you like red wine or white?' or whatever your range consists of.

Sherry as a pre-dinner drink has become almost quaint in the most up-to-the-minute metropolitan circles, but it retains a certain staying power in the country. (A word of warning to guests here: if you ask for or are offered sherry in the backwoods it will very likely be medium dry or sweet, and served at something near blood heat, rather than the ice-cold pale Fino you would expect in town or your favourite *tapas* bar in Andalucia.)

Nicholas Coleridge, managing director of Condé Nast magazines (the publishers of *Vogue* and *House and Garden*), recently wrote an article in which he recorded his surprise at anybody still asking for gin and tonic instead of wine as a pre-dinner drink. But he moves in such advanced metropolitan circles that the rest of us may think his surprise a touch affected. Gin and tonic is certainly

45

the most popular spirit-based aperitif, but you need feel no shame in not stocking it.

Champagne or a good sparkling wine should stifle all criticism over your lack of broad choice. But take care to serve champagne in narrow flutes rather than those galumphing great sorbet dishes – so shallow they spill the fluid easily, not to mention letting the wine go flat sooner – that second-rate caterers try to fob off on their customers at weddings. True, some people dislike champagne, but they will hardly dare admit it loudly and you will have soft drinks on hand anyway to quench the car-drivers' thirst. Alternatively you can serve champagnophobes some of the wine you have put aside for dinner. To avoid your guests' taking alcohol on an empty stomach you should also provide something to nibble on – nuts or cheese straws or whatever – with the pre-dinner drinks.

If you are planning the layout of your drawing room from scratch it is a good idea to install a fridge behind some suitable disguise such as a louvred door, whether at floor or eye level. The enormous success of the parties given by my old (and now sadly deceased) friend the second Mrs Randolph Churchill was in no small measure due to such a precaution. That way you can keep wine cool in the room in which you serve it to your guests. The usual alternatives are far less satisfactory. In hot weather any ice you have on hand in a separate receptacle such as a bucket will melt very quickly and wine bottles in coolers invariably drip water over everything when taken out for pouring, however hard you try to drape them in cloths. Even if you keep a servant to swathe the bottle in a cloth and pour it out, he is bound to spill a few drops of water in the struggle to keep every thirsty guest's glass topped up.

The subject of cocktails is better treated in a separate book all of its own. I would only observe that if you are too poor or mean to stock real champagne – and even real champagne can swiftly pall on your guests unless it is of a very good, hence prohibitively expensive, marque or vintage – an easy way to make Veuve du Vernay or Spanish sparkling go further is to concoct champagne cocktails. Evelyn Waugh, writing in his first travel book *Labels*, gives the standard formula: soak a sugar cube in angostura bitters then roll (it, not you) in red pepper, pop it in the bottom of a glass, cover with brandy then top up with champagne (in the case under discussion just now Spanish sparkling or Veuve du Vernay). I leave the description of how this tastes to the master's pen: read it in Waugh's collected travel pieces entitled *When the Going Was Good*.

Some whisky drinkers detest ice in their glass. Indeed it used to be a sure sign of whether you were dealing with a Britisher or an American that the former would drink his whisky un-iced, the latter preferring his buried under a miniature glacier. Make sure you know which way your guests lean before sloshing in whisky over the rocks.

Almost all red wines are the better for being opened some time, even as little as half an hour, before drinking. The exception occurs with those of enormous grandeur and antiquity, which I assume you will be sufficiently reverent towards to bone up beforehand on the precise method of serving each one individually, having regard to vintage, room temperature, cellarage and so on; if you suspect the wine is a little past its best open it only a few minutes before you drink it.

Unsophisticated people often prefer sweetish wines. (I believe the loathsome Blue Nun is still the top-selling wine in Britain, or somewhere near it.) Beer is popular in hot weather. Another good drink is Buck's Fizz. There was a correspondence in the *Spectator* recently about the correct recipe for this. The barman's lips are

| Champagne flute | Hock glass | Claret or burgundy glass | Sherry glass |

sealed at Buck's Club, which is where the more authoritative of two schools of thought on the subject maintains it was invented. Accordingly, we cannot be absolutely sure. No matter. For ordinary purposes any dryish sparkling wine, even one of the ever-so-slightly sweet Astis from Italy or sparkling whites from Germany, will do provided the orange juice is absolutely fresh. That means you must buy lots of oranges and squeeze them yourself. The proportions of wine to juice are half and half. An anecdotal word of warning: an acquaintance of mine who many years ago was an MP representing a remote part of England once served Buck's Fizz to a party of constituents. The trouble was that the region in question had a long temperance tradition. Not all the guests realised at the time that they were being served an alcoholic drink, and those who did were contemptuous that it was not stronger. He was not returned at the next general election.

Always make sure you have soft drinks to hand for your car-driving guests, for example tomato juice, vegetable juice, cranberry juice, tonic water (my friends who drink tonic water straight tell me nothing but Schweppes will do – no supermarket chain own brand, then). Some even of your most bibulous old friends may suddenly have decided to go on the wagon. Besides, some soft drinks ready in the fridge tomorrow morning will help mightily with your own state of dehydration. Cut slices of lemon, or better still lime, on a dish can be inserted into drinking glasses to improve the appearance of Coca-Cola and glasses of water, whether sparkling or still.

All drinks, whether intrinsically sticky or not, tend to leave dark rings on table surfaces. Guests will seldom remember to use the coasters you have provided after their first swig of alcohol, so bear this fact in mind when serving drinks surrounded by your most precious mahogany tables and either cover them with cloths or resign yourself to many hours with polish afterwards trying to clean the surfaces.

Late Guests

Often, all too often, some guest or other will arrive late. Not just later than everyone else – someone's got to be last unless two or more lots of guests arrive simultaneously, like actors in an under-rehearsed play. I mean scandalously late by absolute

48

standards. My own practice in such circumstances is not to spoil everyone else's enjoyment by doggedly prolonging the pre-dinner drinks but to go into dinner only a relatively short time after you had planned to do so. It is curious how often the act of starting the meal without the tardy guest will conjure up that guest, whereas if you hang around in the drawing room he never turns up for hours, perhaps not at all. The added beauty of proceeding with the timing of the original plan is that the guest who is scandalously late is too apologetic at finding everyone else already eating to reflect how wrong it was of you to have started dinner without him – if it was wrong, which I would always sturdily dispute. If you still feel guilty about going ahead without him you could put all the clocks in the house forward by an hour and point to their faces accusingly if he starts to object. The evidence of several of your clocks will outweigh the evidence of his single wristwatch and he will become too flustered to put up any kind of fight.

Length of Pre-dinner Drinks Session

Forty-five minutes or at most an hour is sufficient for the pre-dinner drinks stage of the evening. Indeed, any longer and you risk producing acidity in the digestive system, to say nothing of extreme drunkenness. Even if you think drunkenness is a desirable state of affairs to aim for at dinner parties, it's only fair to induce it during the meal rather than beforehand. The absurdity of hanging around for long periods before dining is seen in America, where it is, or has been, all too common. I have been at a dinner party there where the hostess was so drunk after four hours of downing whiskeys and Bourbons on an empty stomach that she kept the fire going by ladling raw kerosene on to it from a can kept handily nearby and when it came to sitting down at table to eat she hacked out food from the deep-freeze and plonked it down, still frozen so solid that it clattered metallically on the plates, in front of us. Moreover several of the guests were too drunk to be aware of the rock-like solidity of the food and did their teeth irreparable damage in trying to eat it.

Glasses

You may find you are short of glasses just as you are about to move from the drawing room into the dining room. It's amazing

49

how many households do wind up in such circumstances, what with the inevitable breakages over the years and the way guests put their first drink down somewhere, mislay it, and have to be given a fresh drink in a second glass, one you have had to filch from the dining room. It may therefore happen that your guests need to take their pre-dinner drinks to the table with them, there to have the glasses that held aperitifs replenished with wine. If so, arrange for the glasses to be rinsed out between the pre-dinner drinks session and the meal itself, unless the wine is the same for both. Glance round the drawing room just as you all move into the dining room to make sure everyone has taken his glass.

GOING INTO DINNER
The ritual of men taking women in, and in correct order of precedence, is all but obsolete. Not quite, however. The late Sir Iain Moncreiffe used to tell how his friend Bobby Corbett (a peer's son, as will become apparent) always darted ahead of him through the dining-room door at dinner parties, saying gleefully, 'Hons before Baronets.' However, the very fact that the subject could be raised on such occasions (we are talking of rural Scotland, where as I said earlier precedence is still largely observed) suggests it was seen as early as the 1980s as a quaint survival. Had it been still fully in force it would not have been commented on. For further information see the Appendix on precedence.

The Dinner Party as a Meal
You have chosen the number and identity of your guests. You have prepared the ground for serving them aperitifs in the drawing room. You still have to plan the meal itself. Back, then, to the dining room. Back also in time, to a day or two before the dinner party.

EQUIPMENT

Crockery
You need a set of main-course plates, the larger the better, though always having regard to what your dishwasher or kitchen sink can accommodate, the size of your dining table and the likely number of guests. You need a set of side dishes and a set of soup plates.

Theoretically, either of these may be able to double as pudding plates. If you serve something runny for pudding you will need to use plates like your soup ones, with raised sides. If something solid, flattish plates will do. But remember that in summer what may start as a solid course, ice cream for example, will change into a runny one as the meal proceeds, especially with slow eaters. On the other hand you may have problems if you try to make a set of a certain kind of plate do double duty. For instance, do you have the staff or the energy to take away the side plates, which in any case may be needed for cheese and which will certainly have been used by inveterate smokers as ashtrays from early on in the dinner, wash them and return them later on as pudding plates?

In time you will lose pieces of crockery through breakage. So when choosing a pattern on getting married or otherwise setting up house for the first time, go for something you can be pretty sure you'll be able to match, even though it may be several years before you have to do the matching. If you doubt that any pattern of china will be in stock that long but don't want or can't afford to acquire more than you need for the present, choose a range with lots of intricate pattern and in a colour such as blue, which is popular with china manufacturers. Assorted plates in several patterns can look perfectly acceptable provided they are of about the same size and shape and of the same general decorative type.

Serving dishes, tureens, sugar bowls, cream jugs, gravy and sauce boats and so on need not be of the same pattern as the rest of the crockery. Indeed, if they are of a precious metal like silver they may be far superior. But if money is no object and the design of every single item in the range is good, by all means get everything in the same pattern.

Servant Substitutes

Let us assume you have a fairly generous-sized dining room. In that case it will probably be rectangular. One of the basic items of furniture in such a room is a sideboard placed along one of the walls. Properly employed, that sideboard is worth about two and a half servants, for it can accommodate on its surface cutlery, dishes, decanters, future courses and warming devices to keep said future courses hot where necessary. This means you need not, if servant-less, be springing to your feet every five minutes. It means that, even if you are blessed with servants, they need not be interrupting the flow of conversation every few minutes by interposing stretched arms between couples involved in a delightful tête-à-tête in order to offer vegetables, sauces, bread, wine or second helpings. So few people have servants nowadays that many dinner guests are likely to find them disconcerting, if not downright embarrassing, when they are in constant attendance. If that looks likely to be the case, it is better to confine servants to laying the table, cooking the meal and clearing away afterwards. If, on the other hand, all your guests are among the rich and leisured and above all confident in their membership of both categories the problem does not arise. In such a case you can if you wish strengthen the servant-to-guest ratio to the extent of placing one attendant behind each guest.

A proper sideboard has cupboard doors in it which will be stocked with ice buckets for wine, humidors for storing cigars, cigars themselves, cigar-cutters, brandies, spittoons and song-sheets (I will explain the significance of this last item in due course). Cellarets are usually attractive pieces of furniture as well as useful. Acquire at least two.

There are various types of hot plate. Some work by electricity and may do no more than keep empty plates warm. Others are powered by night-lights or stubby candles. Whichever sort you get it should surely be capable of keeping a serving dish full of food bubbling away throughout a prolonged meal (particularly break-fast where guests may straggle in at all times and dawdle over their food reading newspapers).

Serving food on plates that are heated beforehand is something of an obsession in this country. It is thought less important in France, where they reckon that if the food is hot enough it doesn't matter what the temperature of the dish is. In this matter the distance of your dining room from the kitchen is probably decisive in predisposing you in favour of or – forgive the pun – rendering you lukewarm towards such devices. At Blenheim Palace they inform sightseers that the dining room is 440 yards, or a quarter of a mile, from the kitchens. If that is indeed the case no Duke of Marlborough can ever have had a hot meal without the assistance of hot plates. Unfortunately most of them (hot plates, not Dukes of Marlborough) are desperately ugly objects. Still more so are those trolleys in which one can place a whole meal to be kept warm and which are heated by electricity.

If you live in a London street house constructed almost any time between 1700 and 1850 it will probably have a basement kitchen underneath the dining room. Similarly with a parsonage or glebe house in the country, particularly in Ireland, where the kitchens and sculleries were almost invariably put halfway below the surface of the ground with the dining room immediately overhead and the two connected by a dumb waiter. However quaint you may consider a dumb waiter, I would urge that you think very carefully before blocking off the shaft, assuming that you are lucky enough to live in a house which hasn't been totally remodelled long ago. Dumb waiters can be extraordinarily useful, not just as a means of hauling food up from the kitchen to the dining room but for sending dirty dishes back. Indeed, they can be used for transferring whole hosts of implements, from kindling and coals from the coal hole to the dining room for use in the open fireplace to silver table ornaments which have been polished in the scullery down below. The only trouble with dumb waiters is that they easily conduct any fire that may break out from the lower regions of a house to the upper ones. I heard a short while ago of a house in Regent's Park that was gutted in that way. The owners had had it on the market for £1.4 million just before the disaster. Luckily the property was so sought-after that they still managed to get £1.2 million for what was by then a mere site only a few months later, and this despite the fact that it was a shortish Crown lease rather than freehold. That's Regent's Park for you.

Unless the room is very large, and providing you have adequate central heating, an open fire, no matter how ornamental the fireplace, is inadvisable on the grounds that it will roast the back of whoever among your guests is nearest it. Henry Cecil, whose autobiography I have mentioned earlier, tells how he was once host to the Queen Mother when the lights fused in the middle of dinner. So he suggested a move to the drawing room to finish the meal. There he offered her what he took to be the best seat. She accepted. After a few minutes he noticed perspiration break out on her brow, like one of his own thoroughbreds after an arduous gallop. He had put her too near the fire.

As for lighting, I suppose there can hardly be anyone not aware of the benefits of candlelight. But you should remember to keep a supply of fresh candles to hand. The original ones burn down quickly when one is enjoying a dinner party, and it's a bore having to stumble to one's feet halfway through a piece of conversational raillery just because a candle gutters out, then be obliged to ransack the house distractedly for a replacement. Candlelight softens your own and your guests' facial features, gleams on old silver and jewellery, invests even the most banal oil on the wall with Rembrandtian chiaroscuro and warms the air. But if someone has to dish out food on a sideboard or side table or your guests are asked to serve themselves, that particular spot should be provided with adequate electric lighting, either from a standard lamp or a large table lamp.

Shape of Table

The dining-room table will tend to be rectangular or have curved ends. The latter sort is preferable since it is more flexible. At long and wide tables the people at corners become isolated. The sort of long, narrow table used in the seventeenth century works much better, but this is a relatively rare and expensive item of furniture if genuine. If sham, disguise with tablecloth. Clearly tables with leaves for extending or diminishing the size are preferable to fixed-length ones because within the obvious limits you can seat as many or as few guests as you like. Tables supported by single columns branching out to four or more supporting feet are decorative but can be an infernal nuisance when it comes to drawing up chairs which are constructed with cross-supports placed low down at their front. I mention all this principally for the benefit of those furnishing a dining room from scratch. Most of us have no choice, however. We have inherited some pieces, others are wedding presents, or we must make do with what we can afford to buy, not what we would like to buy. Chairs should be comfortable – upholstered for preference; one spends a long time seated at a good dinner party – but not too heavy to move with ease. When people are seated on chairs drawn up to the table there should be room to move round the room behind them. This is particularly important in the country, where so many of one's friends are permanently confined to wheelchairs as a result of a nasty tumble in the hunting field.

Tablecloth
I have already mentioned briefly the subject of tablecloths. Whether to use one or not on the dining table is largely a matter of taste, though influenced by the quality of one's table surface when bare. An antique-dealer friend of mine still shudders at the memory of a guest I introduced to his house who up-ended a steaming sauce boat over his £25,000 mahogany dining table; all the french-polishers in Chelsea couldn't restore it to its pristine gleam. A tablecloth might have saved the table from much of the damage it sustained on that occasion but would probably not have prevented it entirely. Other factors to be considered, as well as the skill of one's guests in conveying food and drink to their mouths, are the temperature of the dishes to be placed on the table and the greasiness of sauces. Perhaps the single most decisive aspect nowadays is the reluctance of the average householder to launder huge items of linen such as tablecloths at all, given cramped accommodation and the difficulty of drying, starching and ironing the thing afterwards.

Generally speaking, the larger the dining table the less likely it is to be of top quality, hence the greater the need for a tablecloth to hide the imperfections of the furniture. Aesthetic arguments against the use of tablecloths exist as well as those for it. Table settings can be arranged very prettily, but although you would expect it to be otherwise the prettiness tends to stand out less against a tablecloth. A more practical disadvantage of tablecloths is that they cover up unevenness of surface and any dining table that seats more than six is likely to have a join somewhere on its surface, either for a leaf or folding flap. All too often I have seen a wine glass or sauce boat topple over and spill when placed on a tablecloth that covered an unsuspected break in the surface. On the whole, then, the anti-tablecloth faction has it. The one exception is where you are conducting a dinner party at which you know (or suspect) a good deal of amorous intrigue is going to occur. In that case make sure your tablecloth has a generous fall over the edge so that your guests can fondle each other unseen.

Doing without a tablecloth doesn't mean you have to risk your polished wood surface being scorched or stained with dark rings or smears of grease. Bring on the doily. First let me scotch the absurd notion that the doily is somehow non-U, naff, Essex, suburban, *petit bourgeois*. No less an authority than Baron (later Sir) Georg von Franckenstein, whose ancient and noble family dates from the early Middle Ages, who served in the Imperial Austro-Hungarian diplomatic corps and who was later the Austrian Republic's Ambassador to the Court of St James's, records a pre-1939 dinner party at Harewood, seat of the Earl of that name, the King-Emperor George V's son-in-law, where doilies were used.

Admittedly the word sounds unattractive. But the real prejudice against them was got up I believe by John Betjeman. Now although Shelley claimed poets were the unacknowledged legislators of the world, he never meant the social world in the first place and in the second he was *farouche* in his own social behaviour to the point of being uncouth. In short, the claim is mere boyish hyperbole. It is true that some versifiers – Mao Dze Dong, Byron – have passed laws, but Betjeman was neither a revolutionary leader nor a member of the Upper House of this realm. He was wholly middle-class and in the male line a Dutchman (or so he said; Auberon Waugh says the family were probably German), albeit assimilated. So much for his qualifications for telling us what we should or should not use on our dining tables. Obviously, no one in his senses would use a

Table setting using lace place mat cover, or doiley

56

plastic doily, but there exist lace ones of the most intricate workmanship and elegant design which look like giant snow-flakes. Place them over heat-proof mats (which, if at all functional, are likely to be desperately ugly), whereupon you're home and, in every sense of the word, dry. Repeat on a smaller scale with mats and lace coverings for wine glasses.

Table Decorations

The Victorians and Edwardians went in for elaborate centre table decorations – epergnes, statuary, banks of hot-house flowers. It was done mostly on a sort of bullion-broker principle of dazzling one's guests with as much precious metal as possible. A prime example of how absurd this could become is to be seen in the grand banqueting chamber at Apsley House, on Hyde Park Corner in London, where a gigantic gilded *mise-en-scène* – virtu-ally a goldsmith's desert island – takes up 95 per cent of the available table space. Tsar Alexander I of Russia is said to have presented it to the Iron (*mot juste*) Duke (of Wellington). It is very splendid but it is not for entertaining round. You would never see anyone the other side of the table.

Nevertheless, at today's dinner parties there is a place for flowers, rows of decanters and birds and animals in silver and gold, if laid out in moderation. Perhaps there is a limit to the amount you are prepared to spend on table decorations. In that case may I propose you concentrate on providing quantities of silver pepper-grinders, silver butter dishes, ornamental salt cellars, mustard pots and decanters, one for each of your guests? It is far more important to supply everyone with easily reachable accessories to the meal, thus avoiding constant inter-ruptions to the conversation when somebody wants the salt, for example, than to encumber the table with banal silver pheasants and so forth. (If you own a very splendid example of the Italian Renaissance goldsmith's or silversmith's art, that is a different matter; show it off by all means.) It may sound extravagant to provide each guest with his own decanter, but these need not be large. Nor need they contain alcohol, though they can. Water will do. Anything to keep up the flow, not so much of wine but of social intercourse (though this may necessarily depend on the flow of wine). Nothing snarls up social intercourse so much as constant requests for, and the passage to and fro of, condiments, water, wine, bread, butter and so on.

COURSES

The selection and positioning of the cutlery depends on the number of courses you have, also on what kind of courses they are. Accordingly we will tackle the courses and their nature first. I'm afraid to say that three courses are an irreducible minimum if you want to be taken seriously as a host – afraid, because two done really well are better than three done moderately. Besides, three aren't an absolute necessity in terms of the amount of nourishment involved. Whereas the Victorians thought no dinner party was adequate unless there were at least six courses, sometimes more, many of your guests today, possibly a majority of your female ones, will leave a good deal of the food on their plates uneaten. In some cases that is because they were taught it was bad manners to finish everything, though anyone alive during the last war or for the first ten years after it would regard such waste as sinful. Mostly it is because they want to get, or remain, slim. Even in Victorian times it is interesting to note from contemporary diaries and letters how many male guests privately thought a whole array of dishes silly and extravagant. The ladies were not supposed to eat much anyway, so the whole exercise was rather a waste of time whichever sex you were.

Number and Variety of Courses

A fairly elaborate dinner party could consist of a first course, a main course, a pudding course and a cheese course. One can stretch things out almost indefinitely by adding a fish course after the first one (which would be soup, say), an entrée of meat between the soup and the remove (which might be game), a game course in addition to the remove (which would not then have been game but something like veal), a savoury after the pudding, and sorbets in between courses to cleanse and refresh the palate. But this kind of elaboration is getting very rare except at formal banquets and restaurants, usually in France, where the proprietors go in for twelve courses – usually tiny – to show off their prowess.

If you have your meal cooked in-house by a Cordon Bleu girl, you may well feel you can go in for a large number of courses. But

consult her well in advance to see if you have the requisite number
of kitchen utensils. And for heaven's sake test her prowess on a
group of friends before letting her loose on more formal company,
no matter how bleu the reputation of her cordon. Arrange with
her beforehand exactly what her responsibilities are to be. Is she
just going to do the cooking or is she supposed to serve it and clear
away afterwards as well? What hour does she finish? You will
probably have to drive her home or get her a taxi and pay for it. Is
she going to do all the purchasing of food for a dinner party or will
you? If you do it and she decides what you have got is of inferior
quality or insufficient in quantity who is going to have the final
say? Will there be time to rectify any omissions on the night?

The first course – I personally deplore the expression 'starter'
on the grounds that it properly refers to a mackintoshed
gentleman in a bowler hat at a racecourse or point-to-point,
though I'm conscious I'm fighting a losing battle – may be cold
or hot. It is only sensible to serve something cold in summer and
hot in winter, but a harassed host may be forgiven for concentrating on only one hot course, the main one, and serving a cold
first course whatever the season. If that is done, however, the
heating in the house should be well turned up. Sometimes you
can compromise by serving, say, pâté, for pâté is eaten with hot
toast. Perhaps this is the moment to explain that when one says
that a particular food is eaten with another particular food one
is not blindly endorsing some ancient piece of bigotry. If two
types of food go together it's because they've been found to do
so by long trial and error. At the same time, don't be afraid to
depart from custom, substituting fresh grated ginger, say, for
pepper. But test it on your own family before dishing it up to
guests.

It is increasingly the custom to prepare the first course on plates
and set them right in front of where the guests are going to sit,
rather than provide guests with side plates, which they will then
move to the centre of their places at table and heap with the first
course as you pass it round. The first method allows the opening
course to be made ready before the guests even arrive. The only
trouble with it is that it may involve a risk of flies getting at the
food before the diners do, or of the food turning an unattractive
colour or getting hard. So take care.

59

Cutlery

Conventionally the pieces of cutlery for use in the first course are placed on the outside, to left and right, of each diner's place setting, knives and spoons to the right, forks to the left. Oddly enough even left-handed people are catered for in this way, though I know from talking to my left-handed friends that they find other ordinary implements such as potato-peelers and scissors quite hard to operate unless designed specifically for left-handers. Each person dining then works inwards as the courses proceed. A variation of this is to place the spoon and fork for pudding at the far side of the place setting from the person dining, parallel with the edge of the table. A friend of mine was once gently chided by her mother-in-law, whose family holds one of the numerous marquessates created during Pitt the Younger's premiership but is nevertheless of fairly grand lineage, for laying the table with the spoon and fork placed in this way.

But what is traditional in a great house such as a marquess's, where the dining table can accommodate forty or fifty guests, may be inconvenient for us lesser folk since it is obviously going to take up more room round the table, hence reduce the number of guests one can seat. If you place the spoon and fork for pudding on the

Setting for a relatively cramped table

far side of the place setting parallel with the table, you can put the cheese knife parallel with the table too, just inside the spoon and fork, with its handle pointing towards the right. In such cases the spoon is placed beyond the fork, pointing from right to left, and the fork from left to right on the nearer edge of the spoon.

Conventionally knives are placed with their sharp edges facing inwards. Forks rest on the curve, with their tines or prongs pointing upwards. Americans tend to cut up their food by spearing it with the fork in their left hand then sawing away with the knife in their right hand and finally, having put the knife down, shifting the fork across to their right hand and scooping up the food with the fork only. I suppose in a frontier society, which much of America was till only a century and a half ago, it was wise to have one hand ready for defence against Indians or bad men. With pasta it is still the custom in Italy to eat principally with the fork held in the right hand, often holding a spoon in the left hand to concentrate strands of spaghetti scoop-wise so that they can be twisted round the fork tines. In Italy pasta is usually served as a first course, and if in smallish portions can well be dished up in like fashion here, as it is for instance at the fiendishly expensive but chic Orso's restaurant in Covent Garden. Holding a fork in the right hand and using it to scoop up food such as rice or minced meat is catching on this side of the Atlantic (left-handed people tend to hold the fork in their left hand, however). I see no good reason to condemn the practice. And of course at a buffet supper, of which more later, people invariably do it.

Glasses

I mentioned earlier the flutes, or narrow-cupped glasses with longish stems, in which you would be best advised to serve champagne. Hock glasses, in which you will serve white wine, are similarly narrow in shape though usually larger. Claret or burgundy glasses tend to be fuller-bodied; sherry glasses tend to be small and squat. The sherry schooners you see in pubs should stay in pubs not find their way into your glassware cabinet. In Spain sherry is served more usually in glasses like those for port. Port experts maintain that their favourite wine should be served in large glasses which close in slightly towards the top, rather like a full-bodied tulip. That way the bouquet, or scent of the wine, is more fully conveyed to the drinker's nose. The nose is just as much a channel for tasting things as the tongue, if not more so. To prove it, hold your nose when sipping a wine and you will find you lose a great deal of the taste. And, of course, when you have a bad cold your sense of taste is very seriously impaired. The same goes for brandy glasses and those holding digestifs generally as for port glasses, though you can acquire those huge brandy balloons if you wish.

Another point wine-writers make is that wine needs to be drunk in daylight or artifical light, though the latter doesn't have to be particularly bright and often at a dinner party is not. Whether or not it is merely a psychological conviction one develops to the effect that wine doesn't taste nearly so nice drunk from an opaque mug or in the dark hardly matters. The conviction is widespread and that is all the host needs to bear in mind. It is for this reason that glass has been found to be the most suitable receptacle for wine. It shouldn't be too thick unless it is antique cut glass, where the play of light makes up for the rather slab-like feel of the material against one's lips.

If the glasses are antique and heavy it doesn't matter so much if you lack a full set. If you entertain a lot of people at a time fairly frequently you will become inured to breakages of glasses and will regularly top up your collection by buying replacements in the same pattern. If you entertain a large number of guests only once or twice a year you can either mix your style of glassware or hire glasses on a one-off basis from your local off-licence. If you buy sufficient wine from him at the same time he will probably let you have any amount of glasses free.

The order in which you arrange glasses at table is less a matter of form than with cutlery. If you have an enormous table and plenty of room for your guests' place settings you can make it plain to guests which glass they should use in which order by ranging the glasses from right to left at the top right hand of the place setting. You then get the servants to pour the first wine into the glass on the far right, subsequently moving leftwards with each new wine. Most people don't have the room, so cluster the glasses in a bunch. If you have servants they ought to be trained to pour the right wine into the right glass. To this end it is a good idea to have a slightly different shape of glass for each wine, for if a guest refuses one of

The left-hand and right-hand glasses will allow you and your
guests to taste wine to its greatest advantage. The middle ones
are unsuitable, one is too closed, the other too open

The three left-hand glasses will allow you and your guests to
taste port to its greatest advantage. The two right-hand ones are
too small and too open at the top

the wines or has drunk up every drop in one of the glasses, even
the most alert servant may pour the next wine into the wrong glass
when he next comes round. Differentiating your various wine
glasses is not vital, however. If you serve the wine yourself you
may know your own glasses well enough to avoid a mix-up. If you
circulate the wine bottles and decanters for your guests to pour out

themselves they can usually be left by trial and error to pour whichever wine they want into whichever glass. As the dinner proceeds and everybody gets drunker there will be a good deal of muddle as to which glass holds which wine anyway. Don't fret about it; look on it as the sign of a good dinner party.

Salads

There are two schools of thought about how to serve salads. One says put them on side dishes, separate from the main dish. The other says serve them on the same plate as the main dish. I think that whether you do one or the other should depend on what your main dish is. If the latter doesn't go with salad at all, then any salad you provide should be served at a different point in the meal as well as on a different plate. Otherwise you could use the same plate for both main dish and salad, as they tend to do in French restaurants, even if you don't serve the two simultaneously. Ditto with the cutlery used to eat the salad. As salads become more complex they take on the characteristics of a course of their own, so that you can even serve a salad of pigeon breasts or of bacon, rocket and walnut halves, for example, as a first course in its own right. Purist wine-writers maintain that no wine can be drunk along with a salad because the latter contains vinegar. Instead they recommend water. I can see the force of this, but if the vinegar is very faint, and it certainly ought to be as there are few things more horrible than salad drenched in acidity, a robust white goes with it pretty well, especially if your guests have bread or rolls with their salad.

Pudding versus Cheese

Whether you serve pudding before cheese or the other way round depends how Francophile you are, also perhaps on whether the cheeses are French. In France they eat cheese before the pudding, but then their cheeses are softer and on the whole blander than English ones. Quite a few hosts and hostesses over here serve only French cheeses at their dinner parties, a deplorable practice. Cheese is one of the very few things in the food line that this country does really well and even before the joke substance called Lymeswold was introduced we had one of the largest and most diverse ranges anywhere in the world. No other country can come near English cheeses for their characteristic hard consistency, certainly not French ones. The odd 90lb stilton skilfully introduced into a house party anywhere along the Mediterranean coast from Marbella to Ventimiglia will win more friends for the British way of life than any amount of effort by the British Council. Besides, according to recent scientific findings a hard cheese such as cheddar can prevent cancer. Under the present absurd affectation of Gallic sophistication in the cheese line by British hostesses Crécy, Poitiers, Agincourt, Blenheim, Ramillies, Oudenarde and Trafalgar might never have been fought.

Specialised Cutlery

Fish knives and fish forks have come in this century for derision as genteel, and most famously at the hands of the same person as the doily, John Betjeman. Yet in the nineteenth century they had a perfectly legitimate purpose for middle-class households and those members of the upper class who had fallen on hard times and had had to sell the family silver. The old story about grand families having silver cutlery, hence not needing fish knives and forks as the middle classes did seems to be broadly accurate. The purpose of fish knives and forks, and it was perfectly justified, was to shield the person eating from the taint of having to consume fish with cutlery that could not be rendered stainless, for of course fish has a notoriously lingering whiff as well as taste to it.

I was interested to discover during my researches that for a generation or so before the arrival of fish knives and forks some people used a fork and a bit of bread to manoeuvre fish into their mouths, later two silver forks, one in each hand. So few people giving dinner parties nowadays serve a fish course as well as a meat one and still fewer a main course of fish (a great pity, incidentally, since Britain is an island surrounded by delicious fish even if the Spaniards nowadays take most of them). Accordingly such items of cutlery as fish knives and forks have rather fallen into disuse in any case. But there is still a good argument for using them, however much other silverware you can afford. The knives, being pointed rather than rounded and blunt, are shaped better for dissecting fish – and this must have held true even for the nineteenth-century aristocracy, if you think about it. In the course of time fish knives and forks developed elaborate handles, of mother-of-pearl, for example, to the extent that by the 1920s G.K. Chesterton could base one of his Father Brown stories on the theft of a highly decorated set of the things from a private dining club of the most high-toned exclusiveness and nobody batted an eyelid because they thought it *infra dig* for such people to use fish knives and forks. Nowadays, because of Betjeman's artful propaganda poem 'How to Get On In Society', the same theme would convey as little sense of contemporary reality as if one were discussing the hijacking of a sedan chair by footpads on Hounslow Heath.

Other items of cutlery include special implements for extracting the meat from lobsters, pastry forks where one tine is thicker or broader than the other or others and soup spoons. If you have inherited such things you will probably know about them already. But do you really need to acquire them, other than by involuntary means such as inheritance? The rationale for lobster-meat extractors is straightforward: unless you employ a semi-surgical tool you will not be able to get at the lobster meat any other way and as with crabs the best meat is in the claws. Accordingly the decision whether to acquire them depends on how often you are going to eat lobster. Forks designed specifically for pastry I would have thought superfluous. If the pastry is solid enough an ordinary fork will do, and if it is very flaky not even a pastry fork will be able to cope. Soup spoons lie somewhere between the hard-and-fast necessity of the lobster pick and the redundancy of a pastry fork. The idea behind their being round rather than oval in the way ordinary dessert spoons are, is that you drink soup from them sideways, pushing the spoon away from you across the soup bowl, which you likewise tilt away from you. But unless the dessert spoon is shaped in a very narrow oval it will be fairly serviceable as a soup spoon too. And I have come across modernistic cutlery, usually of Scandinavian provenance, where the soup spoon is a quadrilateral with rounded corners. So don't be inhibited from serving soup just because you don't have any round soup spoons of the conventional type.

One relatively specialised bit of eating equipment which I would recommend is a nutcracker with a detachable pick set in one of the handles. With such a pick you can get at recalcitrant bits of brazil nuts, which otherwise are the devil to extract. Nutcrackers of this type come in pretty silver versions. Mine was stolen some years ago. I regret its disappearance often, not just at Christmas.

Variation in Courses
This is not a cookbook and I do not propose to discuss the nature of your menu in any great detail. But it is only sensible to vary the texture of dishes you set before your guests. A great thick broth of a game soup should not therefore be followed by roast pork and spotted dick, unless perhaps you live in an unheated, uninsulated mansion of not fewer than twenty bedrooms on the North Yorkshire moors, minimum elevation 1,500ft above sea-level, and your guests have all spent ten hours between dawn and sunset in the middle of January chasing foxes on horseback at a constant temperature of 39 degrees Fahrenheit in a Scotch mist, humidity around 80 per cent. In summer you can go in for greater uniformity of food texture: gazpacho followed by cold poached salmon followed by sorbet, for example.

Nevertheless, as with so many other notions nowadays, the conviction that rich or stodgy food should not monopolise the menu has been taken too far, even though we now know that a diet deficient in fats can lead to depression. It is sad the way the old heavy food our forefathers feasted on is disappearing. Near-ubiquitous central heating, cholesterol neurosis, increased life-insurance premiums for those with a 'dangerous lifestyle' have seen it off. And of course so many guests have their own little prejudices against stodge, or even red meat. Accordingly one is almost as likely to be served chicken or some bland variant thereof at a dinner party as at a political banquet. It is some consolation that the private dinner party chicken will be better cooked, but not much. Here then is a genuinely useful topic for recording on a card index: the dietary likes and dislikes of your acquaintance. And if you have just butchered a pig, steamed a gloriously suetty pudding and decided your twenty-year-old port needs drinking up, then with a comprehensive list of those among your friends who possess the courage to consume such foods, you may decide that there are just enough convivial souls to help get an old-fashioned John Bull-type dinner party going after all.

Sample table setting

Vegetarians and Diabetics

Vegetarians are defined as people who don't eat meat. Vegans are defined as people who not only don't eat meat, fish or eggs but also shun any animal product whatsoever. Thus a full-fledged vegan guest should not be seated on a leather upholstered chair or be given a mother-of-pearl-handled, bone-handled, or ivory-handled piece of cutlery. To be fair, most vegetarians are uncomplaining. They are often pathetically grateful for a salad into which you have put pine kernels, olives, artichoke hearts and so on to beef it up. Not very many will gag at the mere sight of meat being eaten at the same table, so you can usually invite them along with others. These days increasing numbers of people, called coeliacs, are announcing that they are allergic to wheat. That can pose more of a problem because you may be surprised how many things have wheat in them. But coeliacs seem not to mind being at the same table as unreformed wheativores. Very tolerant of them.

At least they announce their disabilities in advance. Diabetics often don't, perhaps because it is still thought an embarrassing complaint. Actually what is embarrassing is the way it manifests itself. When one of your guests pitches face-forwards straight into his soup one's immediate reaction is to assume he's drunk too much or is on drugs. It may simply be that he is a diabetic who's gone too long without food. Watch for the signs if you suspect a guest may have diabetic tendencies. A leaflet giving guidance for

68

hosts who have to cope with diabetics can be obtained from the British Diabetic Association (071 323 1531). It is particularly important that diabetics eat at a regular hour. This is another good reason for not delaying the start of dinner if another of your guests is late arriving.

WINES

Wine is an enormous subject, and as with food this book is not meant to be a detailed guide. The danger is that I will oversimplify matters by declaring that white wine should be served with fish, red wine with meat, whereas it isn't the end of the world if you break this rule and serve some red wines with, say, red mullet, or some whites with, say, veal.

Providing you do not allow yourself to become hidebound, you may care to bear in mind that in general a light first course involving fish, shellfish, avocado, salad or melon would tend to be accompanied by a light, fairly dry white wine or a none-too-sweetish hock; a more robust first course – game soup, pâté, salad involving bacon or pigeon breasts – with perhaps a claret. The current Countess Alexander of Tunis recommends champagne with soup. She also recommends soup at lunch, which according to some absurd taboos is not done, as well as at dinner. Lady Alexander is on a retainer from the champagne house of Heidsieck to boost its image. She argues that serving champagne with a first course has the advantage of continuing what one was drinking as the aperitif and that anyway it goes well with cold soups, her speciality. I can see that if you serve champagne with a first course you are far less likely to get in a muddle between the glasses your guests were drinking out of in the drawing room and the ones they will start drinking out of in the dining room. The verdict must lie with your guests and depend entirely on taste. Try it and abide by their decision.

Game and the more pungent meats deserve burgundy or, for the poor man, Côtes du Rhône. Don't forget that only the really great years for burgundys are delicious; it can be a disappointing wine, as well as bloody expensive, in other years. With puddings a Sauternes or Muscat-grape wine is perfect. Once you have served port most of your guests will not want to go back to claret or even burgundy; their palates will have become too accustomed to a richer, heavier, sweeter wine.

I do not endorse the various social prejudices (as opposed to those held by wine buffs, which aren't prejudices at all but wise old precepts) that exist with regard to the means of serving wine. But I do believe you ought to be aware of them, in case you want to do the thing absolutely copper-bottomed properly and avoid the terrible slur of being thought middle-class. Here goes then. Don't decant claret; do decant champagne. Do pass all port clockwise (the host having helped his right-hand neighbour first), unless it is the new brand wittily named Starboard, in which case it should be circulated widdershins. I think this is true even below the Equator, where it is said that bath water tends to run out of the bath with the vortex rotating right-to-left (the opposite to what it does in the northern hemisphere), though it may be that Australia is not the best place to drink port. On the other hand Brazil, which was colonised by the Portuguese and is mostly below the Equator, should be awash with port.

Actually the custom of passing the port to the left round the table is peculiar to these islands and derives, I have been told, from naval tradition. A related claim is that the custom of passing it clockwise is a superstition. Presumably that means it was once thought unlucky to pass it to the right. Yet in most cultures the left rather than the right is regarded as unlucky. All in all, we can surely afford to ignore such things as superstitious practices. And are we really so craven that we are going to let the Navy dictate to us how to circulate our wine?

Decanting
Apart from the social imperative mentioned above, when should you decant and what should you decant? There are three straightforward reasons for decanting wine and a fourth rather discreditable one. The three straightforward ones are that wine may have built up a deposit, or sediment, that it allows the wine to breathe and that it gets rid of any nasty smells the wine has developed. The discreditable reason is to disguise the cheapness of the wine. Actually this last reason is an oblique compliment to certain wines, such as the Bulgarian ones, which taste a great deal better than much more expensive wines but which certain of one's friends

70

have snobbish prejudices against. After all if the wine tastes as cheap as it costs to buy no amount of decanting is going to disguise the fact unless your guests are collectively without any palate at all. Conversely, by serving decanted Bulgarian wine which may call forth cries of approval you can then reveal its real origin and shame the snobbish among your friends into judging wine more on its intrinsic merits in future rather than by the fanciness of the label on the bottle.

But to return to the *bona fide* reasons for decanting. Every red wine of any quality and some white wines of quality develop sediment during the years they spend in the bottle. Since the bottle is going to be moved about at a dinner party there is a risk that the sediment will be shaken up and float around in the body of the liquid, though it will eventually settle down again and in the case of port may stick to the side of the bottle. Clearly if you decant the wine so as to remove the sediment you can pass the new vessel containing the wine backwards and forwards among your guests to your heart's content.

Decanting also releases pent-up elements which enhance the flavour and bouquet. It is for the same reason that you will sometimes see tasters swirling their wine around in the glass. Sometimes a wine decanted an hour or two before a meal will develop qualities it might have needed several years to acquire in the ordinary process of lying on its side inert in a cellar.

The third reason is to 'cleanse' old wines of what is called 'bottle stink', when the process of deterioration has set in as a result of their having been allowed to pass their prime. A few minutes in the open air will do wonders, but the wine needs to be drunk quickly after decanting in such circumstances, if indeed it is not too late already.

With port the bottle should be carried up from the cellar horizontally then gently set upright. Remove any wax sealant with a knife and wipe the neck of the bottle with a cloth. Insert the corkscrew and withdraw the cork in one continuous pull rather than with a series of jerks. That way the cork, which may be very fragile in old bottles of port, is more likely to come out in one piece. Next pour the port slowly into the decanter in good light. The purpose of the light is to enable you to watch out for sediment. If you use a wine strainer of silver or some similar precious metal be careful not to pour the wine too quickly because the sediment may become churned up. You can even use a handkerchief to pass the wine through if, say, the crust on the port has become loose and fallen into the wine. (There are two kinds of crust, a thick one found in old vintages and a lighter, powdery one that you will come across in late-bottled and light ports that have been kept in bottle too long.) But make sure the handkerchief is of fine linen and thoroughly rinse it in water first. Once you have decanted the port leave the decanter open, the stopper off, for a few hours.

Vintage port should never be served too cold, though tawny or white ports can be drunk cool or even slightly iced in hot weather. Vintage port, once opened and decanted, will go flat after a couple of days but the lighter ones can be kept in the bottle, which in turn can be corked and reused for several months, rather as with sherry. Mind you, I have come across some wine-writers who maintain that a bottle of sherry should be drunk at a sitting once opened.

SEPARATING THE SEXES

The custom whereby the ladies withdrew towards the end of a meal while the gentlemen gathered together round one end of the table and told bawdy stories while quaffing endless glasses of port or brandy has fallen – some would say mercifully – into abeyance. Of course the conversation may have become bawdy already by the time the port is served. These days the 'ladies' are just as likely as the men to make a few risqué remarks as the wine circulates, flushing out their inhibitions. And why should decent port be confined to the gentlemen? There is as I write an advertising campaign in full flood across the country which employs huge hoardings showing a female model with a slightly smug expression, looking as they say like the cat that swallowed the cream, holding a slice of stilton and glass of port. It is supposed to remind us that port is the legitimate tipple not just of red-faced old buffers of dons and survivors of the Indian Mutiny but of younger and softer beings.

Alternatively the conversation may eschew bawdiness altogether. In Peacock's novels the real business of the evening – immensely learned yet witty dialogue – only starts once the ladies have withdrawn. It's never like that in real life, not even at donnish gatherings.

This business of the ladies withdrawing does not seem to have been observed in any culture other than that of Britain and its subject peoples among the Celts. However, if you follow this slightly barbarous custom you may as well get it right. The idea is for the hostess to catch the eye of the woman on the right of the host, who, it is to be presumed, is the principal female guest, and slowly rise from her seat – slowly so that the other women can catch on to what is happening and get up too. At this point the men should also get up and stand at their places while the woman formerly seated on the host's right leads the way out of the dining room, the other women following her in order of precedence, with the hostess last. The door of the dining room should be held open for them either by the host or by the man nearest the door. He will close it after the last woman has left.

The whole procedure presupposes a good deal of awareness on the part of the guests. It assumes you have ascertained the order of precedence of the guests, that you have first sent them in to dinner in that order and seated them in that order. It assumes your principal female guest will twig that when the hostess rises from her seat at the end of what may have been a long, highly convivial dinner it is the signal for her, the guest, to lead the way from the room. It assumes the men know what is going on, for otherwise they will not rise as one man and stand motionless by their chairs. It assumes that in what may be a large dining room (the manoeuvre is pretentious at a small dinner) the man nearest the door is alert enough to act as doorman for the entire female company. In short, it sums up what has become impracticable in very modern times about much conventional dinner-party behaviour evolved over the last hundred years, that it necessitated the existence of a homogeneous society in which nearly everyone had the basic rules at their fingertips. Unless you can be sure that all your present-day guests are equally expert, you are as likely as not to engender embarrassment.

Alternatives to Apartheid
As the dinner proceeds guests will shed some of their inhibitions, whatever your attitude to separating the sexes towards the end of

the meal. In Ireland we take care of that by winding up the evening with singing. This is where the songsheets I mentioned earlier come in. My good friend Michael O'Sullivan, the celebrated biographer of President Mary Robinson, overcomes the problem of his fellow diners not knowing the words of, say, 'Jerusalem', by enunciating with his beautifully clear diction the words of the next line during the short pause in which singers catch their breath after the preceding one. I like and recommend this technique. Each guest should ideally have a party piece he trots out solo on occasions such as these. In Ireland, oddly enough, they are usually of a melancholy turn rather than celebratory or downright Bacchic.

THE COFFEE STAGE

As the meal draws to a close you will prepare to serve coffee. This should be very strong for those who are manly enough to drink coffee at all. Many people these days voice a preference for decaffeinated. There is no reason why the coffee should not be consumed at the dining table, but most people prefer to have it in the drawing room. If your house is big enough there's no reason to force all your guests to move to the drawing room. You could leave some of them in the dining room and shepherd the others elsewhere. The dining room may have become too full of cigarette smoke for some of your guests, or you may wish to play music and have dancing in another room. Some guests will want to carry on conversation, over wine naturally, for as long as possible, and if they have lit on a fascinating topic which they have been discussing with one of the other guests, to stay in the dining room and do it. Others may be getting tired of all conversation, even if it's as sprightly as in a Peacock novel, and be wanting to dance off the lethargy induced by good food in the arms of a member of the opposite sex, something you don't have to be talking while doing. The division between those who stay in the dining room and those who go into the drawing room need not be along lines of sex, as in the past, but of individual preference. This works well, I find, and in any case guests may drift back and forth between one room and the other, now dancing or sipping coffee, then back for more wine or brandy in the dining room.

In circumstances where the dinner party begins to break up into two or more such sets – the sedentaries and the dancers let us say – the host must be prepared to shuttle backwards and forwards between the rooms, working twice as hard as before to see that everybody's glass is topped up, that bonbons, liqueurs or other digestifs are at hand and so on. I must confess that at my last dinner party, which went on till five o'clock in the morning, I catnapped in an armchair several times in between a series of twirls round the dance floor. If you're capable of waking refreshed after a few minutes' snooze, like Napoleon, you would do better to retire to your study to recruit your strength. Otherwise your guests may think you are trying to send them a subtle message to the effect that your dinner party has gone on long enough.

Winding Up

The best compliment your guests can pay you is to stay on at your dinner party till dawn, or in winter at any rate till 4 a.m. or so. Of course it can be a painful compliment, since unless your stamina is superb you may not feel up to coping with them after 1 a.m. In such circumstances it is perfectly *en règle* to plead fatigue and slope off to bed, perhaps leaving a few extra bottles of wine or brandy for your guests to dispose of in the next hour or two and praying inwardly that none of them sets the house alight by mistake. If a married couple act in unison in this way it is only very bold guests who will stay on instead of sheepishly apologising and leaving within five minutes. But furnish your house with plenty of sofabeds for the drunks who should never be allowed to leave under their own steam anyway, as well as for the late stayers impervious to hints and cajolery who will have to be put up overnight.

General Observations

Smoking

Some people cannot bear to be in the same room with a smoker, even if he's placed at the other end of it and only lights up once throughout the entire meal. Conversely, hardened smokers may well try to indulge in their tobacco habit the moment you have shown them to their seats in the dining room, never mind any taboos about waiting till the loyal toast. (At formal dinners, such as the annual affair at the Guildhall where the Prime Minister or other senior member of the government makes a speech setting out policy, one is allowed to smoke only after the toast to the Queen has been proposed by the Master of Ceremonies.)

The older the friend the harder it is to be severe over his incessant puffing. I fear the only thing you can do is not invite such people at the same time as asthmatics, bronchial cases or those people who detest tobacco in any form. If a new acquaintance lights up early on in the meal and you know one of the other guests is in physical distress as a result you can politely but firmly ask him to put his smoking off till later. If nobody is suffering physical distress, simply make a note of his predilection for smoking and take it into account next time you invite him. In such cases I do not think it is worth making a fuss then and there. If you yourself are the only person who objects I think you do have justice on your side in making a bit of a fuss, for your efficiency as host will be impaired otherwise. If there are servants to do all the menial work, and provided your actual health is not affected immediately, you should grin and bear it, for the old adage that the guest can do no wrong still holds good on such occasions.

Although in the past a host was expected to provide cigarettes for his guests, nowadays this would be thought unusually and unnecessarily generous. Different smokers have so many different pet brands that you could hardly expect to be able to accommodate everybody anyway. Cigars are a different matter. If you are reasonably well-off and giving a fairly elaborate dinner party you should offer cigars to your guests (and some women, as well as men, like them). But if it's a smaller-scale affair and you have been losing money lately it is hardly a crime to keep your hard-won weeds to yourself. Only don't guard a whole box of them in full view of everybody, never offering the box to your guests. Instead place a few cigars in the case you carry on your person, or in the breast pocket of your jacket, before the dinner party begins and take one out from time to time throughout the evening. Some hosts do this with their best Havanas and offer a box of Nicaraguan to their guests. You might as well keep the *foie gras* for yourself and serve your friends cats' meat. Do such people think their guests have no eyes in their heads? I mentioned cigar-cutters earlier. With many cigars they are unnecessary because the cigar has a detachable flap at the end you put in your mouth and this can quite easily be gouged open with a thumbnail. But some cigars don't. And some cigar-cutters are so decorative they make a pretty addition to the dining table as well as furnishing a conversation piece. I have one made from a walrus tusk. It's great fun to use and invariably calls forth cries of pleasure from the guests and queries as to what it is made of. If conversation is flagging it provides a fresh impetus.

Drugs
I think it unlikely that any guest you did not know well would have the nerve to roll a joint at your dinner party. If you have invited an old friend who you know has tastes of that sort you can take him aside before the dinner party starts and ask him not to embarrass you in such a way. If by any chance a guest you do not know well flaunts drugs you must be prepared to crack down hard on him. The very fact he does not know you all that well means you may be a JP, Home Office official or special constable for all he is aware. You might even hint you are one or another of these things in telling him to put his illicit stuff away. When before the meal you caution your old friend who takes drugs you might say that one of the other guests is a JP, Home Office official or special constable.

VARIATIONS: TOP DRAWER
So far I have dealt with the dinner party in fairly mainstream fashion, that is to say on the assumption that you will have some but not much help, either wife, husband or other partner to assist you in preparing and serving it, and that you will not want to conduct the evening with excessive formality. But suppose you are very rich and wish to entertain in top style. In particular, suppose you can afford plenty of servants. There are two approaches, depending on whether your servants are natives (that is, of these islands) or foreigners. There are advantages to having natives. They understand not only your instructions but the nuances of entertaining in Britain generally. For small children a native English-speaker as nanny is essential or the poor mites will end up unable to speak English themselves. And as noted already, if you have children of your own you will find your entertaining greatly hampered unless you acquire a nanny.

Your best bet for obtaining a nanny is through personal recommendation, though personal columns in the quality press and the *Lady* are also useful. It is such a competitive market these days that you may have to entice a good one away from her current employer with extra incentives, just like executive head-hunting. And it is not much less expensive either by the time you've paid for the nanny's own room, own phone, own television, video and CD system, exclusive use of a spare family car, health insurance and whatever else is needed to keep her on your staff. People sometimes say P.G. Wodehouse stories inhabit a never-never land of timeless innocence, but where domestic staff are concerned he shows himself remarkably in touch with today's practices, even if it's by some fluke of prescience. Thus when unscrupulous persons intrigue to lure Anatole the cook away from Tom Travers's employ it is only a foretaste of what you could be exposed to when letting guests see how well you have trained your domestic staff.

When guests with children come to stay they may well bring their nanny too. Consult with them beforehand to see whether when at home she gets a room as good as her employers do. She may not like being put in the servants' wing of your house. Her employers are responsible for tipping any of your servants who have cleaned up after her and her charges. You can hint at this obligation being laid on them when you discuss with them which room to give her.

If you have a good butler or general factotum it may not be necessary to hire anyone else except on a casual basis, for big dinner parties, for example. Since the butler has to make numerous decisions demanding great knowledge of how social life in these islands works he ought to be a native. A married man is preferable to an unmarried one, particularly as his wife may be employed as a cook or housekeeper or upper housemaid. Try to give them separate accommodation from the big house, whether a gatekeeper's lodge, gamekeeper's cottage or agent's or steward's house. It preserves their sense of independence. On the other hand their dwelling may turn out to be too far from the main house. If you put them in the main house try to give them part of a wing separate from your own apartments. Their terms of employment ought to be every bit as good as a nanny's. And don't forget that when your friends come to stay bringing their nanny, the subject of comparative pay and perks is bound to come up when outsider nanny and your resident staff get together for a chat.

Now let us suppose that your servants are recent arrivals from a very foreign country, the Philippines say, and don't know much about how things should be done. I must assume that you can arrange for the actual training of them yourself. My purpose here is to indicate what they should be trained to do, though you must realise that they will probably never approach a native-born manservant for *sang froid* and *savoir faire*. On the other hand they are thought by most people to be more hard-working.

Lady Colin Campbell – not the current West Indian one whom Nigel Dempster conducts a campaign of ridicule against in his *Daily Mail* column, but a much earlier one several generations back – once edited and revised a book called *Etiquette and Good Society*. In it she says that a servant cannot wait well on more than six people at a time. But that was in an era when the paraphernalia of dinner parties put a much greater burden on servants waiting at table than is the case nowadays. I have been at dinner parties of thirty or so where all the waiting was done perfectly adequately by two servants, the butler and his wife. (And here I may say that although in the past it was thought preferable to have only manservants waiting at table, it is not necessary nowadays unless you wish to show off your family livery, of which more presently.) On the other hand whatever servants you use should be thoroughly at home in the house, knowing where everything is and exactly how the hostess likes things to be done. Only let your hypothetical Filipinos loose on your guests when they have been thoroughly trained. And it is no good getting in hired people at the last moment and expecting things to run smoothly unless you turn absolutely everything to do with the dinner party over to them, from shopping for the food to laying the table. In practice most hostesses like to retain a greater degree of control. After all, if the hostess chooses the guests she will be aware of certain fads one or two guests have and will want to retain control of planning the menu too. By fads I don't just mean things such as likes and dislikes in the food and drink line, but favourite conversational topics, a hatred of draughts, love of warmth from the radiator and so on.

Your first task is to ensure you can communicate properly with your servants. Is your Spanish, Italian or whatever good enough? Is their English adequate? Even if they understand basic requests to do with serving food and wine to your guests, will they be able to cope with out-of-the-ordinary ones, to open a window when the dining room becomes stuffy, say, or assemble the equipment to cope with a wine stain in the carpet (something that must be tackled immediately or the stain will prove indelible) without unduly inconveniencing your guests?

A related problem is to get your servants to speak good enough English so as not to seem rude or peremptory when they address your guests. Not many languages make so much use of such honeyed ornaments as 'please' and 'would you be so kind as to . . .' or 'do have the goodness to . . .' or 'I'm so sorry, sir, but . . .' in the way English does. The romance languages in particular – French, Italian, Spanish – sound to native English-speakers curt to the point of discourtesy if translated literally. I will give you an example. I recently attended the War and Peace Ball in aid of a church-building programme designed to benefit the White Russians in Britain. It was held at the Napoleon Suite of the Café Royal in Regent Street, an ironic choice of venue in view of the fact that in 1812 Napoleon was Russia's arch-enemy. The catering was in the hands of the Trusthouse Forte organisation and the reception offered a choice of vodka or champagne. I and one or two people near me asked at one point if there was any more champagne and were told 'No. All finish.' That is not the way to address guests at a reception, certainly not one so munificently funded as the War and Peace Ball, where tickets cost £75. Incidentally, the food at the tables was sometimes handed to one person from the left, as is correct, then swivelled round and thrust under the first guest's left-hand neighbour's nose, which most decidedly is incorrect. THF come in for a good deal of criticism generally. I here add two specific points on which they could improve their performance.

What do you call your servants? In Victorian times some employ-ers called all their footmen by a restricted range of names (James, Jeames, John Thomas, the last of these now having ribald associa-tions, of course) even if the individual had been christened something else. Similarly upper servants when female – housekeepers and the

80

like – were accorded the title 'Mrs' even if unmarried. You may feel that this sort of thing is too despotic. But foreign servants with names that are unprounceable by the average English person might be given temporary aliases by you to enable your guests to address them and this surely is not imposing too much on the servants themselves. In one case I have known the foreign servant actually preferred to be called by the English equivalent of his name – John instead of Giovanni – because it implied he had become English, even though his spoken English was not at all good.

You should train your servants to take your guests' cloaks, coats, gloves and so on when the guests first arrive, to show guests where the lavatories are without having to be asked, to show them into the drawing room and perhaps even to announce them. In the last case your servants must be trained to announce guests properly, according to the correct form of address for the various ranks of society. This last topic warrants a whole book to itself and I have not space to go into details here. *Debrett's Correct Form* is still in print and may be obtained at all good bookshops, even a few bad ones.

Your servants should know how to serve food, handing it from the left of the guest when the said guest is seated at table, and wine, pouring it from the right. Guests can be helped in the order in which they sit, starting with the lady on the host's right then turning to the lady on the host's left and then proceeding round the table. At a dinner with very many guests you should get the servants to duplicate the food and the serving dishes containing the food so that guests each side of a long table can be served simultaneously. The servants should be able to perform their tasks quietly, speaking to a guest only when the guest's attention is so distracted by a fellow diner to whom he is talking that he fails to notice he is being offered food or drink. But when it comes to the port stage the servants should withdraw and allow the guests to pour port themselves. Notwithstanding this I have been in quite grand houses where the servants even pour the port, both when it is served at table and when with brandy and liqueurs in the drawing room afterwards, when coffee also and bonbons in silver dishes were served.

You should train your servants in handling telephone calls while you and your guests are at table. Some rather snobbish hosts of my

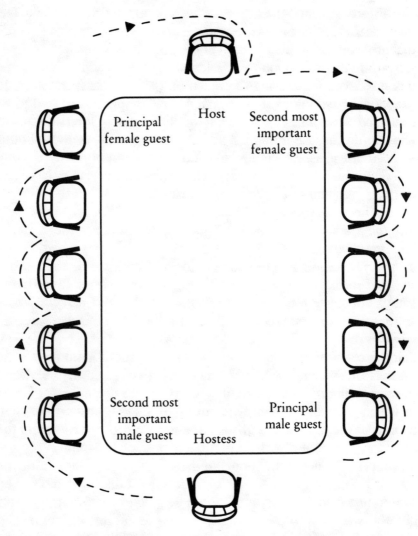

Seating and serving plan for a fairly formal dinner. Arrows
indicate the recommended order of serving by two attendants

acquaintance only permit a servant to enter the room when
company are present and announce that a caller is on the line if
that caller is a peer. Unless you have the Prime Minister or an
immensely important captain of industry to dinner no phone call
made during meal times is likely to be so crucial that it justifies
breaking into your convivial hours spent with guests.

All hosts must stand firm against the importing of mobile phones to the dining table. If one of your guests is in the middle of an important deal with, say, Tokyo, where they start to wake up and trade just as we in the West are going in to dinner, he should not have come at all. I suppose he might claim he thought he had wound things up earlier but that a fresh development had occurred. If so, send him and his mobile phone into another room. He can do his telephoning there. He has by now made the point that he is a personage of transcendental importance. If some wretched little show-off of a junior commodity trader insists on making an exhibition of himself by keeping his mobile phone where his roll and butter should be, get your butler to spill some steaming gravy over it. That'll larn him.

A good servant can freeze out a guest far more effectively than you can. A lady of my acquaintance once stayed at a rather grand house owned by a prominent racehorse owner. She is rather given to complaining loudly about things in general, and this occasion was no exception. Towards the end of the first (and, as it proved, last) evening of her stay the butler came up to her and announced that her bags were packed and waiting for her in the hall. Brutal but effective – far more effective than if the lady of the house had done it.

You should issue guidelines to your servants to cope with drunken guests who ask them for much more alcohol than they would dare do from you yourself, simply because they are servants. You should hint to your servants at the possibility of sexual demands being made on them by some of your guests – or restrict yourself to physically repulsive servants.

From the above it will be seen that a perfect servant needs the *savoir faire* of a diplomat, the discreetness of a cabinet secretary and the flexibility of a bendy toy if he is to be first rate at his job. So unless you have acquired very polished articles from the word go it would be better to start with small dinners of four and gradually work your way up to more elaborate entertainments. A good servant is like a good PA, not to be found easily or cheaply and not to be dismissed without excellent cause.

Formal Invitations
Once your servants have been trained to your satisfaction you can issue invitations. If you use a card for inviting people to dinner

parties you may as well get it engraved, with the lettering raised above the surface of the pasteboard in the font known as copperplate italic. Lay in a stock of cards so that you need only change the date and the time of the dinner party. Instead of filling in the first of the dotted lines illustrated below you could write the name of your guest or guests (the latter if a couple) on the top left-hand corner. The dimensions of the card should be roughly 3ins by 5ins and matching envelopes should be ordered at the same time. The wording of the card might go as follows before it is filled in:

Mr & Mrs Charles Mosley
request the pleasure of
. . . .
company at dinner
on. . . . . .at. . . . . .o'clock

231 Belgrave Square,
London SW1X 4QS   *R.S.V.P.*

Alternative layout for a dinner party invitation card.

There are several possible additions you might make to this, depending on the circumstances. In the old days it was automatically assumed that the dress would be white tie and tails for men, long evening dresses for women. Only when one was giving an informal dinner party did one expect male guests to turn up in the relatively scruffy attire of black tie and short jacket. In such a case one wrote to one's guests in the second person and in the form of a short letter but one didn't actually stipulate black tie and short jacket; it was inferred by the guests. Nowadays, thank goodness, hosts and hostesses are expected to be a bit more explicit. So if you want your guests to wear black tie, say so. Put the two words under the RSVP.

In the old days a formal dinner of the type implied by use of a card was expected to end almost on the dot of 10.30 or 11, rather like chucking-out time in a pub, hence there was not going to be any time for any diversion apart from eating and drinking. Nowadays you might offer additional delights. (Formerly the 'At Home' card for evening receptions catered for this kind of thing, the evening receptions starting relatively late, say around 10.30 or 11.) Accordingly the words 'dancing' or 'music' could be added beneath the rest of the words on the card, centred if you have taken up two lines each side of the bottom section with the address to the left and 'RSVP' and 'black tie' to the right. If you omit 'black tie' you could put 'dancing' or 'music' under 'RSVP'.

After-Dinner Entertainment
I think you can fairly safely assume that your guests will understand that the music or dancing are to come after the meal rather than before (or during) it. Of course, when the word is simply 'dancing' it indicates that the dancing will be undertaken by the guests not by a special performer. Conversely, as regards the single word 'music', it is the other way round: a rendition on some instrument or instruments or by an accompanied voice will be offered up either by a professional person or gifted amateur, not by the guests.

I used to attend a series of parties in Chelsea where after dinner the diminutive (male) South American possessor of an agreeably large block of emerald mining shares performed nude dances solo to his guests in a manner some way after Isadora Duncan. I think it might be a little disturbing to your guests to announce such details in advance, though of course unless they have drunk a good deal at dinner it is likely to prove even more disturbing when they are confronted by such an item unforewarned. Perhaps you could say something like 'Senhor Gustavo Da Silva will give a short interpretation of exotic dancing.' My friend Lady Cusack-Smith, doyenne of MFHs in the West of Ireland, usually announces on her annual ball invitations that 'De Dannan [a traditional Irish music ensemble] are kindly going to give us some music.' It is not customary to offer any other clue as to how the evening will end up other than if bridge is intended, though if you are going to get up a poker session or a few tables of backgammon I don't see why you shouldn't announce the fact, if only so that your guests can then remember to bring their chequebooks or large wads of cash with them.

RSVP

RSVP, literally *'Répondez, s'il vous plaît'*, or 'please answer' in English, underlines the fact that you need to know whether your invitee can make it or not. Unfortunately it is seldom responded to, chiefly because it is so often added that many of one's slacker recipients have come to assume it is as meaningless as a watermark on writing paper (rather than, as the old joke has it, that it stands for 'Remember Send Vedding Present'). Some hostesses get round this with the words 'regrets only'. Better still, though it is appallingly pampering of the invitee, is to send a pre-paid self-addressed envelope with a card printed 'I can/cannot attend your dinner party on the . . . at . . . o'clock', then get your social secretary to ring the invitee up incessantly until you have obtained a satisfactory indication of his movements that evening.

Black Tie

'Black tie', meaning of course the lesser of the two forms of evening dress for men, is a bit of a misnomer. With the increasing variegation in men's evening wear of the last few years it is probable that the ties worn by your male guests will be anything but black. Nor, I regret to say, will many of the men wear proper patent leather black shoes, unless their womenfolk have the whip hand of them. The phrase 'black tie' is really intended for your female guests, for whom it is an indication that they should attire themselves to kill, or at any rate in long dresses.

Formal Table Decorations

For the sort of dinner you will be throwing in Belgrave Square you might as well go the whole hog as regards table decorations, and here you are at complete liberty to indulge your fancy. Not too many flowers, though, because at night they can be a little stifling, breathing in the oxygen which should more properly keep your

Lady Birmingham's Dinner Party
Tuesday 29th February, 1994

Name(s)..

(Block letters, please)

*Has/have much pleasure in accepting the invitation
of Lady Birmingham

*Regret(s) being unable to accept the invitation of
Lady Birmingham

*Please delete whichever is not applicable

Reminder card for lazy correspondents

guests going. Besides, banks upon banks of flowers have begun to suggest ever so faintly the funeral parlour.

Livery

As a Belgravian, or alternatively as the proprietor of a very large landed estate with suitably big house attached, you might care to put your servants into some kind of livery. By custom one's livery reflects the tinctures (heraldry-speak for colours) of one's coat of arms. This assumes you have a genuine coat of arms. If you haven't, now might be the moment to approach the College of Arms, if you live in England or Wales or are of English or Welsh descent, or the Lord Lyon Office, if you are Scots or of Scots descent, for a grant of arms. You may have been using a certain livery already, but it has been suggested that the Officer of Arms in charge of your petition would try to arrange a grant sympathetic to your existing colour scheme.

If you are already armigerous and then decide to put your servants in livery, the following principles should be borne in mind. Suppose the main colour in your coat of arms is sable, then your livery should be black; if vert, green; if azure, blue; if purpure, mulberry or mauve; if gules, red; if or (a metal), yellow; if argent (also a metal), white. Scarlet livery is a royal prerogative, so if you dress your servants in red livery, make the red more like claret or cocoa. Livery buttons, shoe buckles, anything metal in fact, should be black, alternatively the metal (or, argent) of the main metal colour in the coat of arms. Facings (collars, cuffs, piping if any) should match the secondary tincture in the coat of arms, along the same general principles, e.g. sable = black etc. as mentioned above. The waistcoat should be patterned in narrow horizontal stripes of the two colours already used for coat and facings respectively. If a fur constitutes either of the main colours or metals of your coat of arms, you should use the colour that makes up its ground, according to the following principles: ermine (i.e., black spots on white) = white, as does erminites (a form of ermine in which each black spot contains two red threads, more properly hairs since the fur is supposedly that of an animal, but they resemble threads); erminois (i.e., black spots on gold) = gold; pean (i.e., gold spots on black) = black, as does ermines (i.e., white spots on black).

If the field (background) of the shield of your coat of arms is vair, which is a sort of tessellated curvilinear blue-and-white pattern, you can choose either blue or white as the predominant colour of your livery. If the field is vairy, which means the same pattern as vair but of different colours than blue and white, you can choose either tincture as the predominant one.

Your butler should remain resplendent in black tails. But so as to ensure that he is not mistaken for a guest at a formal dinner, kit him out in a waistcoat of horizontal stripes in the same pattern you put your footmen in.

VARIATIONS: BOHEMIA

My second alternative approach is that of the hopelessly Bohemian or merely disorganised host. I say 'host' advisedly as such a person is usually male, either a bachelor, widower or divorcee still in the full stage of disorientation following the collapse of his marriage. Such people are often very generous hosts with drink, perhaps a little over-generous, but they tend to go to pieces where the cooking and serving of food are concerned. And they often, quite wrongly, assume that table decorations and the laying of places are of little importance. The archetypal host of this sort is Mr Badger in *The Wind in the Willows*, of whom Mr Kenneth Grahame records:

> Conversation was impossible for a long time; and when it was slowly resumed, it was that regrettable sort of conversation that results from talking with your mouth full. The Badger did not mind that sort of thing at all, nor did he take any notice of elbows on the table, or everybody speaking at once. As he did not go into Society himself, he had got an idea that these things belonged to the things that didn't really matter. (We know of course that he was wrong, and took too narrow a view; because they do matter very much, though it would take too long to explain why.)

Unconstrained by the need to get on with the story of the river-bank folk in the way Mr Grahame was, this book has the time at its disposal.

What the slatternly single male needs is the help of a good woman, and women being the delightfully maternal people they are, there is seldom a lack of someone among his acquaintance to boss the Bohemian host around and make him run his dinner party more or less properly. She may have to assume the role suddenly, however, even when already inside the house as one of the guests. I now address the problem as if you the reader were such a woman, because in such circumstances you are effectively a co-host, although a delicate form of one. (For instance, you must in no circumstances boss the other guests around, only your host, and him in the nicest possible manner.)

You should indulge the wretched creature, your nominal host, in all fads that don't actually turn the evening into a bear garden. For instance, he may have got the idea that he can pop pre-prepared food into a microwave and serve it up to his guests as if he had cooked it himself. If it's from Marks & Spencer you may as well acquiesce – the first time. Afterwards you can take him aside and tell him it won't really do, though you should be careful not to damage his self-confidence so badly that he retires from giving dinner parties altogether. If the pre-prepared food is from anywhere else, apart perhaps from a delicatessen you personally know and approve of, he must be rapped smartly over the knuckles then and there and told to beef up his act. You yourself may have to be ready to prepare pasta or scrambled eggs at short notice as a substitute for inedible matter.

He may try to serve his guests in the kitchen even though there is a perfectly good dining room in the house. Again, it is probably better to acquiesce just for the first occasion, but you can soften the harsh light of most kitchens by turning out the overhead illumination and sticking candles into every available empty bottle (of which there are likely to be plenty). Find a tablecloth, gingham for preference, and cover the bare kitchen table with it. Aim, in short, for a bistro effect. The disoriented host will try to plonk guests down any-old-where, and here you can be firm and try to introduce an element of correct placement, or at any rate seat the men and women in a less haphazard order.

He will want to retain complete control of serving the drink. Let him. His guests will probably bring bottles of wine as a contribution. This of course is increasingly the custom at more formal dinner parties too. Although I have written disapprovingly of Mary Killen and her 'Dear Mary' column in the *Spectator* earlier in the book, I am now going to make amends and praise her. One of the recent queries she fielded came from a person who wanted to know if it was acceptable for a host or hostess not to serve then and there on that very night a wine of top quality which a guest had brought along. She made the point that it could hardly be tasted to the best advantage within a few hours of having been jogged up and down and side to side while being transported. So yes, it was OK for the host to keep it for another time.

SAYING GOODBYE

On cold nights it is tempting to see your guests only as far as the front door. But a really good host will go out into even the chilliest air and help his guests manoeuvre their cars into the off position. Since one or two drivers will be a little less skilful in handling their machines than usual – not out of any tendency to have drunk too much, heaven forbid, but out of the sheer exuberance of having been to one of your famous dinner parties, topped up perhaps by a lack of sufficient oxygen towards the end of the evening as increasing use of cigars took its toll on the atmosphere – this can be one of the most important duties of a host. It will also pay dividends in that your flowerbeds and garden ornaments are less likely to suffer if you guide your departing guests down the drive, or at any rate away from the sweep immediately in front of the main entrance to the house.

Drunken Guests

If any of your guests really are very drunk and try to drive home you must be very firm in stopping them. There are reports from America of hosts being found legally liable by the courts if their guests drive away from dinner parties in unfit condition due to drink. That has not happened here yet but common humanity demands that you prevent your guests risking their own lives, to say nothing of the lives of pedestrians they may encounter on the way home or of passengers in their cars.

With drunk women guests you can use a number of excuses, such as 'Are you sure you know the way?', 'There have been one or two attacks on solitary women drivers round here recently; are you *sure* you wouldn't rather we put you up for the night?' or 'Darling, they've started digging up the road between here and Blankford [where she lives]. The detour takes you simply miles out of your way and typically of them they only give directions for the first two or three turns. You'll get hopelessly lost. Stay the night and you'll find it much easier tomorrow.' Or even say you've heard on local radio that a jack-knifed juggernaut has closed the main road a couple of miles west of your house – the exact direction your guest was intending to take. I apologise for any bad taste my female readers may think attaches to invoking attacks on women in cars as a ruse to prevent your guest driving, but the circumstances, surely, turn any lie, however vile in itself, into a white one.

With male drivers, particularly if they are of that rather aggressive, vainglorious disposition one tends to associate with a certain type of man when in his cups, your best bet is surreptitiously to remove his car keys. You may subsequently have to join in a pantomime of looking for them with him, so you should be a reasonably good actor. Or you might remove the distributor from his car or let the tyres down, hoping he doesn't know enough about cars to realise what has happened. If he's really drunk he probably won't, however expert a mechanic he usually is. Drastic moves, I agree, but the highly dangerous alternative risk of his

91

killing himself or somebody else or even just losing his licence is justification.

The Aftermath

Once your guests have gone home or retired for the night, it's tempting to throw in the towel and slope off to bed yourself. But before you do that do try to save the wine from getting too much air and going off by plugging half-finished bottles with those grey rubber corks you can get in off-licences and pumping the air out of the bottle with the white plastic plunger that comes with the grey corks in the same kit. It'll taste perfectly good the next day, or even for the next few days. Lady Kilbannock, in Evelyn Waugh's *Sword of Honour* trilogy, is popularly suspected of fabricating her luncheon rosé out of the left-over red and whites of the night before. Well, there are worse drinks. How parsimonious a housekeeper you are is between you and your four walls.

Make sure all candles are snuffed out and that all cigarettes and cigars have been extinguished. Scatter the logs in the fireplace. Clear away any broken glass with a dustpan and brush, or you will have forgotten about it by the time you come to do the main clearing up the next day and risk cutting yourself. Cover up butter and cheese with cloths to prevent them getting hard and discoloured, or put them in the fridge inside plastic bags. Curtains, particularly if made of odour-absorbent material such as velvet, will stink of cigarette smoke the next day unless you have a well-aired room, preferably with an open fire of wood in the hearth. Somehow this negates the process by which stale cigarette smoke infests all hanging drapery, not to mention cushions and upholstery as well. If the proper functioning of your burglar alarm depends on all the internal doors of the house being shut tight and you have no fire guard you had better douse the fire and open the windows for ten minutes to get rid of the cigarette smoke. Otherwise set the guard well in place and leave the sitting-room and dining-room doors ajar. My late father had a chain-mail mesh sliding curtain constructed on a rod across the fire, which he could then pull shut or open up depending on whether he was in the room where the fire was or absent from it. I recommend this feature highly for those of you with working fireplaces.

In a properly conducted civilisation you could expect to get a series of thank-you letters in the first forty-eight hours after your dinner party. Not these days you won't. If you're lucky you may get a few telephone calls, which will probably occur at the most inconvenient time of day (when you are still clearing up after last night's mess, say). From many of your guests, perhaps a majority, you will hear precisely nothing. There is virtually nothing you can do about this. Just accept it as evidence of our having entered a new Dark Age. You might, I suppose, ring up one of your most uncommunicative, hence putatively ungrateful, guests and ask if the set of false teeth you found under a sofa belonged to him (this is a variant of an old ploy recommended by Stephen Potter in his Gamesmanship books). It should jolt the ingrate into stammering out thanks of a kind. You can then airily mention that his letter of thanks seems to have got lost in the post. This is a cheap sort of triumph, however. As with introducing a couple to each other who later get married and later still messily divorce, the consequences of which I mentioned earlier, entertaining must be its own reward.

Collect all strange garments and bits of jewellery you find while clearing up and store them together near the telephone so that when various guests ring up over the next few days to ask whether they have left their sable stole or diamond bracelet with you or the Grandisons (the couple they dined with the following night), you can make some attempt at identifying the items in question.

CHAPTER 2
Lunches

These used to be frequent affairs in fashionable private life. Nowadays they are getting rarer as a purely social activity, at any rate on weekdays, because more and more people have jobs to do, even those in the thick of the social swim. Nonetheless, as regards busy professional activity (in which category I include award lunches, charity lunches and promotional lunches), entertaining people in the middle of the day has its uses. I will deal with business entertaining separately, only observing here that if you live reasonably near your office a very pleasant variation on the business lunch at a restaurant or club is to host a meal in the middle of the day at home. You can hire an attendant or attendants for the two hours or so necessary, and even then it will cost no more than in a restaurant, and probably much less if you are having more than one guest. Moreover, unlike a restaurant it is a totally discreet venue should you wish to discuss confidential matters. Naturally your house or flat should be elegantly furnished, with plenty of flowers everywhere, but provided the table settings are attractive the meal can be very simple from a food and wine point of view. Some of the best lunches of this sort that I have attended consisted of just a soufflé, though perfectly cooked, and fruit. As for drink, lunchtime consumption of wine these days by people who take their business affairs seriously is likely to be minimal.

But for most of us lunch is the supreme event where we can enjoy ourselves in a relaxed way (as opposed to the rather more effortful dinner party) during our leisure hours. For most people 'leisure hours' means weekends, when it can actually be more pleasant to entertain friends during full daylight rather than at dinner, particularly if the weather is fine and one lives surrounded by beautiful countryside. A walk in the country after the lunch, or a game of croquet, tennis or snooker, helps one's guests digest their meal and rounds off the day very satisfactorily by varying the scenery or, if an indoors activity such as billiards, the backdrop.

94

The same argument in favour of a lunch party over a dinner party goes when one is on holiday, if one makes any agreeable acquaintances near where one is staying, or has friends or friends of friends in the vicinity.

Moreover nearly every guest prefers to drive during daylight, and this is particularly true of older people whose eyes may be easily dazzled at night or people coming to your house for the first time who therefore may not know the way very well. Motorist guests may find it a slight disadvantage being entertained at weekend lunch parties in that they are going to have to be careful about how much they drink whereas at a pinch the heavy-drinking motorist guest can plead for a sofa on which to sleep off his excesses overnight after a dinner party. But from the point of view of the host the enforced abstemiousness for motorist guests is no problem. In any case, even at weekends most people drink less at lunch than at dinner.

CHILDREN

Child Guests
It is permissible, or at any rate not unknown, for guests to bring their children with them when lunching out, although they should certainly ask you beforehand. Bringing children may be considerably more of a benefit to the guest than to the host, but all entertaining involves some inconvenience to the host and anyway there is little you can do to prevent it. Even if you, the host, can't stand the thought of having children in the house, it may cause great offence to say so to their parents. But in such circumstances you might invite an elderly party to the same lunch at which your prospective guests who have children are expected, then explain to the latter that old Mrs So-and-so needs absolute repose, so could they please leave their children at home. If a couple nevertheless bring their children you can try putting the children in another room to eat their meal, the kitchen, say, though naturally you will need a helper there to look after them. Alternatively you can set up a separate children's table in the dining room and put them there, but this only works with well-behaved children of, say, four and older, and they are not likely to be a problem in the first place, unless you loathe all children indiscriminately. Friends who persistently thrust their children on you can simply be deleted from

the lunch-party list and only ever invited to dinner, when presumably they will have the decency to leave their children at home.

The Hosts' Children

What of your own children? I am dealing with them principally here, that is to say in the section on lunches, rather than in that on dinners because I assume that you will have got them out of the way completely when you are giving a dinner party, either putting them to bed yourself, handing them over to a nanny or even sending them to stay the night with their grandparents or a schoolfriend. But much depends on your children's ages. I have been to excellent dinner parties where the host and hostess have used their son and daughter as attendants to wait on guests at table. This presupposes that the children are well-behaved and reasonably adroit at handling heavy and cumbersome dishes. But even if you have the most sure-footed, politest children, using them as waiters may put something of a damper on the conversation if your guests like to discuss the latest political sex scandal with full freedom. If your children are too young to be used as dinner-party attendants (I should have thought that twelve was the minimum age for this sort of task), are they nevertheless disciplined enough to stay upstairs rather than creep down and complain they can't get to sleep or want a glass of water? (This may be a genuine complaint or it may be because they are curious about your guests.) Will the babble of conversation on the part of your guests waft upstairs and interrupt the sleep of children who would otherwise be well behaved enough to stay in their bedrooms? The answers to all these questions lie so much with you, the children's parents, who alone know your offspring's characters, that I can give no hard and fast ruling on what to do. Practicality must be your watchword here.

When you entertain during the daytime any children you happen to have are going to be fairly obtrusive. Below a certain age it really is kinder to all guests to have them kept well away from the company, again either by a nanny or a cooperative grandparent. It is not just the noise small children make which can irritate your guests, but the sight of a child drooling food and drink down its front is revolting. And the food small children send flying round the room when they splash their eating implements up and

down in their feeding bowls can make serious stains on guests'
clothes. Any guest, such as a godparent, who genuinely wants to
see the children can be taken into the room they are in and left
with them while the rest of the company get on with enjoying
themselves.

Adolescents
What of adolescents, 'young people' on the verge of adulthood?
They can be a dreadful damper on social activity if at the sulky
stage. Perhaps even worse is the pert, bright adolescent who tries
to take part in adult conversation. He is likely to be a bore at best,
at worst a tiresome cub correcting his elders on points of fact. The
latter state of affairs is made the more unbearable because he is
probably more accurate than his elders over things like statistics
and dates through having more recently been through the educa-
tional process. It doesn't make his opinionated cocksureness any
more attractive socially, however.

The sulky adolescent is unlikely to stay in the room long. If he
does look like mixing with your friends try to arrange beforehand
to get someone his own age along. The precocious, would-be
sociable one is more of a problem. It would be brutal to snub him.
Even pert adolescents are immensely sensitive, though the sensi-
tivity usually acts inwardly, for themselves, seldom for others.
Again, you can only try to get other adolescents along to cope with
your pert one. Alternatively, that is to say if you can't find a lad of
his own age to keep your seventeen-year-old science whizz of a son
occupied, invite the most pompous MP you know, preferably one
professing an interest in aeronautics, the armed services or nuclear
power or something similarly *Boy's Own*-ish, and put them
together. They will at least neutralise each other. And no MP will
dare snub a person who in a year or two is going to be entitled to
cast his vote for the first time and with luck may be impressionable
right now.

Above all watch every adolescent's alcohol consumption. They
have a tendency to drink far too much far too quickly and then
throw up in the most conspicuous and messy fashion. Female
adolescents should be watched closely in case they succumb to the
advances of males of any age, but especially older men. Do not
make the mistake of giving an airy assurance to a young girl's

97

parents that you can easily keep an eye on her while the parents are absent. I once did so, admittedly after being asked suddenly by a girl's mother and saying yes without thinking. I failed miserably. The eighteen-year-old in question ended up blind drunk within ten minutes of the start of the country-house ball our party was attending, then being seduced by a gossip columnist's son and in the middle of the night puking all over the ballgown of a fellow guest whose bedroom, and indeed bed, she had purloined in any case. The above observation applies doubly to convent girls, who, when away from their nuns, are in my experience considerably more ungovernable than their Protestant counterparts. There is one exception to this: it is (just to show I'm ecumenical about these things) C of E vicars' daughters. Get them away from the manse and they become little Messalinas. Looking after girls is a full-time vocation. It isn't possible on a temporary or part-time basis, whether you are the host or simply a would-be chaperon.

PETS
Similar considerations to those pertaining to children apply to pets, the chief difference being that guests tend to be less hypocritical about any dislike they feel for cats and dogs than they are towards children. It is not just that many people cannot stand being pawed by a dog or used as a sofa by a cat; one also has to remember that quite a few people are allergic to cats (less often to dogs, for some odd reason). Yet a cat in the same room as a man or woman with a horror of the creatures will often sense this and sadistically stalk its victim. I have seen humans actually cowering in a corner, sweat on their faces, while some harmless-looking tabby advances towards them or disdainfully arches its back and stretches its claws into the carpet. Other people may simply dislike getting dog and cat hairs on their clothes. So even if you banish your pets from the rooms you entertain in throughout the entire period when guests are present, do not neglect to sweep those rooms free of all cat and dog fur well beforehand. Birds are less of a problem and can probably be left in their usual room unless they are very noisy, but bear in mind that in hot weather a bird's cage can be smelly. Fish present virtually no problem and their tank can be left entirely *in situ* unless you are giving a party for very dissolute or absentminded smokers who will flick ash into the open

top of the fish tank. And if you serve a rather nasty cocktail, you might even get guests pouring the contents of their glass surreptitiously into the tank.

Guests who bring pets are harder to cope with. We are usually talking about dogs here, at any rate when you are having friends to lunch rather than for an extended stay involving overnight accommodation. (More about house parties in due course.) Guests who bring their dog or dogs with them will almost certainly ask to exercise the animals after a lunch even if you have successfully persuaded them to keep the dog(s) in their car throughout the meal. If you fear your neat garden will be damaged or messed up by a rampaging dog you might try to persuade the guest to take him for a walk along neighbouring roads or lanes. You could always claim that the traffic around your house is too hazardous for an unaccompanied dog to be let loose in the garden, stressing the lax state of your fencing or hedges. Anybody besotted with animals is unlikely to be very amenable to reasoned argument to the effect that your distaste for their pet is just a plain old gut feeling, so a little subterfuge on your part is not only permissible but necessary.

You are expected to feed your guests' children as well as the adults, even if the parents of the said children turn up without having told you beforehand that they would be bringing them. No such obligation rests with you to feed a guest's pet. Indeed you can properly expect the guest to come with her own supply of dog biscuits, water bowl, tin of meat and blanket. You may have to provide matting and old newspapers for the wet and muddy dog to lie on after his walk, however, so always keep a supply in stock.

LUNCHES OUT OF DOORS
Sartorially speaking, lunches tend to be more informal than dinner, with little or no dressing up. Personally I prefer whenever the weather makes it at all possible to entertain friends to lunch out of doors, where extreme informality of clothing is customary. Keep plenty of cardigans and other woollens handy in case the sun becomes hidden and your guests get chilly. They may well have neglected to bring warmer clothes of their own. In general when hosting a lunch out of doors do bear in mind that among your guests there may be hay-fever sufferers, those who are so allergic

99

to wasp and bee stings that their very lives could be in danger if attacked by such insects and those whose eyes or skin are excessively sensitive to sunlight. If you live in the country make sure your local farmer's piggery or silage heaps aren't upwind of your house before planning al fresco entertaining. If it's a clement September or early October day, a time of year when lunching out of doors is still just occasionally possible, forbid your own gardener to light his usual bonfire and check beforehand that your neighbours aren't intending to light theirs.

In England even on the finest summer days there may well be a breeze, which can play havoc with tablecloths, napkins, straw hats, sun umbrellas and women's coiffures. But if you choose a good sun umbrella and a well-sheltered spot in the garden, most of these problems can be kept at bay. Alternatively, you could use the conservatory. If you haven't yet got around to acquiring one, now is the time. They are especially good for entertaining in because they can be used all the year round and if you give a big stand-up party or dance or wedding reception at home they may even make the hiring of a marquee unnecessary. Have plenty of power points put in when constructing the conservatory so that you can use a sound system for dancing to when giving a party there. Power points will also make it possible to instal electric fan heaters if you give a dance there during cold weather. If possible site the conservatory well within reach of the kitchen consistent with having a sunny southerly aspect or you will find yourself obliged to traipse backwards and forwards from the place you prepare the food to the spot at which you consume it.

Another problem with eating out of doors is that although you would think in the wider open spaces cigarette smoke would pose less of a nuisance, by some quirk of Sod's Law the reverse is often the case. And be prepared to spend hours after a lunch party picking up cigarette ends from the lawn or patio. Most smokers seem to think their horrible dog-ends are either invisible or quickly biodegradable and even good for the soil.

Barbecues

I have treated al fresco meals so far as if they were invariably prepared indoors then consumed out of doors, but the barbecue is an exception. The word is of New World origin, Caribbean to be precise – *barbacoa* means a large grid-iron – and it is much more feasible in that New World because of the more reliable weather. The barbecue has certain other disadvantages apart from the changeable climate in the British Isles. The high population density in this country means you may cause as much smoke to waft into your guests' faces due to the restricted size of your patio, or over your neighbours' gardens due to their proximity across the hedge separating your properties, as if you were burning a ton of damp autumn leaves in a billowing wind. There are only a limited number of foods that taste good when cooked over a charcoal grill: sausages, steak, chops, halves of chicken. Moreover, they get cold very quickly in our breezy outdoors. In a relatively small garden the barbecue area can easily become a distressingly prominent eyesore unless kept scrupulously clean. Any humidity in the atmosphere may make the charcoal difficult to light. But on the other hand, if you use firelighters or other spirit-based substances to help get the flame going, they can easily give the food an unpleasant taint.

I realise that not everybody can arrange such a set-up, but in Ireland, where I live, we regularly have indoor barbecues. The term may sound absurd, but the weather there is exceptionally fickle. And if you have a biggish fireplace – say a minimum of 4ft across – and a fairly rough and ready attitude to the risk of getting ash all over the floor, you can rig up a grill over a wood fire and cook meat over it. When we have lunches for twenty guests or more we herd them into the lesser hall of the castle and feed them straight from the griddle. As with baking potatoes, use the glowing embers rather than the dancing flames for cooking over. Incidentally, if you are going in for something more elaborate than run-of-the-mill barbecue food – suckling pig or haunch of venison, say – and lack servants, an adroit child may derive amusement from being asked to play at turnspit, keeping the meat revolving over the fire like a latterday Lambert Simnel.

HOUR OF LUNCHING
Lunch is also a flexible meal from the point of view of time. Formerly it tended to be quite late, starting at 1.30 or even 2 p.m. One o'clock would be thought more usual nowadays, though 1.30 would be perfectly acceptable. If you're on holiday and hosting a lunch in one of the Spanish-speaking lands, including the Canary

Islands, and your guests include natives or people from English-speaking countries who have gone native, remember that they will have become used to lunching fairly late.

MENU

In contrast to the form of dress worn, lunch menus tend to be a shade more traditional than dinner. Guests coming out to the country from town for Saturday or Sunday lunch in colder months almost expect roast beef, roast pork or roast lamb, with all the trimmings of horseradish sauce, apple sauce or mint sauce and redcurrant jelly respectively, together with roast potatoes and root vegetables plus Brussels sprouts. In summer you can be more adventurous, however. I imagine this tendency to conservatism is connected with the fact that weekend lunches are more family-related affairs than are dinner parties, and if children are concerned the menu had better be fairly staid. Most children dislike experimenting with new dishes.

Cutlery, crockery, wine glasses and table decorations can be used as if for a dinner party but less plentifully or elaborately, depending on your menu, guest list, wine cellar and the degree of formality of manners.

LUNCH INVITATIONS

It would be almost affected to issue written or engraved card-form lunch invitations unless the function in question is one of those 'Glencoe Whisky High-Flier Women of Achievement of the Year Award' or '*Daily Planet* Parliamentary Debater of the Decade' affairs. But these are essentially official or commercial activities, not private ones. The exception might be if your business activities are so enmeshed in your private life that no hard and fast distinction can be made between the two. Lord Weidenfeld is an example here, and when I wrote a book for him once he launched it at a semi-private lunch party in his flat on the Chelsea Embankment rather than at a stand-up drinks party in some West End club. Much more agreeable for us who were present. On this occasion it was only sensible to send out engraved invitation cards some weeks beforehand.

If you do want to give large formal lunch parties and send out the invitations, even though it's for a purely social event, convention dictates that they should be in the wife's name only, or at any

Countess of Charleville
requests the pleasure of the company of
Mrs Jane Austen and Miss Cassandra Leigh
at Luncheon
on.....**Tuesday 19th April**.....at..**1·00**..o'clock

Headlong Hall,
Loose Chippings,
Shropshire
                                          R.S.V.P

Invitation to a divorced woman and her unmarried daughter
by the first of her several marriages

rate the hostess's only if the woman cohabits with a man.

If you live in one of the more unorthodox *ménages*, follow my advice as to whom to address when sending out invitations for dinner parties, changing the relevant details as if the more feminine of the two cohabitants were issuing the invitation. In all other respects the engraved or printed invitations for lunches can be laid out as for very formal dinner parties. If you want to send invitations for a less formal lunch party you could write a postcard or letter, addressing your potential guest in the second person. For example:

Dear Jane,

I would be delighted if you [and your daughter Janet or whoever else you want as part of Jane's family] can lunch with me on Wednesday 10 June next at 1 pm.

Yours sincerely,
Joan Summers

In the old days subordinate male members of the same family as the fictitious 'Jane' mentioned above, such as brothers or sons of twenty-one (now eighteen) or over, were supposed to be sent their own invitation cards. If you wish to use the card form of invitation I suppose you might as well stick to this convention, but it hardly matters if you don't.

It is strange how many otherwise educated people still start off 'Dear so-and-so' at the top of a postcard. The address on the right-hand side is sufficient indication of who it is being sent to. Adding 'Dear Jane' at the top of the message on the left-hand side (or on the reverse side if the postcard is not a picture postcard) betrays lack of sophistication.

The old-fashioned books on etiquette suggested that an invitation to a lunch party could be extended less far in advance than with a dinner party but in modern life this is nonsensical. In fact many people nowadays have more lunch engagements than they do dinner ones, if only because they commute a great distance from the country to the city, or even within the city, so that much of their contact with people in the same line of occupation or just friends with similarly constricted lives is more easily maintained through the medium of lunch. Besides, their husband or wife may not get on with the old friend they nevertheless manage to see something of at lunches in the middle of the working day. There may be more lubricious reasons for seeing friends at lunch rather than at dinner parties. One old buddy of mine, married now for fifteen years or so, regularly invites women to lunches in inner-city hotels where he has taken a suite upstairs. This is in case they can be persuaded to accompany him upstairs afterwards for a little post-prandial R 'n R.

Days Your Guests are Free
From the purely etiquette point of view it is true that, given the relative informality of weekend lunches, you can invite guests much closer to the actual date of the meal than with dinner. In practice it doesn't work out that way, for the busier people are in the week the further ahead they may have planned their weekends, particularly if they have an efficient secretary, a loving spouse and children. If you are a childless host try to acquire some kind of information as to the length and timing of the school terms

your friends' children are subject to. Parents whose children are away at school tend to be restricted in their weekend movements by the necessity of having to go down and see their children or have them come home to stay overnight. If one of your friends is a father and divorced after a very traumatic ending to the marriage, sneaking down incognito to the school sports day may be the only opportunity he gets to glimpse his child from one year's end to the next. If your friends' children are boarders, are they allowed out every weekend or two or three a term or none at all? When is half-term? When are Sports Day, Founder's Day, St Andrew's Day, the Fourth of June? If your friends' children are at Eton, where the latter two dates bulk large, you can be sure of one thing: the Fourth of June and St Andrew's Day will not be celebrated on the actual St Andrew's Day (30 November) or the 4 June mentioned in the calendar other than once in ten years or so. Eton is so obsessed with getting pupils into Oxford and Cambridge it prefers nowadays to celebrate these important festivals on Saturdays, even if the actual date falls that year on a weekday. You will expose yourself to far fewer disappointments and less frustration in your social life if you do some preliminary research of this sort.

Whereas with dinner parties the guests by and large are not expected to help with serving or clearing away, and certainly not with the preparation, if only because of the greater degree of formality involved, at a lunch they may well pitch in. That is even true of shopping in the local town, and subsequent preparation in the kitchen, as well as the handing out of food in the dining room or transport of food from kitchen to patio, terrace or whatever if you eat out of doors. This is not only because lunches are seen as more flexible events but because a guest who has motored a long way to visit friends either from town or country or from some other part of the country to your part cannot be expected to be quite so accurate in estimating her time of arrival as with dinner parties. Accordingly you may have guests cast up earlier than expected. Or you may have other guests staying in the house already and they will presumably be ready to give some help before and during the meal. But on the whole it is more likely that guests will be late for a lunch party than for a dinner party. I pointed out earlier that most lunches these days were given at weekends and it is precisely on Saturdays and Sundays that roadworks are likely to be undertaken, or engineering works on railway lines. Few guests take a sufficiently military attitude to travel to find out in advance whether there are likely to be hold-ups of this sort on their route, so your timetable for a lunch may be put quite drastically out of joint. Do bear that in mind when drawing up the menu.

CHAPTER 3

Conversation

This is probably the most ticklish subject in all entertaining and I place it at this point in the book because it applies to all the meals I have already dealt with. It is true that nominally you ask friends round to bridge, tennis or dancing, alternatively to drinks, dinner, lunch or stand-up parties where wine or cocktails are served with accompanying nibbles. Talk is never mentioned when invitations are issued, yet it is crucial to the survival of social life.

There is, it is true, a function called a *conversazione*, but it is for promoting artistic, literary or scientific subjects. Thackeray in *Vanity Fair* describes one:

> Mrs Veal's *conversazioni* . . . took place once a month (as you were informed on pink cards, with ΑΘΗΝΗ [Greek for Athene, the goddess of wisdom and learning] engraved on them), and where the professor welcomed his pupils and their friends to weak tea and scientific conversation.

Even today I believe that the Byron Society from time to time holds *conversazioni* (the word is taken from the Italian, hence the plural 'i') and I recently saw a notice in the papers to the effect that the Institute of Marine Engineers had held one. Thackeray would have seen the funny side of that. But in general the various manifestations of socialising through the medium of the spoken word – chat, talk, conversation, raillery, gossip, call them what you will – remain implicit rather than explicit in entertaining. Nevertheless, you would be quite right to regard any guest who came to a bridge evening or tennis afternoon and said nothing as a boor of the first water. Only at a seance is silence on the part of a guest permissible, and not even then if he or she is the medium.

And whereas an expert dancer, bridge-player or even trencher-man is possibly quite a desirable guest if only because of his accomplishments, most of us would exchange any number of such gifted beings for a few sprightly conversationalists where social

107

activity is concerned. Moreover, people who talk agreeably are equally pleasant company whether you are a host or a guest. So good conversation is arguably more important to successful entertaining than food, drink, table decorations, the personal distinction of the guests and the rank of the host.

Although we tend nowadays rather to exalt spontaneity and deprecate the formality of the Victorians, the conversational powers of you and your guests are not always spontaneously deployed. Some people have a favourite anecdote which they trot out on every available occasion, thereby inducing boredom in those who have heard it before. Others prepare the ground for a *bon mot*. Yet others have stooges who supply them with openings and opportunities in the conversation, like a comedian with his 'feed'. But in the main the talk at a dinner table will flow unpremeditatedly.

Nevertheless you, the hostess, can do much to get it going, stop it from dying and turn it from heading off in dangerous directions. If you can't, you had better have a second-in-command, whether husband or *cavaliere servente*, who can sustain, guide and stimulate it. Conversation – or rather its lack, even simply a degree of stickiness in its progress – may become a sandbar on which the skimming yacht of your dinner party comes to the most horrible grief. But if the conversation goes well your entertainments will be borne on the crest of it as if they were surfers on a rolling wave. And so much do we still regard the successful hostess as a species of impresario that simply by gaining a reputation for having amusing conversationalists to your house you will enter the pantheon whose other members comprise the legendary dispensers of hospitality of the past: Mme Récamier, the Duchesse de Dino, Ladies Cunard and Colefax, Mrs Ronnie Greville, Lady Pamela Berry, Ann Charteris/O'Neill/Rothermere/Fleming.

If you wanted to look up the list of names just mentioned, what source would you consult? *Debrett's Peerage* perhaps? Possibly *Burke's Peerage* as well, for although this book is published as one of a series under the Debrett's general title, candour obliges me to say that *Burke's* has more detail on who is related to whom. Knowing who is related to whom is a vital aspect to entertaining. At the risk of sounding like a compiler of an anthology of Thackeriana I must quote from him on this subject, too:

> The elder Pendennis . . . knew the name and pedigree of every-body in the peerage, and everybody's relations. "My dear boy," he would say [to his nephew], with a mournful earnestness and veracity, "you cannot begin your genealogical studies too early; I wish to heavens you would read in Debrett every day. Not so much the historical part (for the pedigrees, between ourselves, are many of them very fabulous [this is no longer the case and the accuracy has been greatly improved since the early nineteenth century]) as the account of family alliances and who is related to whom. I have known a man's career in life blasted by ignorance on this all-important subject. Why, only last month, at dinner at my Lord Hobanob's, a young man, who has lately been received amongst us, young Mr Suckling (author of a work, I believe), began to speak lightly of Admiral Bowser's conduct for ratting to ministers, in what I must own is the most audacious manner. But who do you think sat next and opposite to this Mr Suckling? Why – why, next to him was Lady Grampound, Bowser's daughter, and opposite to him was Lord Grampound, Bowser's son-in-law. The infatuated young man went on cutting his jokes at the Admiral's expense, fancying that all the world was laughing with him, and I leave you to imagine Lady Hobanob's feelings – Hobanob's – those of every well-bred man, as the wretched *intrus* was so exposing himself. *He* will never dine again in South Street. I promise you *that*.

Mind you, guests can be almost as bad to you as host when you are trying to make pleasant conversation as part of your duties. A man I have known for many years used to spend several months a year in his villa in Spain. From time to time he and his wife would have other English-speaking visitors to that part of the Mediterranean coast over for drinks. One evening an Irish family came along. One of the ladies in the party paying the call had a dog with her. 'Fond of dogs, are you?' the host asked. His guest grew noticeably disdainful. 'We keep a pack of foxhounds at home, actually,' she said.

The old etiquette books laid down quite strict rules on what could or could not be discussed at dinner parties and the various other forms of entertaining listed and described in this book. Religion was out lest it gave offence. Politics was often out lest it led to unseemly altercation (remember Lady Prowche's house party?). Many regiments and similar institutions forbid any talk of 'shop', that is, subject matter of direct interest or importance to the conversationalist from a professional point of view. Clubs discourage business talk and actively forbid members to wave around documents that might have to do with business, even though many clubs would have to close down from lack of revenue if not used incessantly for lunches where business is talked over and for launches of commercial undertakings at drinks parties in the evenings.

If we all obeyed the above strictures there wouldn't seem to be much left to talk about, especially if you have at your table one of those tiresome goody-goodies who says: 'I never listen to gossip about my friends,' which rules out anything about people's personality traits and activities. The problem used to be compounded by the fact that the older books on etiquette had precious little that was helpful or positively informative to say about what *should* form the subject of conversation. One author would advise 'keep conversation general;' another 'keep conversation light and avoid personalities,' both of which are as much practical use as a sick headache.

So what is there for modern hosts and guests to discuss? Politics affects everybody's life sooner or later and although some people claim to be wholly uninterested in the subject they usually mean that a blow-by-blow account of the passage of Clause 42 of this year's Finance Bill through the Standing Committee on Public Accounts is not quite their cup of tea. When it comes to personalities and backstairs gossip about leading public figures they are likely to be as avid for news as anybody. Accordingly, you can have politics discussed as long as it's done fairly frivolously. Journalist guests are best at this. The professional politicians themselves tend to be a bit too prosy, didactic or detailed. In fact, now that politicians are so single-minded, in contrast to the happy amateurs of the past who combined being an MP with a busy practice at the bar or a prolific literary output, it might be best to avoid the discussion of politics and the presence of politicians at the same dinner – if you can.

And don't forget that the old nineteenth-century problems can crop up even today. For instance, a friend you know reasonably well as a parent of schoolfriends of your child, but whom you are not terribly well acquainted with in other contexts, may see eye to eye with you and your MP guest on education but differ sharply about nuclear deterrents or Europe. I cite the last two subjects deliberately as nuclear deterrents can still get people extremely hot under the collar, although less so than a few years ago, and Europe currently holds the position that Suez or the Spanish Civil War once did as a watertight method of breaking up old friendships because of differing views. Even people you know much better and whose souls you think you have explored to the depths where current events are concerned may develop considerable irritation with what they see as the government's foot-dragging over Bosnia, say, and berate your Conservative MP friend who is sitting opposite them at table. Then again, your homosexual friends may dislike the attitude of the governing party to Clause 28 of the Local Government Act which forbids gay proselytising in certain circumstances, especially if the MP you have to the same dinner party is a closet homosexual himself and they know or suspect such to be the case.

Racism is now held by most people to be so disgusting that you would probably exclude automatically friends with hostile attitudes to blacks or Asians or whoever. But remember that an old friend who has never shown signs of such an attitude before tonight might have been mugged by a black man last week and developed distressingly illiberal views as a result. Of course a nimble-minded guest may be able single-handedly to head off any racist unpleasantness directed against him. I recall a dinner party at which a somewhat uncouth young man started making mildly disparaging observations about Jews. One of the other guests quickly chimed in with: 'As my Jewish grandmother used to say . . .', which effectively shut the youth up. That sort of thing only works if the person who has made the unpleasant remarks retains some vestigial sense of shame, however.

Religion sometimes crops up at dinner parties, usually in the form of metaphysical questions such as is there an after-life? Discussions of this sort are likely to stay fairly good-humoured. But doctrinal differences can be fiercely contested among some of your guests once more precise religious beliefs are aired. There, too, the Victorians were not necessarily wrong in steering clear of the topic. Clearly you wouldn't invite a strongly Presbyterian friend to dinner at the same time as a Catholic, but then one of

111

your oldest friends might recently have gone over from the C of E to Rome and even within Catholicism there are various cliques and jealousies so that two Catholics at your dinner table may get into a squabble about something.

As a general rule never discuss, or permit to be discussed, the Irish Question. Irish people who have lived for several generations on the mainland of Britain may still regard any talk of their native turf as just another sign of ignorance and insensitivity by the Sassenach. Ditto Scottish matters. Any guests you have from Ireland or Scotland who actually live there are likely to be more tolerant. Incidentally, natives of either country who still live there can be rather prim about raunchier matters. Bear that in mind. Elderly people can still be shocked by what you and your friends in middle age or youth take for granted and discuss freely.

Another fairly obvious topic to avoid is losses by names at Lloyd's. Even in the past, when the going was good, you could never be absolutely sure who among your guests was a 'name'. Nowadays it is only a very attention-seeking person who advertises the fact. You have slightly more chance of knowing if one of your guests is a Lloyd's broker or agent, but this is all the more reason to avoid the subject of Lloyd's generally since one of your other guests may regard him as the embodiment of her misfortune. Any Lloyd's broker or agent who dines out regularly is probably going to have learnt over the last few years to keep information about what he does for a living to himself in case he gets involved in altercation at social gatherings. You cannot expect to know all about your friends' lives to the extent of being aware who is a member of which syndicate, who is on the verge of bankruptcy as a result of being called on to meet huge insurance losses or who is being sued by one of the persons facing those losses. But if you do a lot of entertaining you ought to keep an eye on the gossip columns to see who is suing whom and who is being cited in a divorce suit. And if you have any barrister friends who specialise in libel, say, or fraud, try to keep up through the press with what they are currently involved in lest you have to the same dinner some person they have cross-questioned in court recently.

Probably the best way to approach the problem of what can be safely discussed is to look at it in terms of your friends' characters. If they have a *bête noire* the chances are that, whatever its nature, it will surface sooner or later. Here is where you may want to have another guest of enormous diplomatic skills. He need not be a professional diplomat, just a natural peacemaker. Possibly your own special talent is defusing awkward situations and if you can be sure you'll be on hand throughout the entire evening by all means rely on yourself to keep the peace. But unless you have servants to do all the menial work there are bound to be moments when you are out of the room supervising developments in the kitchen or elsewhere. Similarly, if the dinner party is a very big one you cannot guide everybody's conversation simultaneously.

I fear I am beginning to make it sound as if every dinner party is likely to end in bad blood, which of course is not by any means the case. Nonetheless, perhaps 10 per cent of dinner parties exhibit at some point signs of distinct mutual antipathy between two or more of those attending. The longer the dinner parties go on and the more there is to drink the greater the risk. But don't rush your guests through their meal or let them die of thirst for fear an altercation may blow up.

Where conversation is likely to tread on sensitive issues, consider having people to a buffet meal. They will be milling around throughout the reception rooms or even upstairs, so altercation is less likely to be a danger. And conversations between a knot of two or three people aren't overheard by others to such an extent as they are at dinner parties.

CHAPTER 4

Buffet Lunches and Suppers

The buffet style of entertaining is more flexible than a sit-down dinner or lunch. It allows you to play host to more people than you might be able to seat at your dining table and it largely dispenses with the need for servants or constant attendance by yourself on your guests if you have no servants. Nevertheless you will find yourself pretty busy in a more intermittent way than at a sit-down dinner party and more peripatetically too. You must be prepared to dart around the room or rooms, urging on the shy to help themselves, helping your short-sighted or merely confused guests find various dishes and condiments, replacing a guest's dropped fork here or spilled glass there.

Because the guests stand up to help themselves then walk around eating their food, or sit down on chairs and sofas throughout the room or even the entire house, there is inevitably more spillage, more breakage, more muddle than with sit-down affairs. If you have very good carpets you may want to consider very seriously whether the saving in convenience with a buffet is worth the danger of food and drink getting trodden into your kelims and Aubussons. A halfway house might be to serve dinner in the style that used to be called *à la russe*. Here the guests are seated at table as at a conventional dinner party but the main dishes are placed on a sideboard and carved there, if they need to be carved at all. In the variant of the *à la russe* method which I have in mind the guests queue up at the sideboard and serve themselves, taking their plates back to their respective places at the main table to eat. As the meal wears on they will be more likely to change places than at a conventional dinner party, which may save you having to swap them around yourself (see the chapter on dinner parties). This, of course, still hampers you as to numbers if you have a dining table that is less than enormous. An alternative is to set up a series of smaller tables, possibly collapsible ones of the pembroke or card table type, in the sitting room as well as the main one in the dining

114

room. You do not have to use tables exclusively: at country-house balls guests often sit on the stairs to eat their buffet suppers, even when attired in white tie and tails for men and ballgowns and tiaras for women. Or you could extend the separate table principle indefinitely and set them up all over the house, wherever there is room. Clearly the layout and size of your house will dictate tactics here.

With a buffet the fork is the supreme instrument, being held in the right hand while the left grasps the plate on which the food is piled. Nobody manages successfully to grasp their wine glass as well – not, at any rate, for any length of time – and although one quite frequently comes across little plastic grips which are supposed to clip on to the side of one's plate and hold a glass in them alongside the food, they never really seem to work. The average glass is too heavy for one thing, certainly when anywhere near full, and the resultant structure too cumbersome and top-heavy. People cannon into each other at buffets and a wine glass precariously attached to the side of a plate at right angles to the plane of inclination of the plate is a recipe for disaster. Plastic drinking vessels, though lighter, invariably come in tumbler shape, whereas the clip works well only if the drinking receptacle has a slender waist which can be slotted into it. I have come across very light wooden drinking vessels of proper wine glass shape – some Balkan countries and the Japanese have been known to manufacture them – and these would be ideal except that they tend to be painted in garish peasant colours. Furthermore, they are hard to find.

Of course, if one is to face facts in a brutally honest state of mind, one would have to accept that the best method of providing your guests with drink as well as food if they are obliged to stand up and eat simultaneously would be to give them wine in leather water bottles which they could sling over their shoulders on cords and suck at through straws. But even in our present relaxed state of civilisation this is unthinkable unless you throw a fancy-dress buffet to which everyone is asked to come as an irregular skirmisher or *vivandière* of any European war between the Middle Ages and the Napoleonic period. Or as one of a band of Italian *banditti* of Byron's time.

BUFFET FOODS

In view of the foregoing considerations, you need to think very carefully about what food to serve at a buffet. Soup is fine, provided you hand it round in cups, preferably with handles since it ought to be piping hot. Plastic cups may be fine for wine-drinkers unencumbered with food on plates, being unbreakable, but they conduct heat too easily to the fingers to be acceptable for soup. Rice and rice-type dishes – risottos, pilaffs, couscous – are fine in theory but the smaller-grained the food the greater the difficulty of cleaning the carpets of all the spilled bits afterwards. And any meat dish with gravy can turn into a nightmare once spillage occurs. Because people are holding their plates with their left hands and eating with a fork in their right the use of a knife becomes almost obsolete. So meat must be very tender and cut up beforehand into small chunks – almost minced – but at the same time rendered fairly glutinous by adding a suitable sauce, which mince rarely is, otherwise bits of the mince or whatever will be spilled too.

Salads are theoretically ideal at buffets, but you should either cut the lettuce very fine (the iceberg or cos variety is preferable to the standard floppy one) or replace it with a smaller, more compact green vegetable such as fagioli beans. Otherwise your guests will be unable to cut the lettuce into smaller pieces with the forks they hold in their right hands and in spearing it and lifting it to their mouths they are likely to spill dressing down their clothes. The really ideal piece of cutlery for a salad would in fact be the teaspoon, but convention forbids this.

BUFFET CUTLERY AND CROCKERY

Serving your guests at a buffet has the great advantage that it allows you to use disposable tableware: paper plates and napkins, plastic forks, spoons, cups and knives. But try to procure tough paper plates. (I haven't ever come across any that allow one to cut up meat properly without the plates buckling or, even worse, being cut open so that the food seeps through on to one's trouser leg – assuming that one has been able to find a place to sit down and balance the plate on one's thigh in the first place.) Ditto plastic forks. All the ones I have come across break as soon as you encounter any really solid bit of food. Plastic knives are never sharp enough. I have already referred to the disadvantages of plastic cups when filled with hot fluids.

TIMING OF BUFFETS

You will perhaps have begun to suspect from the above paragraphs that I don't much care for buffets. Certainly, whether speaking as host or guest I have usually found them more troublesome than they are worth from the gluttonously restricted point of view of the out-and-out epicure. Their justification, then, lies in the fact that they allow you to serve lots of friends simultaneously, that they save you having to hire servants and wash up afterwards, and above all in the flexibility they offer where the time element is of paramount importance. By this I mean that they are perfect for feeding guests soon after a performance or a ceremony – wedding breakfasts, funeral baked meats, theatre suppers, or receptions for a special friend who has just given a song recital, danced the role of Giselle at the ballet or fiddled her way manfully through Max Bruch's Violin Concerto. In such circumstances it would take too long to prepare a formal meal, seat the guests and serve them, if only because the dinner party is predicated on everyone arriving at once, or at any rate being seated and served at once. With buffets it does not matter so much whether the full complement of guests you were expecting all turn up or not. When several contingents of guests are struggling back from a church, concert hall or opera house in terrible traffic this is again an advantage. Nor need there be so much inhibition about starting the meal before every guest is present, unlike with a dinner party.

You may be so punctilious you nevertheless wait until all your guests have arrived before letting them loose on the food. But punctilio can be a false kindness. With friends who have that evening been earning their livings as performers – usually one's star guest – it is often most important to nourish them as soon after the show as possible, otherwise their adrenaline dies away, their blood-sugar level drops alarmingly and they get very peevish. Maria Callas was once being put up at the house of a Washington hostess after a performance she had given in the American capital, and when not handed her fodder within minutes of getting back from the opera house became distinctly stormy, moaning: 'Food –

food – food' until her hunger was assuaged. Those who were there say that until she was fed her stage interpretation of Medea was as a cooing dove in comparison.

I do not propose to deal with the specific problems engendered by weddings as these are covered in Jacqueline Llewelyn's *Debrett's Wedding Guide*; nor with those arising in the case of funerals, as I shall be covering them in a companion volume to this book. Let us first tackle the post-performance supper, then. Late that afternoon you have prepared the food – either concocting dishes that can be served cold or ones that can quickly be heated up in microwave or on hot plates – laid out the crockery, cutlery and drinking vessels in the appropriate room(s) and provided seating for the hard core of distinguished or infirm guests who must on no account be obliged to stand, even though it is a buffet. If even the seated guests are not to have a small table at which to eat you may want to think about providing them with trays. Certainly elderly or infirm guests should at the very least be supplied with plenty of cushions. The rest of the guests will presumably stand or perch on window seats, other cushions on the floor, sofa arms and other unorthodox sites.

BUFFET INVITATIONS
The method of extending invitations, and to whom, needs forethought. Are you going to invite everybody several days prior to the night or walk round the groups of your friends at the recital, theatre, opera house or ballet in the interval or while everybody is congregating before or after the show and whisper, 'Would you like to come back and have a little supper? Madame Castafiore [or whoever the star performer is] said she would look in.'? The trouble here is that even the best-controlled whisper will be heard by some other person, one of your acquaintance you didn't have room for or didn't want to invite, and can thus cause needless hurt.

Similar considerations operate if the performance has taken place in your own house. You have artfully to shepherd the guests you wish to entertain at a buffet in the direction of the dining room while readily allowing, if not actually discreetly encouraging, the others to depart. If you have a big enough house it would be wiser to prepare the buffet in the morning room or library rather than the dining room, as to do so in the latter would give the game away to the unfortunates you have not asked to stay on. Some billiards tables have detachable hard covers which make excellent impromptu buffet tables. You might therefore think of using the billiards room.

The trouble is, the essentially informal nature of a buffet is spoiled if you send out invitations in advance. In any case the problems of timing that I mentioned earlier operate with any kind of advance invitation. So, for instance, if you send out an invitation to the buffet saying 'from 10.30 on' and several of your most important guests get held up by traffic until 11.30, you find yourself in the dilemma of whether you start without them or risk your other guests, who have arrived on time, fainting from hunger. That is more the case nowadays than formerly because very few people will aim to tuck into a dinner then take some supper a few hours later, in the way they once did, so that by 10.30 you will have some pretty ravenous guests on your hands.

On the other hand, if you invite people at the last minute a number may already have made arrangements to eat at a restaurant after the show; others may need to get back immediately to the babysitter, before the latter's overtime rates soar into the stratosphere. Nevertheless, from the point of view of your guest – and this should always bulk large in the minds of practitioners of successful entertaining – there is something delightful about being asked *sotto voce* to drop in for a little buffet supper the same evening as one has undergone a heavy dose of culture, whereas being asked to a formal dinner at equally short notice is near to being an insult (is one only a stop-gap, one asks oneself).

CHAPTER 5
Other Meals

Tea

If luncheon parties during the week have fallen rather out of fashion, tea has dropped out of sight altogether – as a social function, that is. Presumably farmers and similar outdoor folk gnaw on bread and butter and hunks of rich Dundee cake, washing them down with strong cups of Indian, once the afternoon milking is done. Indeed, the only family I know who still invite their friends to afternoon tea are a mildly impoverished gentleman farmer and his wife. But this is a book about entertaining, not folkways, however interesting a cultural survival examples of the latter may be.

The key word in the above paragraph is 'impoverished'. If you look at the older etiquette books such as those by Lady Troubridge and her circle you will find that dinner-party giving is decreed as being restricted to those with substantial incomes and tea is the recommended mode of entertaining for lesser beings. It was not just the cost of alcohol but that of employing cooks to prepare the dinner, serving men to hand it round and scullery maids to wash up afterwards. Tea parties required none of these things, though if you had a butler he could be used to distribute sandwiches, cakes, biscuits and teacups.

Now that wine has become cheaper in terms of average disposable income than for many decades, and now that all the aids to convenient entertaining I mentioned in the Introduction are within every middle-class person's reach, the distinction between the tea-party-giving classes and the dinner-party-giving ones has disappeared, at least as regards an income qualification. Not only that, but the great mystique attached to tea has disappeared. I do not, of course, refer to the drink but the meal, for there undoubtedly was a mystique and tea at its best seems to have been a very British sort of ceremony, perhaps the supreme example of the genre. It was also bound up with At Homes and other obsolete forms of social activity. Thus one had the *thé dansant* whereas a '*déjeuner dansant'* sounds an absurdity. Tea in its heyday tended to be more a favourite with women than with men. P. G. Wodehouse in one of his short stories has Jeeves getting rid of an obnoxious female friend of Rosie M. Banks, the novelist wife of Bingo Little, by fomenting a quarrel between the ladies. The quarrel is the more bitter because they have been deprived of their tea through the means of an apparent mechanical fault in their car during an all-day trip by Little, Wooster, Banks and obnoxious female friend to the races. The party has had a scanty lunch in any case, but when explaining his tactics afterwards to Bertie Wooster Jeeves observes that the mere deprivation of her lunch would not of itself sour a woman, it is the absence of tea, especially on top of no lunch, that does the real damage. Nowadays that *aperçu* seems even more dated than Bertie Wooster employing a valet. I do not actually know whether Jeeves' analysis of the female sensibility in the twenties and thirties has any basis in fact, but tea certainly did bulk large in a general way in those days.

Tea must be the most flexible meal. It can consist of a single cup of jasmine-scented hot water at one extreme or at the other extreme a huge spread comprising not just a strong sergeant-major's brew in which the teaspoon stands up unaided, together with bread and butter, sandwiches, crumpets, muffins, toast, toasted buns, biscuits and cake, but also ham and eggs, scrambled eggs, shrimps and other cooked delicacies. In the latter case it is known as high tea or meat tea and as with fish knives and doilies a certain suspect quality attaches to the concept. The snobbish disdain investing high tea seems to have arisen because it is somehow considered working-class, high tea being the sort of meal a manual labourer would demand on getting back from the coal mine or road-building site. The upper classes, this theory goes, having not soiled their lilywhite hands in the same way, can wait till dinner at 8 or 8.30 at night, whereas the navvy has his substantial repast at 5 p.m., 5.30 or 6.

Yet in fact even the grandest afternoon At Homes of sixty and seventy years ago involved lobster and wine cup, both of which are suspiciously close to what we might call a 'meat tea'. And in our own time children and adolescents of all classes frequently eat high tea, both because their bedtimes are earlier than adults' and because they have quite often spent the afternoon in strenuous physical activity. Schoolchildren of as old as eighteen enjoy a good blow-out after an arduous game. In the same way if people have been out hunting ever since breakfast at 9 a.m. they may well be ravenous when they get back in the mid to late afternoon of a winter's day. In such circumstances you can offer your guests scrambled eggs, or at the very least a lightly boiled one, without incurring any reproach.

Other guests might also appreciate something relatively solid, hot and savoury at that time of afternoon. For instance, you might be hosting a house party in some remote corner of the country and one of your guests arrives several hours late because of incompetent time-keeping by British Rail, or a car breakdown. He could well have had nothing much to eat since breakfast. Don't let the pundits frighten you into never offering a highish tea whatever the circumstances just because the concept has been tainted by 'low' or 'genteel' associations.

Breakfast
Like weekday lunches in private houses, this meal has rather fallen into abeyance as a method of entertaining one's friends. The reason is similar; more people have jobs to go to. I suppose an exception might be an undergraduate, the sort of consciously anachronistic young Oxford blood up at 'The House' who hunts with the Bicester and dines with the Bullingdon. But there's no reason why more run-of-the-mill students shouldn't go in for breakfast parties, too. The crucial factor with undergraduates or students is that when up at a university most live within a short distance of each other and can call round on each other without recourse to crowded public transport, as would be the case in a big city. Nor do they have to be at an office at nine or thereabouts. Of course, the working breakfast has a certain vogue too, particularly among international statesmen or more run-of-the-mill politicians on foreign jaunts. This class of person likes to give the impression to electorates watching them on television as they confer over hot croissants at some unearthly hour that they are not just abroad on a junket but firmly committed to furthering world peace or some similarly specious nonsense. (I will deal with working breakfasts later, under business entertaining.) Back in the sixties, Sir (as he then wasn't) David Frost once invited to breakfast the Prime

Minister of the day, Lord Wilson of Rievaulx (as he then wasn't), along with a clutch of other celebrities of the age. The menu comprised kidneys, bacon and eggs and caviar with sour cream, washed down with champagne. It was served at the Connaught. The host told the press that it was a private party – 'a chance for a few friends who don't always meet to gather and chat'.

The Rev. Sydney Smith said he liked breakfast parties because no one was conceited before one o'clock in the day. I can't say I've noticed it myself, but perhaps things were different in his lifetime (1771–1845). In Sydney Smith's day there was a ceremony called the wedding breakfast, and if you get married in the morning, as I did once, you could stage a slap-up meal with plenty of champagne afterwards. Most people's weddings take place in the afternoon nowadays and the meal afterwards is called a reception.

If you give a breakfast party it ought to be relatively elaborate. There's little point in serving up nothing more than a bowl of muesli and a carton of low-fat yoghurt, even though that may be more typical of most people's breakfast menu than kedgeree, devilled kidneys, champagne or Buck's Fizz, ale, beefsteak and onions. If you go in for anything like the last three items your guests will need exceptionally strong systems to be able to cope with such fare early in the day, or they will have spent an hour or two beforehand in strenuous physical activity. They might have been wildfowl shooting, for instance, or have hacked across country to your hunt breakfast. When I was at Eton we had a breakfast of beefsteaks and ale on the day of the annual Wall Game match between the Oppidans and Collegers, and very welcome it was, too, if one had been out in Thames Valley mud early on a late November morning getting in the last few hours' practice before the match itself. This, then, was a deliberate throwback to high Victorian custom, and significantly it is among fashionable young bachelors in nineteenth-century novels that one most often comes across the breakfast party.

PART 2

Parties

CHAPTER 6

Parties

If dinner parties are at the same time the commonest form of entertaining and entertaining raised to its highest power, parties are more Dionysian. By that I mean less restrained, more loosely structured. I was almost going to say more fun, as if fun could be measured or reckoned to be more in evidence because people were dancing rather than sitting quietly conversing over a dining table. 'Boisterous' would perhaps be a more accurate word.

Nevertheless boisterousness is relative, and parties range from sedate sherry symposia to wild extravaganzas costing hundreds of thousands of pounds. But they tend to have a few things in common all the same. First of all, the guests stand up – at least initially – and move about, talking now to one person now to another. Secondly, the food and drink are either served while you stand up to consume them or, if you sit down, you do so without being allotted a particular place. Or if you are – at a catered coming-of-age birthday party or elaborate dance in the country – dinner is a secondary feature compared with the band, the disco, the cabaret, the lights, the fireworks and so on.

As regards the menu generally, see the section on buffet suppers. If you are having servants to hand the food round, you can be less constrained as regards menu than I suggested in that section. If you are getting the food catered by one of the masters of colour coordination like Lorna Wing (tel: 071-731 5105), it would be absurd to worry about crumbs getting trodden into the carpet. It would be like persuading Rembrandt to paint your portrait and then fussing because there was a smell of turps in the studio.

A dinner party in a private house for x people is only going to set you back a sum of money within a fairly narrow range. At its most expensive it is unlikely to cost more than three times what it would do if organised on a shoestring for the same x people. A really elaborate party could cost a hundred times what a modest affair for the same number would do.

Your guest list is bound to be more comprehensive with a party.

127

You can afford to have more duty guests and bores at it than at a dinner. They won't stay long, or if they do they'll congregate together in one room while the non-bores take over the others. But when you give a party with someone else there is a risk that your guests may not mix enough with his. The good hostess does her best to stir the ingredients thoroughly on such occasions, taking round key personnel to be introduced to new people every so often. To get a party moving you may have to break up quite cosy conversations and tow one of the people involved in it away to be introduced to somebody else. To begin with you should do that, at any rate; towards the end of a party it is bad form to break up couples, particularly if they are coupling (something that will happen at the best parties, or in my experience happens at the best parties rather more than at other ones).

In fact you may find yourself tempted when giving a big party to work off every social obligation you have built up in twenty years. Don't do it – or don't do it without thinking. Parties are much more flexible than dinners, but also much more volatile, one might even say fragile. One wicked fairy who has not been invited and who crashes it, or a wicked fairy who has been invited and still manages to dispense bile, wild behaviour or offensive language, can ruin the evening. Talking of gatecrashers, the party caterer Andrew Chance (tel: 071-376 5995) maintains that the swiftest way of guaranteeing disaster is to economise on bouncers.

Whether you are having your party catered or doing it all yourself, decide what you want to spend on (a) drink, (b) food, (c) music, (d) other entertainment (fireworks, a cabaret, for example), (e) the premises (can you do it all at home, must you add a marquee in the garden, or should you hire somewhere else altogether?). Then work out how many people you can afford to invite, bearing in mind that an elaborate affair is not going to make much sense unless you have fifty people minimum attending. Then allow for people not turning up, say 10 per cent. Party-giving is one of the few activities where you make no economies of scale. If you manufacture 1,000,000 cars it costs you less per unit of raw material, power and so on than if you manufacture only 1,000. If you invite 2,000 guests to a party it will cost you four times as much as if you hire 500 – probably a great deal more than four times as much.

If you throw the party at home invite your neighbours, assuming

128

they live sufficiently close to you that they would be disturbed by the noise otherwise (or perhaps just made jealous by being excluded). If you throw it locally in the country and invite some but not all of local society, be prepared with a very good excuse for those who are not to be on your list. For instance, you could say that you wanted to have people from further afield. But if that is supposed to be the case why have anyone local at all? You see the difficulty, I trust.

Rather than annoy your neighbours you may decide to have your party at a local hotel, assembly rooms, restaurant or private club. It is also more convenient if it is someone else's building that gets turned topsy-turvy before the party, to say nothing of clearing up the mess afterwards. Many people, even when having a party at home, prefer to have it catered. But the costs sky-rocket and you tend to lose something in atmosphere. And though your guests may not say so outright, they do appreciate a party organised at your own house rather than in the anonymity, however well dressed up for the occasion, of a restaurant, or the local 'stately home' hired for an evening.

With large numbers of guests it makes even more sense than with dinner parties to send out the invitations by post. Ring ten people and half will be out or the line engaged. So write to them and follow up the invitation with telephone calls if necessary. Invitation cards vary enormously. I have come across many an amusing magazine article listing the various styles in that line, with an illustration of what sort of party one can expect from what sort of invitation. Issuing facetious invitations is a phase we all go through, usually as teenagers. But all types of invitation, as with dinner invitations, ought to supply basic information such as time of kick-off, date, dress, location of function, location and identity of people to whom to RSVP (if different from you, the host), identity of guest and identity of host(s).

The size of an invitation card is thought by most guests to be a guide to the degree of elaboration of the party. The larger it is the more the host will be spending on the party and the more worthwhile it is for the guest to go. So by sending out large cards you are likely to push up the acceptance rate by 10 to 20 per cent. I would have thought that 9ins by 6ins would be the absolute maximum for an invitation card, but some may be folded in two, particularly if the party is to take place in the country and the

Lord Sebastian Flyte and Mr Charles Ryder

Mrs Stuyvesant Oglander
at Home
for Diana
Saturday, November 2nd
The Assembly Rooms, Plumstead Episcopi

R.S.V.P.
Matching Priory,   Dancing 10.30 p.m.
Hogglestock, Barsetshire   White Tie

Invitation to a dance sent to both parties in a *ménage*

invitation gives details of where the guest down from the big city will be staying, how he should get to wherever it is and so on.

If you buy a set of At Home cards pre-printed, you lose the ability to have them larger or smaller depending on the size and luxuriousness of the party. But the wording 'At Home' on any card can be used both for the meanest little potato crisps and vin ordinaire session of a dozen people in a basement flat in Earl's Court and a Lucullan masked ball in a Venetian *palazzo* for 2,000 people flown in at your own expense from all over the world with entertainment that includes lion-tamers, jugglers and performing elephants. It is one of the paradoxes of modern entertaining that 'home' is more and more often the place you won't be 'at' when you give a big party, because you don't have any or enough servants living in or you don't have a big enough house. Never mind.

Your name and the name(s) of any co-hosts can be engraved. The name of your guest can either be written in the top left-hand corner or filled in where the blank is, if the invitation is of the type 'Mrs John Smith requests the pleasure of the company of'

130

followed by an empty line. Write either the first name only or the first name and surname, depending on how well you know your guests. Avoid ambiguity. If you are sending an invitation to a Mr David Jones who has a son Dennis, an initial only will not suffice; make it clear whether you mean father only or father and son. Likewise with the wife and daughter. With couples who live together unmarried it would be best just to write their first names, unless they have hordes of children some of whom use the father's surname and others of whom use the mother's. (I have known this confusing state of affairs to happen.) *Debrett's Correct Form* has numerous examples to assist with sending invitations to titled personages.

As our basic form of party invitation we have:

Mrs John Smith
At Home
Monday 23 April 1994

RSVP	Drinks
2414 Park Lane	7.30–9.30
London W1	

You could put 'Cocktails' instead of 'Drinks', though unless you really are going to serve cocktails it would be a misnomer. With drinks you usually specify a time of starting and one of finishing, even though some of your guests may stay on well after 9.30 and then go on to a restaurant (to which they ought to have the decency to take you, the hostess). You could start at 6.30 and finish (notionally) at 8.30, but people will tend to straggle in some time after 6.30 if you do, and without having gone home from the office to bath and freshen up generally beforehand. Hence it is kinder to put 7.30 to 9.30 rather than the earlier time.

These days people would expect champagne as the form of 'drinks' if sent an invitation like the one illustrated above. If you can't afford champagne you have no business hosting parties in Park Lane. If you want to serve still wine, distribute invitations by phone and have the party somewhere less exalted. Some people try to serve non-champagne sparkling wine at their parties well wrapped up in a napkin and distributed by a waiter, but few sophisticated guests are fooled. I don't say you shouldn't try it, and some of the best sparkling wines that are nevertheless not allowed to call themselves champagne are better than those minor products of the champagne district which are. With the drinks at any of the aforementioned parties you should serve things to eat. But 'eats' are never mentioned on invitation cards unless a business is doing the entertaining. On such an occasion it is wise to let the freeloading journalists you hope will write you up know that it is worth their turning out in force. Hence businesses seeking a favourable press should also specify the marque and year of the champagne, assuming it is a good vintage – which it had better be, or you'll find yourself the target of waspish remarks in the columns of the more epicurean business journalists.

Notice that Jane Smith sends her invitations out under the first name of her husband, John. If she is unmarried she can of course use Jane Smith. For a big party both husband's and wife's names can be mentioned, though the older writers on entertaining deprecate this, saying the wife only should issue invitations to evening parties.

The Chairman and Directors of
Scrooge, Marley & Company Limited
request the pleasure of the company of
Thomas Creevey and partner
at their Annual Reception
on Thursday, 28th February
at the Vander Plaza Hotel, Berkeley Place, London W1

R.S.V.P. to the Secretary
Scrooge, Marley & Co. Ltd
852, Mincing Lane, London EC1.11 2JD

Pol Roger

7.30 – 9.30 p.m.

Corporate invitation to a gossip columnist. Note the strategic mention of the champagne marque to procure a friendly write-up

If more than one person is giving the party, all or both names are listed, either vertically one above the other or horizontally, which is usually only possible with two names at most.

Some women like to give parties for younger people, usually but not always their daughters or sons, goddaughters or godsons, nieces and nephews and so on. In such cases they might add the line(s) 'for Miss Annabel Smith' below the line 'At Home'. Alternatively you can put 'for Annabel' if the relationship of hostess to beneficiary is well known, usually only if they have at least the same surname.

Instead of 'Drinks' you can put 'Dancing', but of course then you would specify a later time of starting, at the very earliest 8 p.m., and omit any mention of a finishing time. The later you start a party the later it is likely to go on, assuming the drink holds out. Even if you put 'Breakfast 9.30 a.m.' or 'Breakfast from 5 a.m.' as some indication that the party, having gone on all night, should start to wind up about then, it will make no difference to most of your guests. Once guests have survived to 3 a.m. or later nothing will fell them in their tracks except sheer physical exhaustion. It would be wise to have a secret cache of extra drink somewhere, rather like the auxiliary petrol tank in a car, for guests with unusual stamina and drinking capacity. Do not, on being asked for yet more champagne, say something like, 'I do have some Dom Perignon tucked away, but . . .' looking round the company, '. . . I don't think it'd do for just now,' or, almost as bad, 'I do have some bottles of champagne but they aren't on ice.' Both the hosts who have said that at a party I attended were millionaires.

I have come across invitations with 'Carriages at dawn' printed in the bottom right-hand corner, but they are no general indication of when a party is expected to end since when dawn is depends on the time of year. By and large any party that starts after 8.30 in the evening can be expected to continue till the early hours of the next day at the very least.

When you are hosting a big dance in the country you really should organise some sort of accommodation for your guests if those guests have come far. By far I mean more than twenty miles, though with the police making a nuisance of themselves to drivers the way they do these days all your guests would be wise to arrange overnight accommodation. My point is that it is no responsibility of yours if your guests are near neighbours. Nevertheless a thoughtful hostess ropes in her neighbours to provide a preliminary dinner party for up to eight guests before the party starts, if it is a big one (and therefore starts about 10 p.m.). She will also try to arrange overnight accommodation, for convenience's sake with the same people as are giving the preliminary dinner party. This needs patient groundwork carried out months in advance and of course the friends providing accommodation and a dinner must be put high on your guest list.

Send full photocopies of route maps, a separate card with the invitation for the invitee to fill in and say if he wants accommodation, plus full directions as to how to reach the house of his overnight/dinner-party hosts as well as instructions on how to get to yours. You have every right to say that if you haven't heard from your invitee by such-and-such a date you will assume he doesn't need accommodation.

In addition you should create a boys' and perhaps also girls' dormitory in an attic or, in summer, outhouse at your own residence. That way you can put up twenty or more of your guests yourself. In summer quite light bedclothes will be sufficient. Camp beds with sleeping bags are preferable to sleeping bags only, but the latter will do at a pinch if placed on plenty of cushions.

If you are celebrating your own or your wife's, son's or daughter's birthday, or your wedding anniversary, do for heaven's sake say so to every one of your guests or keep quiet about it altogether. It is acutely embarrassing for friends who are not informed in advance to find that half the rest of the guests have turned up with birthday presents. For a big party you would stipulate dress on the invitation, 'black tie', 'fancy dress' or whatever, as with dinner invitations. If you want your guests to dress up in period costume by all means say so, but do not expect any great historical accuracy.

If you get the party catered, agree in advance with the hired servants exactly how long they are supposed to be working. Ditto the band. Most musicians need at least half an hour off in the middle of a party for their own supper, as well as rest. It is a good idea to send your guests into supper while the band is resting. A former MFH I know locks her guests out of the dining room till around midnight then gets her huntsman to blow a few blasts on the hunting horn to indicate that it's feeding time. After half an hour the first sitting is shooed out of the dining room and the second contingent is allowed in. This works well. Two sittings won't be necessary if your dining room is very large or your guests number no more than 200 or so.

Arrange to have a substitute band play during the principal band's rest interval or put on a disco. Don't use live rock musicians for dancing to at parties; they're no good at it. A well-managed disco firm will test its equipment at your house well before the party starts to ensure that it gives out the best sound in terms of volume and beat and clarity of vocals for whatever room it is in. Remember that if you erect a marquee in your garden the sound will carry much further than if the music comes from within the house, though if it is summer the windows of the house will be open and the sound will carry pretty far out of doors even when generated inside the house. Even if you invite close neighbours, you should in common courtesy also alert further neighbours. Noise carries far on a still, hot summer night. It is best to alert the police beforehand wherever you hold your party, whether at home or in a local hotel, so that they can direct cars and arrive promptly to break up any fights or arrest violent gatecrashers. (Gatecrashers who commit no damage to property the police will probably not have the power to arrest.) A letter of thanks to the local police would not come amiss. *Douceurs* or outright bribery of the police must not even be contemplated. You may have the police calling anyway, either because some guest has parked his car in a dangerous position on the high road or left his lights on or because the neighbours are complaining of the noise. The police will be much friendlier if warned in advance of what is going on.

If you are organising a table for friends at a charity ball or any kind of ball where guests pay money for the privilege of attending, make it clear to all your party well in advance what is to be paid for by them, how much it will cost and so on. Remind them as tactfully as possible to bring the wherewithal to pay for items that are put up for auction or drinks, if drinks are to be paid for separately.

Children's Parties
Among children's parties I include adolescents' ones. The overriding criterion is that you, the adult, are paying for it. In such circumstances the difference between a children's and a teenagers' party is negligible. Children, of course, can never be left to get on with

135

enjoying themselves at a party, whereas adolescents dislike any hint of supervision.

Indeed the ultimate entertainment that revolves round a child is his own christening and at this he usually has to be supervised completely. Accordingly it is only if you baptise your child somewhat later in life, as Isaac Disraeli did with his famous son, Benjamin, that the principal actor is going to be mature enough to play a major role. At most christenings the child contributes nothing more than a few yells and a flood of tears. From the adults' point of view, the party after the ceremony is much like any other. It may be a sit-down lunch or a stand-up buffet, a few glasses of champagne or a more substantial repast. But as with ordinary children's parties, the giving of presents to the child bulks large.

Unlike babies at christenings adolescents are likely to cause real chaos, as anyone can testify who has gone away for the night and rashly given their teenage children leave to throw a party in their absence. The very day I was writing the above paragraph I came across yet another report in the papers of a mob of youthful gatecrashers looking for a 'rave' party and terrorising the teenage daughters of a property developer who were hosting a quiet knees-up for selected members of the local philosophical society – or that's what it sounded like when the girls were interviewed. I wonder. There'd be fewer gatecrashers and fewer wrecked suburban houses if adolescents learnt the most sensible way of distributing invitations: to send out selected ones by post. It is not to go down to the local pub and bray loudly within earshot of the local ne'er-do-wells to all your friends that they're invited. A nastier element is bound to hear about it and try to gatecrash. Half the trouble is that many teenage girls find the rougher element distinctly attractive.

At least with children's parties the adults can choose the guest list. Remember that children are as capricious as tyrants where friendship is concerned. Last week's favourite may have become this week's non-person, as was once the case with bigwigs under Soviet totalitarianism. If you send out the invitations now, your child's current enemy number one may have got back into favour by Thursday of the week after next, when the party is to be held. Be prepared to take other parents into your confidence and issue invitations on your own initiative fairly late in the day so as to remedy this sort of volatility.

Children are also less hypocritical than adults. They will tell you

Dear Theodore...
Come to my Party
at the London Zoo
outside the flamingo house
Date 24 April Time 4 p.m.
From your friend Angela
RSVP

if the party you threw for them doesn't come up to scratch. Although some of them have a well-developed social sense, their criteria for whether a party was a good one or not has far more to do with their stomachs than in the case of adults when they socialise. And visual effects bulk large in children's estimation of the quality of a party. At the same time they have even less sense of historical accuracy than their elders and none whatsoever of irony. One of my earliest recollections is of the puniest boy at my kindergarten coming to a fancy-dress party as Superman. No one under 10 saw the joke at the time.

The buzzword with children's parties is 'theme'. Under closer examination the word turns out to mean little more than an old-fashioned craze: in 1993, for example, it was dinosaurs (yawn) because *Jurassic Park* had just been released. So different from my own schooldays thirty-five years ago when the hot topic for Jennings, Darbishire and me was – dinosaurs. Frog Hollow, the 'in' children's party shop in Kensington, offers tableware, balloons, hats, masks, crackers, dressing-up clothes, games and tricks. I have just been looking through some old *Punches*, 1851 vintage (the year of the Great Exhibition). What do I find to be the accoutrements of 'juvenile' parties, as the Victorians called them? Why, tableware, balloons, hats, masks, crackers, dressing-up clothes, games and tricks. The Frog Hollow spokesman claims that boys like 'cowboy and pirate parties, too . . . and the girls like our "Ballet Shoes" theme', as if this were a revolutionary change in what boys and girls respectively have been keen on since the dawn of time.

The reporter from whose articles I have culled all this stuff about 'themes' and Frog Hollow says that at a children's party the cake is still the table centrepiece, while the human centrepiece will be an entertainer. I began to sit up at this point, wondering if children had got so blasé as to want strip-o-grams. No, what they want and get is apparently magicians, clowns and puppets. So you see, throwing a children's party in the 1990s is very much like throwing one in the 1890s, even in sophisticated Kensington.

What has changed since the late nineteenth century is the tariff. Entertainers cost £75 for three-quarters of an hour to £105–15 for the duration of the whole party. If you have the whole thing catered and arranged by outside experts it will cost £200 to £600.

At children's parties you are supposed to supply the guests with little going-away presents, and on the whole the guests are much more punctilious about bringing presents for the birthday boy or girl than when they grow up and attend a birthday party for someone in his forties. Yet as adults become more infantile when it comes to entertaining, in the way they do at charity balls or New Year's Eve festivities – theme parties with entertainers, fancy dress, funny hats, streamers – so the going-away present has come back in again for them too.

In the country, where parents may have driven their children forty miles or so to a party, do please provide some refreshment for the adults. When distances like that are involved there is little point in going away again then coming back two hours later to fetch the child home. The mothers may be happy playing with the children, but the fathers should be left to themselves in a room and given plenty of liquid refreshment.

CHAPTER 7
Country-dwellers Who Entertain

If you live in the depths of the country your entertaining has a completely different dimension from what operates with townies or suburbanites. I mean the real country, where the nearest railway station is at least ten miles distant and the nearest delicatessen or reasonably well-stocked supermarket probably a minimum of twenty miles away.

You will, of course, throw dinner parties, just as if you were living in Chelsea. But you will tend to have a smaller stock of guests to draw on. Moreover they will know each other to a far greater extent than if they are city-dwellers. That means you must watch out in case a feud has erupted between one set of acquaintances and another. Feuds may not last long, but they can be very bitter while they are in spate. And in a district where not much else is going on nearly everyone may find themselves drawn into supporting one side or the other. Keep an ear to the ground for which side all your friends have taken and be wary about inviting members of opposing factions to dinner simultaneously.

If you like to make a practice of introducing new people to each other at your dinner parties you may have to import a certain proportion of your guests from further afield, possible even one of the big cities such as London. Do consider to what extent townies will mix with country-dwellers. Fox-hunting is a fairly contentious subject just now. Ascertain your towny friends' attitude to the subject before inviting them to meet the local MFH. Vegetarians may not get on with the local proprietor of several thousand acres of prime shooting country. Even if there are no obvious differences in attitude, townies may find locals parochial, locals find townies supercilious and superficial. On the other hand a contrast between one viewpoint and another can be highly beneficial to social life. The late Joanie de Vere Hunt used to get a particular kick out of taking bespangled, pink-suited proto-punks down to Oxfordshire and shocking the locals, but that is probably carrying things too far. All I say is, don't reject out of hand the possibility of fruitful cross-fertilisation between two cultures.

Country-dwellers have to stock their larders and wine cellars with what is available when it is available. They cannot so easily pop out to an all-night delicatessen to replenish a comestible they have suddenly run out of, nor to an off-licence that stays open till 11 p.m. when the burgundy has been drunk up rather more swiftly than expected. But on the other hand they tend to have bigger houses. They may be able to buy certain things in bulk, and they have access to an almost unlimited supply of game and fresh vegetables, eggs, honey and cream from neighbours, whether landowners or market gardeners or farmers. Home-made jams, chutneys and cakes are beginning to be cracked down on by the health inspectors, which is a great pity and entirely unnecessary, but for a year or two more you may be able to lay in a store from village fêtes. Buying wine several cases at a time can represent a saving over a piecemeal purchasing policy – if you have the capital and the space to store it in. Wine merchants will deliver to your house free, even if you live up to a hundred miles away from them, provided you order enough at a time. So the towny doesn't have it all his own way.

Country-dwellers must be prepared to put up their dinner guests for the night more frequently than if they live in a town. Taxis to take guests home from your house are either unheard of late at night in rural areas or prohibitively expensive. And since you are likely to have at least one spare bedroom if you live in the country, whereas in a city flat you may be quite short of accommodation for your own everyday needs, let alone for an overnight guest, the moral pressure on you to put up a guest becomes overwhelming. That means you must always have fresh sheets and blankets in readiness, to say nothing of towels and the wherewithal to provide breakfast next morning, even if on ordinary days you may not eat breakfast at all yourself. And when neighbours in the country give a big dance you may be asked to accommodate some of their guests overnight. Your spare bedrooms should be well equipped with bedside reading matter against such an eventuality as an overnight guest at short notice. If you do not keep the radiators on all the time in spare bedrooms, remember to turn them on before a dinner party in case a guest needs to stay the night. Ditto the hot water in the spare bathroom or bathrooms. Anybody not used to the cold of the average country house – which means almost all townies – ought to be given a hot-water bottle as well. In addition, some authorities recommend a dog or two for extra warmth or a cat to keep the mice from disturbing a guest's sleep.

The true country-dweller, like the boy scout he should come to resemble in resourcefulness, is always prepared. One of the things he must be most prepared for is what Alex in *A Clockwork Orange* wittily calls 'the surprise visit', though I hope to God none of my readers ever has a surprise visit such as the droogs in *A Clockwork Orange* inflict on the writer and his wife in the film. This paralleled an incident to which the author, Anthony Burgess, and his first wife were exposed in real life. No, I mean something much more prosaic, simply the turning up of unexpected guests. I don't know why they won't use the telephone to ask you in advance if it's all right to drop in. More and more people have mobile phones these days. There seem to be fewer vandalised public call boxes than a few years ago. Phonecards are now freely available so that the excuse of not having any spare change with which to feed the call box is untenable. Yet people still insist on motoring up the drive and ringing your doorbell without even five minutes' warning.

Perhaps they slyly calculate on your being so infernally bored in the country that you will put up with anybody. More probably they are passing somewhere in the area and on recalling that you live nearby think it would be nice to take up the thread of an old acquaintance. Clearly the nearer you live to major routes of communication the more exposed you are to this kind of behaviour. But even if you are as much as ten miles away from a motorway – and who isn't within ten miles of one these days, at any rate in the south of England? – you are regarded as fair game. It is even worse if you live in a beauty spot. I once inhabited a pretty little village in the middle of the Sussex Downs. It had no post office, no shop, no school and consisted of a single street only. Even that petered out in a cart track once it had left the combe in which the village nestled and soared up on to the downland again. Nevertheless, from March to October, every weekend without fail, we were besieged not just by tourists motoring out from Brighton and clogging up the little street – that was understandable, perhaps – but by friends down from London who brought two or three complete strangers with them, dropped in unheralded for tea (which had a way of prolonging itself to take in supper as well) and prevented one doing any gardening, reading of the Sunday papers, housework, clothes-mending, car-washing, shoe-polishing, goat-feeding or any of the other 1001 chores which constitute the very backbone of the English day of rest.

There are two approaches to this problem. You can get a few fierce dogs and let them roam loose within the bounds of your garden, meanwhile resolutely refusing to answer the doorbell. If your car is kept in a garage well out of sight with its doors shut this may convince your unheralded guests that you are out. It is clearly impossible in summer, however, or even if you spend any time whatsoever out of doors. An alternative is to exit from the front door just as your friends get out of their car. You should be all dressed up in coat, gloves, hat, umbrella etc. (though use of an umbrella is always slightly suspect in the true country-dweller) and say something like, 'So sorry. We're just going out. We'd have loved to stay and have a chat. You could have stayed to tea. But we're going to a christening/drinks party/dinner party/lunch/ garden party [whatever seems most plausible given the time of day and the season]. *Why* [slight emphasis here] didn't you ring in advance and say you were coming?'

The other approach is more stoical and as I am supposed to be writing a book on entertaining rather than evading one's duties as a host perhaps it would be wiser to add that this second approach is more ethical. You may be in dressing gown and slippers when the unbidden guests arrive; you may be in the middle of making love to your wife (or, worse, someone else's); you may have jam on the boil, children you are trying to catch and put to bed, chickens you are in the middle of feeding, outhouses you are in the process of painting. It doesn't matter. If in a state of undress slip on a tracksuit, go out into the driveway and ask your guests to step inside. If you're very filthy or paint-bespattered you are permitted to have a bath after the guests arrive, which means leaving them alone for a minimum of a quarter of an hour, but only after their first drink, in which you will probably join them, if only because their arrival has so put you out in your plans for the day that you are feeling a bit irritable and need alcohol to counter your peevishness.

142

Always keep the freezer stocked with pizzas and soups against the day when you have to prepare a scratch meal for up to half a dozen unexpected guests. Always have at least a dozen bottles of wine put aside for the same eventuality, even if your house has no cellar. Always have biscuits, nuts, some cake, milk, tea, coffee etc. as a minimum level of refreshment. In summer always have some cans of beer in the fridge. Always have some magazines available in the sitting room which your guests can look at while you go and have your bath. Or get one of your children to show them round the garden while you are cleaning yourself up. One of the things you are perfectly within your rights to do with unannounced guests is risk boring them into the ground by expatiating on the latest improvements you have made to your garden, outhouses, conservatory, stables, pigsty or whatever. After all, the least they can do is politely hear you out on a subject that is dear to your heart. If you really want to get rid of them you can try boring them into leaving as soon as is decently possible with incessant talk of local matters. But I rather assume that if you are reading this book you are of a more hospitable disposition and even if you were a bit tetchy when your guests first rolled up you will enter into the spirit of the genial host after half an hour or so.

If you have a swimming pool you will never be left alone for a single day throughout a warm summer, and only slightly less so if you have a tennis court. Therefore you must not acquire either of these things if you are not of a highly sociable disposition – unless you are prepared to snub importunate friends and neighbours throughout the summer. Swimming pool owners are considered particularly fair game by those of their friends with children. The advantage to being a tennis court or swimming pool owner is that people are slightly more ready to ring in advance and ask if they can come over to use it rather than turn up unannounced. But you should keep a good supply of tennis shoes in all sizes for both men and women, also tennis racquets and balls, because even the most shameless exploiters of your hospitality seldom have enough of these things themselves. Likewise a good supply of swimming costumes, goggles, flippers, waterwings, lilos and sun-tan lotion if you own a swimming pool. I assume that you will have laid in a good supply of sun umbrellas and easy chairs anyway.

One policy you can be fairly firm about if you own a swimming pool is no eating or drinking by the poolside. You can claim that your insurance company insists on it from the point of view of your negligence liability in the event of an accident. But the real reason is that you don't want the pool to become polluted by broken glass from drinks that your smashed guests have smashed, or the filter system clogged by soggy crisp packets their children have abandoned in the water, or simply that you don't like bits of food floating on the surface of the water.

No matter how hard you try you will not be able to stop guests smoking by the poolside, and some ash will inevitably find its way into the water, perhaps whole cigarette ends. There is nothing you can do to stop that either. Just make sure your filter system is efficient.

CHAPTER 8
House Parties

So far I have concentrated on the improvisatory side of social life in the country. But there is another side to it and this is perhaps the single most arduous activity for the hostess. I refer to the country house party. There are of course variations on it, such as the holiday villa party in the sun or the winter sports chalet party in the sun and the snow, but many of the problems to be surmounted as well as the strategies with which to surmount them are common to all forms of house-party entertaining, which may be defined as a situation where you have a minimum of three other guests staying under your roof, whether freehold or temporarily rented, for a minimum of two nights.

The chief difficulty is that you have to be permanently on your toes to ensure that your guests have a good time. Literally so, in fact, since in any reasonably large house your guests will become scattered and you should patrol the property incessantly to make sure they are all enjoying themselves. Ensuring that others have a good time can be exhausting enough for the four or five hours of the average dinner party. For forty-eight hours or more it can be utterly draining. You must provide at least three meals a day, indeed four if you count tea, and ensure that the table is laid beforehand and cleared away again afterwards on each occasion. You must somehow ensure that the washing up is done. You must provide sleeping accommodation, bedclothes and changes of bed-clothes if guests stay for longer than three nights, heat and light, conversation, reading matter, sporting opportunities and travel guidance in case your guests want to make short trips to local beauty spots or sites of archaeological interest. You may have to act as a doctor, or at any rate a paramedic, if they injure themselves or suffer from a hangover or a sleepless night.

A good host puts lots of writing paper and envelopes and perhaps a pen or two in each guest bedroom. This is not because guests these days are great letter-writers at a house party any more than they are at home. It is partly so that if the house is a grand one your guests may let their friends know just how exalted their surroundings this weekend are. I believe that otherwise uncommunicative people who go to stay at Windsor Castle or Balmoral may develop quite a fit of epistolary activity. The most eloquent thing about a letter from such a place is not so much the writer's prose style as the address on the heading.

Even in the case of lesser houses letter-writing has its place. Saying, 'I'm just going to my room to write some letters,' is the perfect excuse to slip away from the rest of the company in the middle of the afternoon for a snooze, or to make love to the maid or a fellow guest's wife or even sometimes the hostess.

Because your guests are thrown together for a good deal longer than at a dinner party you must take much greater care in selecting them. It may be desirable to ask a stop-gap at the last minute, but it isn't necessary in the way it can so often be for a dinner party, where you may want to make up round numbers, let alone even ones, balancing the sexes and so on. What is vital is to make sure the guests mesh together comfortably. I have been to a house party where one guest – a remarkably pretty girl, as it happened – sat silently and presumably miserably out of it all because she knew nothing of politics, which everyone else was discussing almost incessantly.

Good looks, even if unfortified by learning, wit or intelligence, constitute an adequate passport to a dinner party. But their possessor is unlikely to fit in with other guests of more intellectual bent in an extended stay under the same roof. Even if your aim as host in inviting her is sheer sexual gratification you would do better to sap her defences in quieter circumstances. And even in those circumstances she may have her own ideas on the subject. I knew a host, later an MP, who invited a girl to what he represented was a weekend house party in the country. So it proved, but there were no other guests. She was obliged to cook dinner and afterwards discovered that there was only one bed, which her host unceremoniously took possession of and indicated she should share with him. She declined. He did not offer to drive her to the nearest station – admittedly a long way away. So she curled up unhappily and uncomfortably on the sofa and early next morning hitch-hiked back to London. Her host had not even offered to give up the only bed.

The other side of the coin is that hostilities between two or more guests which may smoulder away fairly harmlessly at a dinner party could threaten to get out of hand during an extended stay. To cite a Saki story again, I would refer the reader to 'Excepting Mrs Pentherby'. It tells how Reggie Bruttle has inherited a big house but not enough money to keep it up. He invites seven or eight married couples to stay there with him throughout the winter on a day-to-day sharing-living-expenses basis, a little hunting and shooting, but not much because they're expensive; more golf, dancing, some mild gambling (auction bridge in those days) and so on. He is warned by an old friend with whom he talks over his plan in advance that it will work well enough with the men but that the women will quarrel if confined together for so long. Yet despite the gloomy prophecy the experiment turns out to be rather a success. The couples agree that by and large they have seldom enjoyed themselves more. With one exception. The women have all taken a dislike to Mrs Pentherby, a member of the house party whom nobody has met before. Reggie's sister-in-law even speculates that she has some hold over him; she cannot conceive why Mrs Pentherby is there otherwise. In agreeing on their dislike for Mrs Pentherby the other women of the house party have of course achieved a degree of unity.

After the close of the winter a second house party is suggested for the next winter. None of the original women can make it, but Reggie is unperturbed. He has laid his plans well in advance and has several other candidates eager to join up. Notwithstanding the defection of the original set of women, the house looks like being filled for the next winter. Reggie's sister-in-law discovers that of all the women originally involved only Mrs Pentherby is to be of the second party. She asks Reggie why. He explains that Mrs Pentherby is his official quarreller, his lightning conductor, as it were. Because the hatred of the other women is focused on her they have no energy left to quarrel among themselves. And as she is a poor relation in ordinary life she has enjoyed getting her own back for once by telling the other women what she really thinks instead of meekly keeping her opinions about the rest of the world to herself.

Because having people to stay at a house party eats more into their spare time than a dinner party, you will probably need to plan it further in advance. This is even true of weekends, as I made plain earlier when suggesting that you check on your friends' children's school term times before arranging weekend lunch parties. You might therefore write as much as several months in advance to invite people to stay with you, particularly if you are restricted to a certain number of weeks in the summer, as where, for instance, you are renting a shooting lodge (see Shooting Parties). Always specify the exact duration of your guest's stay.

It is only fair to your guests to tell them exactly what clothes they should bring. For daytime during weekends in the country many guests can safely be left to make their own choice, though even here it might be wise to specify subdued colours to non-sporting guests in case they want to accompany the guns when they go out to shoot the coverts. If you are having a grand black-tie dinner party during your guests' stay with you, say so. Do not indulge in that typical piece of understatement to the effect that the weekend is going to be 'quite informal'. Similarly, if you are having a garden party, or taking your guests to one, during the summer, make sure you tell them. If your house party is arranged round one of the great sporting events such as those mentioned in the following pages, you should give quite detailed instructions to your guests. Of course they might be insulted if you spelt out to them that for a visit to Ascot men should bring morning coat and top hat. It depends how well they themselves know the procedure, or perhaps I should say how well you judge that they know the procedure.

At the end of a stay of two nights or more, and by this I include weekends even if the overnight stay is just Saturday, your guests ought to tip the servants. If there are several servants a guest might give the butler or other head servant £10 minimum and ask him to share it out with the others. A married couple should tip around £15–£20 unless they have palpably caused more than twice as much work (for example, the wife needing to get her evening dress ironed before dinner since it has come out of her suitcase rather wrinkled). These sums, like all other specific economic figures, are subject to inflation and were judged about right at the time of writing in early 1994.

If your guests don't tip you can try the ploy resorted to by a friend of mine when he had a villa on Corfu years ago and a notoriously mean baronet came to stay. The latter left nothing for the house boy. Subsequently his erstwhile host informed the baronet that he had given the boy £10 on the baronet's account and would charge it to him when they next met to have lunch together at a restaurant. For such a manoeuvre you have to be on fairly old friendship terms with your guest, though.

SPORTING FIXTURES

Certain house parties have specific themes or are arranged around specific events, usually sporting, such as Ascot, Goodwood, Henley or Wimbledon. From the point of view of the composition of the house party they are simple to plan for. Any of your friends are eligible who like racing or regattas or tennis or just being seen in public at fashionable gatherings at the height of the Season. (The securing of tickets for the Royal Enclosure at Ascot and other purely technical aspects of taking your friends to the races is outside the scope of a work such as this; see instead *Debrett's Etiquette and Modern Manners* and *The Harpers and Queen Book of the Season: An Insider's Guide*.)

Dons used to arrange reading parties, and characters in the novels of Iris Murdoch still attend them. They are the intellectual equivalent of the Ascot house party, and just as at an Ascot house party guests should be racing enthusiasts, they ought in kindness to be restricted to those who like reading. Holiday house parties, where the principals club together to rent a house or villa or chalet in some exotic spot abroad, can be more mixed. A taste for pursuing pleasure is sufficient qualification. But get it absolutely straight at the beginning who is the person in charge of (a) negotiating with the landlord, (b) hiring the maid or other servant(s), (c) persuading the other tenants to cough up their share of the rent and other expenses, and (d) hiring the cars. Clearly the person or persons who do the bulk of the work involved should have priority in choosing the best bedroom. But everyone should have his or her own power of absolute veto on who is invited as a guest by the house party as a whole, even if it's only to a single lunch. The principle operating here is that where you have a degree of collective responsibility you must allow collective powers to invite, or disinvite as it were. That does not mean that all members of the holiday house party must do the same thing every day. You will find that there is a natural split between those who are content to lie by the pool all day and every day, dozing, sunbathing, swimming, reading or playing Travel Scrabble, and those who want to sightsee in the surrounding historic towns and villages.

Chalet parties are more homogeneous because you would hardly go on a holiday in one if you weren't keen on winter sports. But even then there will be advanced skiers who may wish to go on excursions to neighbouring resorts which could involve an overnight stay away, or cross-country skiers, or off-piste skiers, or those who prefer tobogganing, or those who like skating. Ascertain who likes doing what and plan where you intend to rent your chalet so that it is in reasonably close reach of facilities that suit everybody.

Country House Parties
The standard house party is still the one you host in your own home. Which bedrooms to allocate to which guests used to be a favourite preoccupation of Edwardian hostesses, but those were the days when adultery was highly stylised, yet divorce relatively rare, so that a knowledge of which husband was currently sleeping with which other husband's wife was a basic qualification for a hostess. Nowadays the position is in some ways easier. You put the married couples in double bedrooms and everybody else in a series of single ones. If an affair starts up on the premises, that is to say during the actual duration of the house party, it is no business of yours as a hostess, still less of fellow guests, however prudish they may be. If a couple who are not married but an 'item' are coming, you can put them next door to each other. I don't see that there is any more difficulty to the bedroom side of it than that. If you have other guests who are elderly or prim their susceptibilities will have been taken care of by your giving the members of the 'item' separate bedrooms. Oddly enough, it amounts to coming full-circle back to the practice in Edwardian times. For in those days one separated many couples even when they were married to each other, putting the husband in one room and the wife in another, precisely so that the husband could go his separate way during the night, while his wife was on hand to receive a visit from the King or Harry Cust or one of the other bucks of the day.

150

Let us go through a typical day in a house party. Unless you have a horde of servants you are well within your rights to set your face against providing guests with breakfast in bed. It is not that the preparation of a tray is a great nuisance – in some ways it is easier than having people coming downstairs at all hours of the morning and breakfasting in the dining room. The objection to breakfast in bed for guests is more that crumbs, tea, coffee, jam, marmalade, egg and bacon grease are bound to get spilled over the bedclothes. On the other hand you are unlikely to get everyone downstairs at the same time in the morning. Accordingly you should arrange a kind of buffet breakfast, with hot food kept bubbling away on the sideboard and the guests helping themselves. Cereals they can help themselves to entirely. They can also be left to make toast for themselves if you have a toaster in the dining room.

In fact, if you have breakfasted yourself before most of your guests descend from their bedrooms, all you need to do is look into the dining room once every ten minutes to check that the hot food doesn't need replenishing. You do not need to be present all the time yourself, though it is much appreciated if you are. But you are likely to have 101 other tasks to attend to – tasks which are directly connected with your guests' comfort later in the day. It is a good idea to supply your guests with as many of the daily or Sunday newspapers as possible at breakfast, including rags you would normally refuse ever to have in the house. Even the most intellectual guests at weekends delight in scandal-sheets such as the *News of the World*.

After breakfast you can more or less leave guests to their own devices. You can show them where the weekly magazines are in the sitting room, advise them of nearby tourist attractions or towns for shopping in or quaint country pubs. The rest is up to them. (Major local sporting activities are a different matter and need more organisation on your part as well as discipline on your guests' part; I will cover these presently.)

At about 12.30 you can serve drinks, doing so in the sitting room or drawing room as if for a lunch or dinner party. Some hosts leave out a drinks tray complete with spirits, sherry, ice, angostura bitters, nuts, madeira and so on all day in the main room where guests assemble and urge them to help themselves. It depends on the sobriety of your guests. Some of them may nip away at the drinks tray throughout the entire weekend or longer if the house party is of greater duration. In one case I know of, the wife of a visiting couple drank so much during the Saturday pre-lunch tippling session that she had to retire to her bedroom and was not seen again for thirty-six hours. Moreover the hostess noticed a trail of blood going up the staircase to the bedroom of the couple in question. She expressed polite but real concern to the husband, who made light of it. Presumably the spouse knows best in such circumstances. You should certainly assume so and, apart from having the stains cleared up, overlook the matter. If it turns out he has murdered his wife he will hardly be able to cover up the crime when it has been committed in your house.

If you're having an elaborate dinner party that evening, whether with guests coming in from other nearby houses or just amongst yourselves, it is acceptable to provide a very light lunch, a bowl of soup, salad and cheese or fruit, say. Perhaps weekend lunches might be rather more solid than weekday ones, but of course you will probably be having outside guests to those as well as to dinner. In the afternoon you can urge the guests to go and play tennis or croquet in summer or go for walks or drives in winter. The ideal hostess accompanies some of her guests on an expedition to a nearby cathedral or ruined castle but it is no great sin against hospitality not to. The fact is, you cannot be everywhere at once in the house and grounds, but if you stay at home you can keep a general eye on events more easily than if you set out on a jaunt with certain members of your house party. If there is an immensely distinguished individual among your guests, one who stands head and shoulders in achievement or social eminence above all the others, it would be wise to devote yourself to him, going wherever he wants to go, doing whatever he wants to do. Otherwise your time is liable to be taken up checking your stores and supervising any servants you have.

EVENING ENTERTAINMENT
Tea and dinner can be served as advised in the preceding chapters on those specific meals. It is after dinner that the house party comes into its own. You may have dancing, bridge, poker, private theatricals, charades or just conversation. It is a good idea to vary

the activity from one evening to the next unless your house party consists exclusively of fanatical dancers, say, with no card sense and a loathing of private theatricals. You can ask generally what everybody would like to do and, acting on the consensus of the gathering, provide what is generally desired. But often you won't encounter unanimity and may have to decide the question on your own. For your peace of mind you will probably do better to plan things in advance, for example devoting Tuesday to bridge, Wednesday to dancing, Thursday to charades and so on. The house party is a much better occasion on which to have an outside entertainer come in and perform than a dinner party. You can have opera – Pavilion Opera or the European Chamber Opera (telephone: 081-806 4231) both perform in private houses, either with piano accompaniment only (which makes a surprisingly satisfactory sound) for a mere £3,500 upwards, or with an orchestra of up to twenty pieces, which naturally comes more expensive at around £8,500. Entertainments on this scale need to be booked well in advance. An indoors room around 40ft by 40ft will be sufficient for a chamber opera. Most largish houses have a room somewhere about that size. If yours isn't quite big enough, you would do best to wait till summer and hire a marquee.

Gambling

If you have gambling on the premises, either during a house party or after a dinner party, lay down the ground rules very firmly well before play gets going. Stipulate a time for ending the session and stick to it rigidly. If there is to be a maximum stake, say so, and tolerate no attempts to exceed it. All gambling debts must be settled the very evening they are contracted. I would refuse to allow IOUs myself, but some people regard them as almost as good as cheques. How good are cheques these days, though? Cash or cheques backed by a bank card are the only currency unless your guests wager specific items, Sheikh Bab El-Ehr betting his gold-plated Rolls-Royce, for instance, against the Marquis di Gorgonzola's Derby-winning racehorse. Women should only be put up as gambling stakes with their permission, though this may be tacit. Their husbands' or 'protectors'' decision alone to stake them is not enough.

153

Bridge

Bridge is so special a game that it deserves a section all to itself. It is the queen of card games, rather as theology used to be called the queen of sciences, wholly distinct from one of those frankly rather buffoonish pastimes such as charades that can be taken up by anybody. I suppose it sounds rather smug and wisdom-of-hindsight to say so, but I could tell the royal family was never going to be a match for the Princess of Wales as soon as I heard that she played bridge, whereas the royals allegedly prefer dumb crambo (see page 158).

Bridge is a game on which enthusiasts tend to concentrate to the exclusion of anything else. At the same time there will always be one of the four players, the dummy, who is not actively participating once the bidding is over. If the bridge players are all very enthusiastic he will probably get enough enjoyment from watching his partner play the hand for it not to matter that he is temporarily a supernumerary. If he is merely a sociable bridge player he will be at a loose end for five minutes or so. It is only kind to all concerned to arrange a bridge evening so that all four players at any one table are either unanimously 'serious' players or unanimously 'sociable'. Best of all, try to arrange for there to be a minimum of two tables of bridge so that whoever is dummy has some other dummy to talk to while the other three people at his table are engaged in play. Some dummies use their period of leisure to make drinks for the other players, but serious bridge players don't drink much as to do so clouds their brains.

If only four players go in for bridge during a house party numbering more than four, the spare person, or dummy, can temporarily be drawn back into the rest of the company. But talk should be relatively low while the card players are at work at the other end of the room, or you can set aside another room entirely for cards. Whoever is dummy can pop back into the drawing room when not actively engaged in the card room.

Some bridge players may be indifferent performers but take the etiquette side of the game superlatively seriously. It is best to humour them. You as host should supply at least two new packs of cards every evening bridge is played and more than two packs still more frequently, perhaps a new one every hour, if a game such as poker is going on. For bridge remove from the pack any jokers and

154

cards giving bridge scores when you rip away the cellophane. A proper card table with a green baize surface and bridge scorecards are also essential for devoted bridge players.

As a host player yourself you should to a certain extent supervise the correct form of play. To begin with the four bridge players cut one of the two packs for partners, either the two highest cards playing together as partners against the two lowest or the highest and lowest against the two middle cards. The person who has cut the highest card is the dealer for the first hand. He shuffles the pack thoroughly. He then passes it to the person on his right, who cuts it back to the dealer. The dealer places the lower half of the cut pack on top of what was the upper half and deals, one to each person in a clockwise direction till the pack is exhausted. (Some types of poker are dealt three cards at a time, two cards at a time then three cards at a time, or a variation thereof; you as host should insist that agreement on exactly how to deal is reached before play begins.)

At bridge the person sitting opposite the dealer 'makes' the second pack, that is, the one not in immediate use, shuffling it thoroughly. He then passes it across the table to the person sitting opposite him, who is of course currently the dealer. For the next hand the dealer will eventually cut the shuffled or 'made' pack to the person on his left. This latter person becomes the dealer for the next hand. And so on round the table.

As host you should throw the weight of your authority behind such rules of the game as are sometimes waived on the grounds that only a pedant would insist on their being obeyed. Such a rule is the one obliging whoever is playing the hand (the declarer) to play any card from dummy that he has touched. Another rule that sometimes gets waived by sloppy players trying to pass themselves off as anti-pedantic is the one about having to play a card that becomes exposed as soon as possible.

ROUND GAMES

Here are a few more flexible, physically active games you might care to try out to vary the evenings. These games can also be used not just for adults but for children's parties and even for adolescents who are not too self-conscious or knowing and blasé to appreciate their decidedly period flavour.

155

I have given a very short list of games because in my experience these are the ones that work best for adults or adolescents. If someone among the assembled company is good at telling fortunes you might care to bully her into reading people's palms or tea-leaves or predicting the future from cards. But anyone who is any good at that sort of thing is going to be sick to death of being asked to perform at gatherings all over the country. It isn't therefore fair on her. Many of the other games were designed to further sexual selection in an era when people couldn't be expected to get on with it by themselves. Nowadays it is all a hostess can do to stop her guests getting off with each other. Besides, dancing is better for that sort of thing.

Charades
The best known game, surely. Nevertheless, there are variations on it. One rather elaborate version is virtually a form of private theatricals. This calls ideally for costumes, lines to be spoken (hence rehearsals, however perfunctory) and even a small orchestral accompaniment to remind the more stupid members of the audience what the setting is (such as by playing Oriental music when the performers are dressed in Turkish costume). Readers of Thackeray's *Vanity Fair* may recognise this as the type of charades performed by Becky Sharp at Lord Steyne's London residence of Gaunt House when she is at the height of her social success, just before the disastrous crash. On that occasion, however, there was no question of any competition between two teams, but instead a continuous series of performances by the more theatrically inclined guests of Lord Steyne for the amusement of such guests as were not inclined to dress up and make guys of themselves on the stage.

A better version, because it is more competitive, is when two teams take it in turns to perform playlets. The team not in action at the time fills the role of audience and tries to guess the word the first team has chosen. A word of two or more syllables is chosen by one of the teams. The word must be capable of being split in two (or more) syllables, each of which itself has an independent meaning, even if only phonetically. Examples are 'popinjay' ('pop', 'inn', 'jay'), 'catastrophe' ('cat', 'ass', 'trophy'), 'perfunctory' ('purr', 'funk', 'tory'). One school of thought says you can jiggle with the words a bit, so that 'repository' could be split into 'reap' 'pose' and 'tory', although the 'e' of repository is short and the 'ea' of reap is long, likewise the 'o' of 'pose' is long and that of 'repository' is short. The stricter faction says the constituent parts of the full, polysyllabic word should be pronounced more or less as they appear in the full word.

In this version a dialogue is fashioned and each short, monosyllabic word appears somewhere in it. There is also a last scene where the whole word is introduced into the dialogue. Clearly the first three scenes are not going to be difficult for the acting team to pull off. It is the last scene that is going to risk giving the game away, because the word is going to be one of the longer ones. Therefore the composer of the dialogue is going to have to stuff the final scene with polysyllabic words, thus sacrificing verisimilitude. Of course one can improvise the dialogue in each scene, but if so the last one will pose even more of a problem than if the passage containing the whole word is carefully crafted in advance.

A version of charades which gets round this difficulty in the final scene, the one that portrays the whole word, is for each scene, tableau or playlet to embody in its very theme the meaning of the whole word. The drawback is that the entire exercise may become too subtle for the audience. But let me illustrate what I am getting at with an example. If you are lucky you will have a competent friend who as 'playwright' is composing the dialogue, and indeed making up the entire playlet or series of playlets which contain the clues to the word. Such a person might choose for the word 'catastrophe', for example, three well-known cases of a sudden reversal of fortune. ('Catastrophe' doesn't need to be a reversal of fortune in a downwards direction, from good fortune to bad, merely a sudden reversal in either direction.) For instance, the playlet embodying the first syllable, 'cat', might consist of Dick Whittington hearing the London bells and deciding to return to the city, being encouraged tacitly or otherwise by his cat. The second tableau might have a reference to Balaam's ass or the fable in which Midas, asked to choose whether Apollo or Pan is the better musician, rashly gives Pan the prize whereupon Apollo changes Midas's ears into those of an ass. (Now that so few people have a classical education I admit that this might pose something of an enigma to your younger guests.) The third might have a reference to someone winning a trophy in some competition or other, say Bobby Fischer the World Chess Championship, but then having the trophy confiscated for an infringement of the rules. All three episodes, you will observe, embody sudden reversals of fortune.

Mime Games

There is a fairly similar game, virtually a mime version, sometimes called dumb crambo. It can involve two teams, one of which goes out of the room and selects a word which one of the team then mimes to the team that has stayed behind in the room. Alternatively a single person can be chosen to mime a word of his own devising, then the next person among the company is chosen, and so on round the room. It is better to have two teams because if the individual is left to choose his own word to mime he will go for something easy. Conversely his team-mates can be relied on to choose something nice and inappropriate to his character for him to mime. But try not to let them get too sadistic. Shy people need more understanding than extroverts in this kind of situation.

You can stipulate that every participant must use polysyllabic words which have to be guessed after being broken down into constituent syllables, or you can insist the whole word is mimed at once. Or you can allow either method to be used. But speech cannot be employed by the mime artist at any point. There are various conventions used to signify that the word – or phrase, for it is sometimes a catchphrase or the title of a work of art using more than one word – is a book, a play, a film or whatever. The mime lets his audience know how many syllables there are in the word or words by holding up the requisite number of fingers to denote the total number, then one finger, which he tells off with two fingers of the other hand, to show that it is the first syllable/word in the phrase, then two fingers to show it is the second syllable/word, and so on. If it is a book the mime holds the palms of his hands together and opens them once or twice to suggest that a book is being opened. If he wants to let it be known he is miming the title of a film he makes winding motions with his right hand close to his head, which suggests a very old kinematograph of the early years of this century rather than state-of-the-art technology (but then, dumb crambo is a very old-fashioned game). With a play the mime makes the gesture of drawing curtains apart. Ballet and opera have to be left to the individual mime's ingenuity.

Putting a hand to one's ear and bending forward in an exaggerated pose of listening means 'sounds like'. The mime uses this convention to hint at a single syllable of a complex word which doesn't have any meaning in itself and for which he therefore has to find a one-syllable rhyme with its own meaning, hence one that can more easily be guessed. For example, let us suppose you are the mime and have been given 'antidisestablishmentarianism'. Impossible to get across by gesture as a single word, I would have thought – even if you were Marcel Marceau. So you break it down into 'ant' . . . but what then do you do about '-i', or '-idis' and so on? Back to the drawing-board. Try 'anti', 'dis', 'establishment' (or 'establish' and 'ment'). 'Anti' shouldn't be too hard. You could suggest 'anti-fox-hunters', which should have a reasonably good chance of being guessed if you are in the country, or 'ante' as in poker if you're in a hard-gambling set. 'Dis' is not mimeable unless you're surrounded by a host of classics dons, to whom the word is familiar as one of the alternative names for the ancient world's Hades. So you mime 'sounds like' and try 'kiss' or 'hiss' or whatever. For 'ment' you can of course mime 'meant', but here you begin to get into deep water as after you have mimed a number of syllables successfully your audience will begin to forget what has been built up so far. That is why 'antidisestablishmentarianism' is such a fiendish choice, though if it is obvious a very long word is being mimed then the audience might guess it simply because it is famous for nothing so much as being a long word.

In general, if you can do anything else, miming 'sounds like' is not recommended because it confuses most of the audience. Where games such as dumb crambo are concerned, people tend to think in analogies or free association rather than in rhymes – perhaps they always do when involved in mental exercises. Certainly even with the best will in the world, as a character in Anthony Powell's novel *Agents and Patients* puts it, you can't film a man subconsciously hating his father. Likewise you can't mime a highly abstract book title such as *The Critique of Pure Reason*.

Mime is arguably preferable to speech in round games as it throws everyone into an unfamiliar medium. If speech takes a major role then the person who orates every day of his professional life – a barrister, politician or salesman, say – has an unfair advantage. Here is another mime game. Its actual operation is brilliantly described in Kingsley Amis's novel *One Fat Englishman*. Somebody goes out of the room and the rest think up an adverb – swiftly, slowly, proudly, humbly, adroitly, clumsily. The absent person is then called back and he is empowered to ask each person who has remained in the room to perform an action in the manner that the chosen adverb sums up. After it has been performed a few times he tries to guess it. In the book Roger Micheldene, anti-hero par excellence and the fat Englishman of the title, is staying in America. Everybody else in the house is either American or Americanised. He asks various members of the assembled company to perform an action in the way that the adverb would describe. He cannot guess it because they all seem to be doing a different adverb. One performs an action stolidly, another effeminately, yet another insouciantly. Finally he asks the married woman he is in love with and with whom he is having a highly frustrating clandestine affair to make love to a standard lamp in the manner of the adverb. She advances towards it and gives it nothing more than a chaste peck. The adverb is 'Britishly'.

Consequences

Consequences is better played by people with a vaguely literary turn of mind. Stolid, unimaginative types don't shine, but then what do they shine at? The company sit round a table. Each person takes a sheet of paper and writes the name of a man, either real or fictional, historical or current, near the top. The sheet of paper is then folded over so that the name can't be read and passed to the next person to the left (or right, it doesn't matter which). The word 'met' is then written down – it doesn't matter by whom since this is purely a piece of linkage – and the name of a female, again either real or fictional, historical or current, is added by everybody to his or her sheet of paper, which of course has just been passed to him or her by a next-door neighbour. Again the paper is folded over, so that there are now two folds, and the paper passed on again. The next item to be written down is 'at', followed by a place in which the two people already featuring on the piece of paper are deemed to have met. The other items are: 'He said to her' – fill in anything vaguely amusing that comes to mind; 'She said to him' – fill in as before; and 'The consequence was that' – fill in. You can add other items, such as 'He did' and 'She did' before the final consequence.

Effectively you end up with several short stories written by the entire company in a joint effort, each person contributing a line or so of the narrative. At its best this sometimes achieves a truly surrealist result. Mere obscenity is not enough, so eschew it when contributing your own lines. Do make sure that everybody who reads out the completed narrative puts in all the linking phrases such as 'met' and 'He said to her' and above all 'in' or 'on' instead of 'at' if the meeting place was a bath or roof instead of Plumstead Episcopi. Stupid people sometimes read out only what is written down and without the right linking phrases the result sounds like gibberish. You will find that unless a spark of inspiration is struck early on this game soon palls, so don't persist in it for long.

Cardinal Puff

This is probably a thoroughly irresponsible game in these neo-temperance times. Actually it's less a game than an excuse for drinking – not that people who like drinking need any excuse. I suppose you might argue that it develops concentration. Anyway, it is an elaboration of the various types of ritual which used to be observed in college dining halls in universities, where any incorrect use of a piece of equipment such as a snuff box entailed the guilty party having to drink off his wine glass in one go, then refill it ready for the next round. Each person round a table drinks to the health of Cardinal Puff in the correct manner. If he makes a mistake, and the more he drinks the more likely he is to make a mistake, he must start again. Once he has completed a round the turn passes to the next person on his left (or right, depending on which way you want to circulate).

Each participant fills his glass with whatever wine is being consumed. The first person to take his turn stands up, says 'I drink to the health of Cardinal Puff,' and with one finger of each hand hits the table surface lightly, first with the left finger then with the right, or with both simultaneously, then the underside of the table in the same manner, then his left thigh with his left-hand finger and right thigh with his right-hand finger, then his left breast with his left-hand finger and right breast with his right-hand finger. Then he grasps the wine glass with his right finger and thumb only, raises the glass to his lips, takes one sip and taps the glass once on the table as he sets it down. Clearly there are numerous variations on this; I have sketched the most common only.

He then says 'I drink to the health of Cardinal Puff for the second time,' and repeats the performance, this time using two fingers of each hand and two taps whenever one tap was used before. He must take two sips and knock the glass gently twice against the table when setting it down. He repeats the performance a third time and in the course of the process finishes the wine in the glass, which he then upends on the table, hitting the table as usual with three light taps as he sets it down. Any mistake in the ritual – and a mistake can include saying 'drink the health' rather than 'drink *to* the health', for example – means that the participant has to start all over again.

CHAPTER 9

Entertaining Royalty

British Royalty

You may be having royal guests to any of a number of social events
which have already been covered in this book. For instance,
members of the older generation of the British royal family are
rather famous for their love of round games after dinner. It has
been suggested that this is partly to get their own back on the
politicians they are from time to time obliged to have staying in the
house. It is the only occasion when, if one doesn't have the vote or
if one is prevented from exercising it by constitutional considerations, one can humiliate a politician. The rest of the population
can at least vote for the other lot every four years or so. What
better sport than to watch the Home Secretary writhing around on
the carpet imitating the mew of a seal while you studiously pretend
not to have twigged what he's portraying?

I have thought it advisable to devote a whole separate section to
entertaining royalty since they are still very much a race apart from
the rest of us.

Above all they are still looked up to with immense awe in a
social context. Most people come over weak at the knees at the
thought of meeting a member of the royal family. It is, then, a bold
host or hostess who contemplates entertaining any of them.

First, however, you must decide whether you are on sufficiently close terms to extend an invitation to a member of the
royal family at all. Much the same considerations apply here as
with any other guest. Some of us are forward hosts, others are
so shy or lazy they cease to make new friends after early youth
and never have new faces to the house. Moreover the royal
family are like any other family: they include both shy and
outgoing people. In wondering whether to invite a member of
the royal family to one's dinner party, ball or house party one is
bound to fear rejection, but so it is with asking anybody who
you (or they) think are more important than you to a social
function. At least shops pre-empt the matter by putting out

163

placards saying 'Do not ask for credit as a refusal may cause hurt.'

Don't take your courage in both hands so much you go off and importune every celebrity you bump into, royal or otherwise. But on the other hand if some of these breezy showbiz types one reads about in the papers as 'a friend of the Prince of Wales/Edward etc.' had never edged themselves forward, the royal family's social life would doubtless have been the poorer too. The right mixture of deference and familiarity is so rare nowadays in any social circle that it is harder than ever to give the recipe in print for dealing with royalty. Clowning may be a swifter route to social success but the role of court jester has always been one of extreme precariousness. Indeed, ditto that of courtier (I use the term in its older sense of one who attends on royalty regularly and in a social context rather than the more modern connotation of a paid member of one or other of the royal households).

When dispatching an invitation to royalty I would have thought that you should use the post rather than telephone because it gives your invitee more time to mull over the invitation. Some authorities say it is acceptable to phone the lady-in-waiting or private secretary but this is likely to result in just as much delay as if you had written. Neither the lady-in-waiting nor the private secretary can make a snap decision over the phone on behalf of their master or mistress. And it is in any case the royal personages who are your true quarry rather than their staff, who simply relay your message, though they may also perhaps advise on whether to accept it or not, if asked for their opinion. Write to 'The Private Secretary to Her Majesty The Queen' [note the obligatory capital T for The Queen and The Queen Mother even though it comes in the middle of a sentence] or 'The Private Secretary to His Royal Highness the Prince of Wales' or whoever. In the letter refer to the royal personage in the third person as 'Her Majesty' the first time and subsequently as 'The Queen' or 'His Royal Highness' and subsequently as 'the Duke of Clarence', 'Princess Mary' or whatever their names are, as appropriate.

A full guide to coping with royal guests at official ceremonies, receptions etc. is given in *Debrett's Correct Form*. For the greatest degree of information on protocol during visits to private residences, consult the private secretary to the specific member of the royal family. As with ordinary human beings, royalty tends to be less formal the younger it is. Nevertheless, when you as hostess are planning to present a guest or guests of yours to a royal personage it would be wise to submit the list of names in advance to the private secretary.

You and your guests are supposed to address the Queen and Queen Mother as 'Your Majesty' the first time of being presented and as 'Ma'am' (to rhyme with 'ham' rather than 'harm') thereafter. 'Ma'am' pronounced to rhyme with 'harm' seems to have been superseded some time between the Crimean War and roughly around the end of the Second Afghan War in 1880. With the rest of them, start off with 'Your Royal Highness' and continue with 'Sir' and 'Ma'am', depending on the sex.

There is not the same rigidity of etiquette in dealing with royalty that there used to be. For instance, someone who is a guest at the same function as a junior member of the royal family need not now regard herself as being obliged to wait to speak to royalty till after she is spoken to. Indeed the junior member of the royal family might quite like to be approached. All too often most fellow guests, other than those known to royalty already, hang back through shyness. As a hostess you should apprise your prospective guests of this. And you should always let your guests know that they are going to meet royalty, for example, by adding 'To have the honour of meeting His Royal Highness [engraved in full, not just HRH] the Duke of Clarence [again in full, as for instance "Princess Alexandra, the Hon. Lady Ogilvy" rather than just "Princess Alexandra"]' on any invitation card you send out – but only after you have ascertained from the private secretary to the duke that His Royal Highness is coming to your little do. It is true, as some sources point out, that the phrase 'Decorations' on an invitation card to a private party hints that royalty will be present. But why add to the complexity of modern social existence by dealing in nods and winks? If royalty is to be present, say so.

So far I have dealt with junior royalty, which for the present purpose may be defined as comprising all HRHs. The Queen and Queen Mother are another matter. Your guests ought to wait to be presented to the Queen herself, also to the Queen Mother, on the grounds that one is the actual head of state and the other was once a reigning queen, a crowned head if you like. So even within the royal family there are distinctions. Again, should either of the last two members of the royal family be attending a social function hosted by you, your guests should be warned and told not to intrude uninvited upon the royal personages in question in the way they perhaps did last week when it was merely HRH the Duke of Clarence whom you had to the house. Incidentally, whether fishing for royal guests at a single party or a series of parties, start at the top and move downfield if responded to with a polite regret of unavailability to begin with. In other words, don't try for Princess Michael of Kent first and then, when it appears she is unavailable, make an approach to the Queen Mother. See the Appendix for royal precedence.

You may have to advise your non-royal guests on the approved method of consorting with royalty. Where fluidity of conversation is concerned, matters ought to be relatively straightforward. Apart perhaps from diplomats, no class of human beings has had such practice as members of the royal family in putting at ease people introduced to them only a moment before. Nonetheless it takes two people to keep up a conversation. And while the old rule about not changing the subject when involved in a conversation with royalty is less sacrosanct than it was, for one of your guests to launch unilaterally into a boring, egotistical, inappropriate or indelicate subject, or even into an interesting one if with vehemence and wild gestures and at great length, would be unpardonably rude. That again would especially be the case if you don't know the person you're addressing well, or even at all, and would go just as much for ordinary people as for royalty. Other things being equal you will probably want to invite to meet royalty chiefly, or only, those of your circle who can converse cheerfully and courteously and who can be amusing but do not overstep the bounds of good taste.

When entertaining members of the royal family at dinner you should follow the rules of precedence, as set out in the Appendix to this book. That goes not just for seating but for serving them. An unmarried hostess would do well to have a male relative acting as temporary host, but then so she would in formal company anyway. It is now permissible for other guests to leave the function before the royal personage does, though only really at big functions. At private dinner parties where the ladies still withdraw from the room before the gentlemen so that the latter may drink port, the hostess should nod to the senior royal female present, even if it is the Queen herself, and the royal guest will troop out with her hostess, leading the way of course as described in the passage on port earlier in this book.

Remember that the test of your loyalty, even when host to the sovereign herself, is not, and has not been for many decades, how near you can drive yourself to bankruptcy. Undoubtedly it once was, or was thought to be (see the Introduction to this book). The Christopher Sykes who was a member of the Marlborough House set clustered round Edward VII when he was the Prince of Wales is said to have gravely impoverished himself in keeping HRH amused, but there have not been many like him for some centuries. In practical terms this means that you need not feel you have to accommodate a host of courtiers and servants, but that is equally true of entertaining generally now that so few people have servants, and virtually nobody has valets, grooms and coachmen who attend on them everywhere they go.

But there is one very important aspect of entertaining royalty which is quite new. I refer to the personal protection officer, or in plainer English the detective. Each member of the royal family who undertakes public duties has one in constant attendance. (At the time of writing the Princess of Wales has just shed her detective, however, unless she is with her children, who being close to the succession warrant close guarding.) Before a royal personage comes to your house the detective will almost certainly want to view it to see how secure it is, how easy any alternative means of exit are, whether it is overlooked by high buildings, flyovers, bridges, viaducts, woods which might harbour assassins and so on. He may make suggestions for temporarily modifying the way you arrange your furniture, fixtures and fittings, though clearly anything too drastic may make you want to think twice about the whole business of entertaining such guests. These islands still contain large numbers of houses and castles where in the past whole walls were erected or demolished, wings of buildings put up or pulled down, gardens landscaped, mounds and hillocks bulldozed to accommodate a visit from the sovereign or his near relation which might last only a few hours, or which was sometimes called off at the last moment. But they are essentially relics of a more elaborate style of entertaining generally. Security, not opulence for its own sake in receiving your important guests, is the overall consideration.

If you entertain a member of the royal family you must provide some kind of accommodation for the detective, although at a pinch he may be prepared to sit outside in the car for a few hours, rather as some rich men's chauffeurs are obliged to do. It would be kinder to let him use the kitchen or the scullery or a guest house if you have either of the last two things. He'd probably like some refreshment too, though it needn't be terrifically elaborate and it certainly shouldn't include alcohol. Notwithstanding which, I have heard of a case – it took place overseas, I hasten to add, so no member of the British police force need hang his head in shame – in which the local special branch man attending an international VIP to a private dwelling got a bit too merry on drink and tried to get off with the lady of the house. With great presence of mind she whispered to him that she'd meet him outside in the shrubbery in twenty minutes and once he'd gone out of doors to search for their trysting spot she locked the front doors behind him.

At a house party you ought to present every guest to the royal personage. Ditto with a small or medium-sized dinner party. At a ball or country-house dance or garden party or buffet supper, or perhaps even a sit-down dinner to which a huge number of guests are bidden, you as hostess will probably want to be more selective, though you should bear in mind that if you present forty out of fifty guests to HRH the other ten are likely to be terribly disappointed, perhaps even bitterly hurt. But you will probably have exercised more discretion than usual in drawing up your guest list beforehand so that there can really be no excuse for not presenting everybody. But bear in mind that the royal personage may not enjoy meeting shoals of people; after all that is what their 'job' consists of every day. So give them a break for once.

When you come to present one of your non-royal guests to your royal guest of honour you would say, 'May I present Robert Carr, sir?'. If you are presenting a relative of yours, make the degree of relationship clear when giving the name. Thus you might say, 'May I present my cousin Abigail Hill, ma'am?' In one-to-one conversation with royalty it is safest to refer to other royals as 'His/Her Royal Highness' rather than 'he' or 'she', initially indicating who it is you are talking about by mentioning 'the Prince Edward' or 'the Princess Royal', for example, by name. Only children of a sovereign take the definite article before their style of Prince/Princess. Accordingly

Prince Michael of Kent, who is only a grandson of a sovereign, does not.

If in the least doubt about how to style your royal guests, enquire from the private secretary of the royal personage, or if the royal personage has no private secretary, as may be the case with impoverished former ruling families, enquire directly. This is clearly particularly important with foreign royalty, as there are so many variations.

Foreign Royalty

Most other female crowned heads or former female crowned heads you present your guests to should be addressed in the same fashion as Queen Elizabeth II, for example, Queen Beatrix of the Netherlands or ex-Queen Anne-Marie of Greece. (I use the term crowned head deliberately since it covers not only queens regnant but queens consort and queens dowager as well as ex-queens.) With kings and ex-kings you begin 'Your Majesty' and continue with 'sir' thereafter. Otherwise you behave exactly as with queens and ex-queens.

There are other kinds of sovereign apart from kings and queens, for example, emperors and empresses, who tend to rank above kings and queens. But three of the four imperial dynasties – Russia, Austria and Ethiopia – that reigned until well into this century have become ex-reigning ones. (The Japanese emperor remains on his throne of course.) And the Brazilian imperial family, which constituted the fifth such major dynasty, has not reigned since 1889, though there were reports from South America of a resurgence in its fortunes last year. Nonetheless by no means all members of these deposed imperial families have renounced their claims to the thrones of their respective countries, and those who maintain claims ought to be addressed correctly – in a social context at any rate. (Foreign Office protocol might blanch at use of imperial style at official functions.)

An emperor or empress would be addressed initially as 'Your Imperial Majesty', subsequently as 'Sir/Ma'am' and referred to as 'His/Her Imperial Majesty' or less formally as 'the Emperor/ Empress', unless you have more than one in the room when, to avoid confusion, you add the realm of which the emperor/empress is, or maintains a claim to be, sovereign. The Russian and Ethiopian imperial dynasties were relieved of their thrones in 1917 and 1975 respectively. The Queen Mother is a former empress (of India), but since Indian independence in 1947 she has never been addressed by the style 'Your Imperial Majesty' or referred to as 'Her Imperial Majesty', and even before 1947 that usage seems only to have applied in the Indian sub-continent. The children, grandchildren and brothers or sisters of a Tsar of All the Russias were addressed directly as 'Your Imperial Highness' and referred to as 'His/Her Imperial Highness'. Nowadays it is suggested that members of the Russian imperial house apart from its head, His Imperial Highness (HIH) the Grand Duke Vladimir, his wife and their children, each of whom is 'HIH the Grand Duke/Duchess Alexei/Tatiana' or whatever, should be addressed in the lower ranking form as 'Your Highness' and referred to as 'His/Her Highness Prince Ivan/Princess Anastasia'. This seems a sadly Jacobinical attitude, especially in an era when the ancient name of St Petersburg has been restored and associations of the nobility flourish back in Russia. On the other hand, many members of the Russian imperial family have in recent generations married commoners, particularly Americans, who as citizens of a republic sometimes drop their titles. It is possible that the children of such a marriage may not use any title at all, even if directly descended from a tsar in the male line. You should try and find out what the position is before inviting such people and introducing other guests to them. Great-grandchildren of tsars were addressed directly as 'Your Highness' and referred to as 'His/Her Highness'. All descendants in later generations, unless products of morganatic marriages (unequal in rank, as between the royal personage and someone of lesser rank) were addressed as 'Your Serene Highness' and referred to as 'His/Her Serene Highness'.

The correct form of address for members of the Ethiopian imperial families is more complex, owing chiefly to there being more than one royal house and partly to the protocol that existed in Ethiopia, which was somewhat haphazard (at least in European eyes). The emperor himself and his empress or empresses were addressed as 'Your Imperial Majesty' and referred to as 'His/Her Imperial Majesty'. So far so good. And the children of an emperor would be addressed as 'Your Imperial Highness' and referred to as 'His/Her Imperial Highness'. But the siblings of an emperor might be of the whole blood, the half-blood through a subsequent marriage or by the same

170

father out of concubines. And whereas grandchildren of an emperor in the male line would tend to be addressed as 'Your Imperial Highness' and referred to as 'His/Her Imperial Highness', grandchildren of an emperor in the female line would tend to be addressed as 'Your Highness' and referred to as 'His/Her Highness' only. But sometimes the prefix 'His/Her Imperial Highness' seems to have been conferred on connections of an emperor who were much more remote even than a grandchild.

The position of the Austrian imperial house is less complex than that of Ethiopia but less easy than that of Russia. Dr Otto von Habsburg, its head, has renounced any claim to the throne of Austria but has not done so for Hungary. I am informed by a spokesman of his household that he doesn't care how he is styled, being more interested in substance than surface. This raises the interesting question of whether it would not be lop-sided, to put it at its most diplomatic, to address one of his near relatives formally if you address him as just 'Doctor', given that he is the head of the house. Archdukes/archduchesses of Austria, who latterly were also princes/princesses of Hungary, were addressed as 'Your Imperial and Royal Highness' and referred to as 'His/Her Imperial and Royal Highness'. As with the Romanovs, there have been several morganatic marriages and descendants of such a marriage often have had a lower-ranking style granted them, for instance the style 'His/Her Highness'.

The head of the Brazilian imperial house and his eldest son are addressed as 'Your Imperial and Royal Highness' and are referred to as 'His Imperial Highness'. Other descendants of the Princess Imperial Isabel (regent for her father, the last emperor, before his deposition), which in effect comprises all the other members of the imperial house, are addressed as 'Your Royal Highness' and referred to as 'His/Her Royal Highness'.

Members of the French royal houses have not renounced their claims to the throne of France and are permitted to reside on French soil. (There are three lots; Legitimists, Orleanists and a branch that claims to be descended from Louis XVI.) All except the head of the Legitimist house, the Comte de Paris, who is addressed as 'Monseigneur', are addressed as 'Your Royal Highness' and referred to as 'His/Her Royal Highness'. The head of the Prussian royal family is addressed as 'Your Imperial and Royal

Highness' and referred to as 'His Imperial Highness'. All other members of the Prussian dynasty, and all members of the other major royal German dynasties (Bavaria, Hanover, Saxony, Würt-temberg) are addressed as 'Your Royal Highness' and referred to as 'His/Her Royal Highness'. For the form of address for members of ruling families of the lesser German principalities and former kingdoms, which is complex and variable in the extreme, see *Burke's Royal Families of the World*, Vol. I (1977). The head of the Italian royal house is not permitted to reside on Italian soil and has not renounced his claim to the throne. Members of the Italian royal house are addressed as for the French one, but there is no equivalent to the position of the Comte de Paris.

The current Pope (John Paul II at time of writing) prefers not to emphasise his temporal status as sovereign. Three monarchical sovereign states remain in Europe that are neither kingdoms nor republics: the Principality of Liechtenstein, the Grand Duchy of Luxembourg and the Principality of Monaco. Princes and prin-cesses who are members of the ruling families of the two princi-palities are styled 'His/Her Serene Highness' and princes or princesses of the ruling family of Luxembourg, technically Princes/Princesses of Luxembourg, Bourbon-Parma and Nassau, are styled 'His/Her Royal Highness'. Further details may be gleaned from *Debrett's Correct Form*.

A friend of mine who has regular dealings with Arabs finds it best to call all princes 'Your Royal Highness' unless advised otherwise in advance. Actually, the Sultan of Oman is addressed as 'Your Majesty' and referred to as 'His Majesty', as is the King of Saudi Arabia. The Amirs of Bahrain, Kuwait and Qatar and the sheikhs of the United Arab Emirates are addressed as 'Your Highness' and referred to as 'His Highness Sheikh Blank Ruler of B'lanq' or whatever. There are so many members of the ruling houses in the Gulf and other places in the Middle East that it is almost impossible to keep up with them. The Foreign & Common-wealth Office may be able to provide some assistance if consulted before you know you are to deal with certain foreign dignitaries. *Burke's Royal Families of the World*, Vol. II (1980) gives some guidance as to who is who among them, but of course that would be rather out of date by now. By and large it is better in such circumstances to err on the side of excessive formality.

CHAPTER 10

Sporting Events

Shooting Parties

There are two extreme approaches to hosting a shooting party and a whole bushel of grades of grandeur or simplicity of approach in between. It can be done at a cost of thousands of pounds or for comparatively little money. Shooting is not necessarily a rich man's sport, nor need it be a rich woman's (females are in fact taking to it in increasing droves), though in recent years it has been seen as one. In Ireland, where I live, anybody can join a gun club and pot away at hares, rabbits, rooks, pheasant and snipe. Some of these creatures are shot during certain seasons of the year; others are fair game all the year round. The historic distaste on the part of most people in Ireland for game-preserving landlords means there are fewer large landlords, fewer still who successfully preserve game to the exclusion of sporting opportunities for the man in the street and less snobbery about taking up a sporting gun. There is less population density and consequently more chance to go shooting on a casual basis, what in Britain would be termed 'rough shooting'.

In Britain shooting, which has come in effect to mean game bird shooting, has for centuries been connected in the popular mind with the upper class or would-be upper class. Accordingly it has an enormous snob value, so that the first thing a prosperous hairdresser does on retiring from the salon and buying a country place – from the shears to the shires in a single generation, as it were – is to get a pair of tweed plus-fours run up for him and take to blasting pheasants out of the sky between 1 October and 1 February every year. If he is more prone to the death wish he can get himself a pink coat and take up fox-hunting, but among your true *arrivistes* only pop musicians seem to have the requisite daring.

In fact, by the nineteenth century shooting was available, often over a wide area locally, to anyone with a gun and a bit of plausibility as to manners. The nineteenth-century satirical sporting novelist Robert Smith Surtees is a useful witness to the truth of this observation. In *Facey Romford's Hounds*, his anti-hero

Romford gets as much shooting as he likes, yet he is the proprietor of no acres and possesses no money other than what he can get by horse-dealing and cheek. It is a paradox that over the period in which shooting has been seen increasingly as an establishment sport the old necessary condition for participation, being a landowner or close friend of a landowner, has been eroded. Nowadays anyone with sufficient cash can take part. You don't even need that much cash if you go shooting in an out-of-the-way corner of the country with farmer friends rather than in one of the fashionable areas such as East Anglia.

At the more rough and ready end of the spectrum the host need only provide the terrain over which to shoot. As little as 200 acres make a satisfactory area. And it need not be woodland: farmland interspersed with copses will do at a pinch. The host here will typically arrange perhaps eight shoots a season and let half of them to outsiders so as to provide him with an income to meet the costs of having his friends over on the other occasions. The total cost per day of this scale of activity is about £4,000. As host you would send out invitations to your more elderly and distinguished guests well in advance, a minimum of three weeks before the actual shoot or even before the start of the season, naming several dates and giving them some choice of which to take. Write in the second person, as you would an ordinary letter, then back up the initial approach with a phone call. The advantage of sending the initial invitations by post, as with dinner parties, is that the guests can refuse politely. But in any case if you don't invite them again for some time, or even never, they ought not to feel particularly hurt. As with other social functions you can invite bachelor guns (a 'gun' in shooting parlance meaning a person who wields a gun, even though it may be a pair of guns, one in use at a time while the spare is being reloaded) very much at the last minute, obviously as a stop-gap, and be pretty certain they will take no offence.

Clothes for shooting need not be conspicuously old, though you will come across all kinds of snobbish remarks to the effect that your Barbour, tweed cap and plus-fours should be well worn in that new clothes betoken the *parvenu*. It is a ridiculous attitude because if you come to think of it even the Duke of Devonshire, proprietor of God knows how many thousands of acres of moorland and other shooting country spread over England and Ireland, must occasionally wear out his old togs and need to buy fresh ones. Malicious stories abound regarding his late brother-in-law, Harold Macmillan, to the effect that the famous actor-manager, on noticing how His Grace always shot in a shabby old set of clothes, made haste to discard his own newer ones and procure costume every bit as moth-eaten as a true gent's. The only truly important principle to bear in mind is that you should wear clothes which blend in with the landscape as regards colour and texture – russets, greens, autumnal yellows or heather mixture in woollens and tweeds and home-spuns rather than lycra or day-glo. Get your valet to wear them in for a few months first if you must, but don't feel you have to hire a valet simply to act as an ageing mechanism for taking the sheen off new items of sporting wear. If you wear a jacket rather than Barbour or similarly more generously cut garment, make sure that it sits loosely on you, particularly about the armpits, as you will be stretching upwards much of the time to shoot almost perpendicularly into the air. Mittens are a must on cold winter days otherwise you will lose all feeling in your hands and shoot much worse. They should be supple enough to let your left hand curl round the stock of the gun and with holes in the end of the right hand (or left hand if you are left-handed) so that you can squeeze the trigger effectively rather than fumble for it.

Normally the early shoots are the plum dates, but some of your friends who are really good shots can also be asked to shoot the woodcocks on the last day of the year, woodcock being a bird that only arrives in Britain from Scandinavia around the first moon in December. Pheasant rather than woodcock are the standard game bird. They are mostly reared by gamekeepers specifically for shooting, sometimes in very elaborate – one might even say pampered – circumstances such as feeding bins, straw-strewn patches of ground, wired pens for protection against foxes and so on. But you do come across wild ones, or at any rate semi-wild ones that have escaped from preserved land. Pheasant are not native to these islands but come originally from the East. Sometimes they fly high, sometimes low, depending both on the weather and terrain. Wet weather makes them fly low because the moisture weighs down their feathers. In dry cold weather they fly high. In windy weather they may fly less straight than in calm conditions. The altitude of their flying path will affect where you site the stands. A stand is the place where each gun stands to shoot at the birds from; the spot is usually marked with a peg, that is to say a stake about 3ft high with a number attached to it and then inserted into the ground; the gun stands just behind the peg. In big, open, flattish terrain such as Norfolk the stands would be placed 25 to 30 yards apart. But in more enclosed country, such as parts of Lancashire, where the birds fly high, one would place the stands rather closer, say as little as 15 to 20 yards apart. The line of stands will be in a straight line or curved or whatever, depending on the contours of the particular bit of woodland straight ahead of you from which the pheasants are expected to emerge. If the birds come over a ridge ahead of the guns the stands would fit the horizontal shape of the ridge, U-shaped if the ridge curves away to left and right, straight if it is straight. A competent gamekeeper will take into account such things as terrain, hence the distance apart of the stands, but the more you know about it yourself the better.

For partridge, which fly lower and flatter and therefore can see the guns more easily, you will want to provide stretches of hedgerow or similar cover for your guns to shoot from behind. Although woodcock are late arrivals in Britain proper, in the Scilly Isles and Ireland they are considerably more plentiful and it is in those parts that they are shot on a large scale. Some authorities think it unkind to shoot them because they are said to be monogamous and to kill one of a pair may lead its mate to pine. They can fly very low in rather darting fashion and trying to shoot them when they do this can be dangerous for other humans nearby. As a general rule, never permit a gun to shoot below the level of the tops of the trees, nor at a horizontal angle of more than 45 degrees to right or left. Accordingly never be tempted in the middle of a drive to shoot at an earth-bound creature such as a rabbit. A useful precept is 'sky behind bird', meaning that you should only fire at the bird when it is silhouetted against the sky. You as host must impress such rules on any of your guests you suspect of ignorance or carelessness in these matters. At the same time you must be courteous. It can make hosting a shoot a nerve-racking business.

You should go round the area to be shot in advance of the day itself, placing the pegs yourself, though in consultation with your gamekeeper. Each peg is allocated to each gun by drawing lots for the first drive. For the second drive, move everyone along two pegs. For the third drive move everyone along another two pegs, and so on. That way everyone sooner or later gets whatever may be the best stand as well as the worst one. There is an old saying that for sons and lovers you should monkey with the draw. I leave it to your conscience whether to follow it. Perhaps only when you have been a substantial figure in the county for fifteen years.

The four or five hours that make up a shoot are divided into drives, or sessions, when beaters advance through the woodland stirring up the pheasant so that they fly towards the guns, which then do their best to bring the birds down. The duration of a drive is measured from the moment when the guns take up their positions at the pegs. Some time later, perhaps as much as three-quarters of an hour, the keeper blows his whistle to signify that the beating is about to begin. At grander shoots each gun may use a pair of weapons, also a loader to stuff one gun with cartridges while the employer uses the other. As a result a gun who has the services of a loader can keep up a steady fire. At less elaborate affairs each gun may have no more than a single weapon. You as host are under no obligation to provide any of your guests with a weapon, but if you had a very young man without much money staying with you who had not yet acquired his own gun or guns, you might lend him a spare one of yours. Women are so new to the business of shooting that they are expected to bring guns on all occasions when they are asked to shoot. This is not particularly fair, but that is how it is, nevertheless. If your keeper is good at his job he will slow down the beating progress when there are only single guns shooting so that the birds do not come through to the guns all in a crowd. Not even the best shot can keep up with a rush of birds. In old-fashioned circles it is considered a bit off for a gun to count the number of birds he has brought down. Indeed, a good shot doesn't show off his prowess as a marksman but has it as his intention to 'give the birds a good salute'. Of course from the pheasant's point of view it doesn't make much difference whether you're shot dead by an arithmetically inclined oik anxious to tot up as many corpses as he can or a gentleman of the old school who merely wishes to salute you, albeit with lead.

177

You can send a couple of walking guns along the flanks of a wood, one to the left of the wood, the other to the right. Their task is to take out any birds that fly sideways from the line of fire. Assign this task to a young relative or young unimportant guest. Sometimes a walking gun is sent out behind the beaters to take care of any birds that fly back when stirred up.

As host you should employ a few chaps with dogs to pick up all the birds the guns have brought down before moving on to the next drive. Ideally you would use only gamekeepers as beaters, borrowing those of your neighbouring landowners for the day. Otherwise use as many local gamekeepers as you can and top up the numbers with local lads. You will hear it said in some quarters that the guns' wives and girlfriends will do as beaters. Don't you believe it. (Though I have heard that at Lord Carnarvon's shoots the Queen has been prevailed upon to pick up pheasants.) More and more non-royal women are rebelling against such menial tasks and either staying at home over a hot fire and a hotter Jilly Cooper novel or taking up shooting themselves. Besides, you cannot impose any discipline on them in the field by threatening to sack them. If you live in a strongly male chauvinist part of the country you may get reasonable results by inspanning the womenfolk under a ferocious gamekeeper. And of course you can shout at dogs to your heart's content, though whether it will make any difference in the case of a giddy and headstrong animal I rather doubt. One of the curses of hosting a shoot can be indisciplined dogs belonging to your guests. To get yourself and your guests to the next drive you can provide Land Rovers or any other four-wheel drive vehicle, or even a tractor and trailer. Some big estates employ buses.

In the north of England the winter days are substantially shorter than in the south. Accordingly, if shooting above the Trent one would tend, having started off from the house or other assembly point at 9 a.m. and begun the first drive about 9.45, to shoot continuously through to about 3 p.m., when one would have lunch. The great advantage of this is that no matter how much people drink at lunch there can be no danger of them getting trigger-happy afterwards. In fact people who go shooting are fairly abstemious during the day's sport, however much they may make up for it that evening. But there are accidents from time to time, and the less these can be attributed to drunkenness the better for the reputation of all concerned.

The shooting lunch should consist of warming drinks such as sloe gin, cherry brandy or port. Nor need it be good port. In fact shooting lunches are the ideal venue for getting rid of all that ruby-type stuff that has accumulated over the years. I do not recommend mediocre port out of meanness but because in the chill open air of a game lunch your guests will be in no condition to savour really good stuff. As far as solids are concerned, thickly cut sandwiches full of ham, chicken or pheasant are recommended. You might also serve game pie, giving the biggest bits to those who have shot best. In the most exalted circles not a million miles away from east Norfolk a little bird tells me that first courses are never served at game luncheons. Well, it saves money.

Talking of money, how much should your guests tip gamekeepers, loaders and beaters? They are bound to ask you if they don't know already. The standard tipping tariff for a gamekeeper is 10 per cent of the total bag in pounds sterling. Accordingly if you down 1,000 birds the tip would be £100. The beauty of this is that it imposes an automatic sliding scale depending on whether the shoot is a grand one or a modest one. A loader would be paid about £30 for serving a double-weapon gun, £10 upwards for serving a single-weapon gun. If your guests are shooting at clay pigeons, which is sometimes arranged, for example for inexperienced shots or shots who are out of practice, on the first day of a shoot lasting several days, the trappers (i.e., the people who operate a clay pigeon trap, the device that releases the clay into the air for your guests to shoot at) would expect £15 upwards a day. The same tariff operates for beaters at a live-bird shoot. Pickers-up, whether they work with or without their own dog, though many people would argue that one's own dog is essential, rate about £10 to £20 a day; more, however, if they have more than one dog of their own.

Big shooting estates will consist of at least 1,000 acres and cater for at least eight guns, at most sixteen guns. Very rich people might shoot the same acreage that normally serves eight guns with as few as six guns in all. With each pheasant costing around £20 to kill, taking into account all the expenses, that represents a substantial outlay since each gun might reckon to kill 250 birds with a single weapon and much more with two weapons and an efficient loader. Relatively inexperienced guns at that level tend to like having the same loader every time; regular participants in the sport of shooting probably will bring their own loaders with them. A good host will bear that in mind.

At a small shoot the lunch may take place inside the house around which the shoot as a whole is arranged. That assumes the coverts are within relatively easy reach of the house. If they are, shooting may continue after lunch. But herein lies the danger that somebody will take too much to drink at lunch and bring about a nasty accident afterwards. Clearly the smaller shoots are likely to be less meticulously planned and run, but they may compensate for this by being more intimate. You as host must decide which atmosphere suits your temperament more. Probably the depth of your pocket will turn out to be the decisive factor.

GROUSE SHOOTING
This is a slightly different sport from pheasant, partridge or woodcock shooting. Grouse are unique to these islands and are found on bleak moors rather than in lowland woods. They are wild, not reared. Worst of all, there are not many of them just at the moment. Many have been killed off by the strongylosis worm. Others have succumbed to foxes and in 1993 an unusually cold snap in May. On the moorland behind where I live in Ireland we flushed only a single brace when out hawking the September before last and none at all last September. But in Ireland, although private individuals may retain the sporting rights to tracts of land that otherwise have passed under the heavy hand of the Forestry Commission, they cannot always enforce them. Accordingly several brace may have been taken by unauthorised persons. In Scotland and England matters are more firmly under the control of big landowners. A typical estate would comprise many more thousands of acres than one further south or nearer sea-level which specialises in pheasant.

You shoot from butts, primitive little cairns constructed of wood or stones, and the grouse are driven towards you by beaters and dogs. Or you can walk across the terrain and shoot the birds as they get up. Grouse fly rather like a cruise missile, dipping and soaring in much the way the contours of the land do, and not much

180

slower than cruise missiles either, at up to 80mph. They are therefore a good deal faster than a pheasant and being smaller as well are a great deal harder to hit. Unlike with pheasant you are therefore likely to shoot at them as they come on at you or as they fly away. Impress upon your guests that they should never shoot as they swing the gun round. That is how fatal accidents occur.

Well, of course it's very nice in theory to be a landowner – less so in practice – but not all of us, however well heeled, can manage it just at present. If you nevertheless wish to host a shoot, what do you do? You take your guests to one of the estates owned by other people that for a fee will allow you to shoot their land. Prices range from £220 a gun for a sixteen-gun day for clays to more than half as much again per gun for an eight-gun shoot. For live shoots you will probably negotiate direct with the estate owner. Three of the leading commercially run shoots within reasonably close reach of London are Catton Hall, Derbyshire, run by Mr and Mrs Robin Neilson, of an old landed gentry family (see *Burke's Landed Gentry*, 1972 edition); Kirby House, Inkpen, Berkshire, the seat of Mr and Mrs Richard Astor (see *Debrett's Peerage*, 1995 edition, under Astor of Hever); and Salperton Park, Gloucestershire, where Mr and Mrs Victor Watkins are in charge.

The above are suitable if you want to take your friends to shoot pheasant or partridge. For grouse try the small-ads pages of the *Field*, *Country Life* or the *Shooting Times*. The Game Conservancy, of Fordingbridge, Hampshire (tel: 0425 652381), the British Association for Shooting and Conservation (tel: 0244 570881) or leading estate agents can help you locate an estate on which you can pay to go shooting on either a daily basis or a weekly one. Driven grouse cost around £35 a bird, ones you shoot as you walk up on them around £27 a bird. But since grouse moors are more remote and further from London and other big urban centres you will have to spend more on getting there and accommodation once there. If you fly to Scotland the journey from the airport may be another hundred miles or so. Grouse shooting can cost up to £30,000 for a week's sport for a typical number of guns.

Lawn Meets
It's always pleasantest to host an entertainment in your own home, at least from the point of view of atmosphere, even if it's a chore

181

clearing up afterwards. If you have no more than twenty acres or so you might care to have the local hunt meet at your place during the season. This is usually called a lawn meet. It doesn't mean you have to have a host of horses, hounds and hunt followers, to say nothing of horse boxes, Range Rovers and other wheeled vehicles churning up your putting-green-like greensward. The term lawn here is used in the older sense of an open space of smooth level ground covered in grass, derived possibly from the French word *lande*. Old-fashioned country people still refer to any expanse of flattish field within fullish view of an old mansion or manor house as 'the front lawn'. Parkland might count as lawn in this sense if not too heavily encumbered with mature trees. So if you have a field or reasonably generous-sized paddock in front of the house, preferably separated from your garden proper by a ha-ha, though railings or stud fencing will do, you are in a position to host a lawn meet.

You do not yourself have to hunt to mount an operation of this sort, merely to support the practice of fox-hunting. If you live in the country and have ever kept chickens, ducks, geese or even small cats and kittens, you will know better than to get steamed up about killing foxes, for they do the most appalling damage to creatures that are smaller or weaker than themselves. They are the lager louts of the animal world, in fact. The fox-hunting season starts usually on 1 November and continues through to about early March. That said, I know of at least one pack that has its opening meet in mid-October and the Devon and Somerset Staghounds start work in August. You should get in touch with the Master or secretary of the local hunt well before the season starts, when they are still making out their programme. There is hardly any point in having the lawn meet on any day other than a Saturday, as except for the fashionable packs in the East Midlands of England there won't be many people out on weekdays. (Most hunts don't go out on Sundays, though again I have known at least one that did.) Besides, you have to think of the enjoyment of your house guests and it is probable that they will be with you principally over the weekend.

Let us assume that about forty people will turn up. Perhaps a quarter to a third of that number will arrive in cars, mostly of the shooting brake or four-wheel-drive variety. Plan parking spaces for as many as possible. Signpost where on your paddock or field you wish those attending the meet to park, bearing in mind the location of any boggy bits in which vehicles could get stuck. You might want to use one of your teenage children as a steward for visitors' parking. Perhaps a quarter of your notional forty will bring their horses in boxes; more if the meet is on the periphery of the country (the area hunted by the local pack), fewer if it's in the middle of the country.

Leave a large open space in one part of the 'lawn' in which any excitable horse can be ridden round and round in circles till it wears itself out. It's a terrifying spectacle when a powerful animal like a hunter needs to be rendered calm. I have seen this happen at a lawn meet and even though the rider in that case was a superlative horsewoman it was decidedly alarming. Everyone, but everyone, who turns up must be considered a genuine hunt follower, provided that your hunt is sufficiently far from centres of urban-based subversiveness to escape the attentions of 'sabs'. If it is, to operate a policy of discrimination against, say, foot followers as opposed to the horse-owning classes on the grounds that the latter must be gentry whereas the former are probably peasants is about the shortest route to unpopularity I know. In addition it's almost certain to be a false appreciation of the situation. Some of the gentry may have given up hunting on horses, whether due to old age or declining finances, and follow the hounds on foot out of abiding enthusiasm. Some of the most oafish yobs I have ever come across ride to hounds. Actually, country sports usually involve the least snobbish gatherings of human beings conceivable. It is more usual to serve one's guests refreshments out of doors, but indoor gatherings are not unknown, and if you have frail townies from London for the weekend and the weather is bad you might want to gather some at any rate of the hunt followers inside. If nevertheless, you fear lest your bibelots are heisted, lock the rooms in which they are kept and serve your guests in the conservatory, kitchen, barn – anywhere that will hold large numbers. If the weather is fine you can probably manage the whole thing out of doors. People dress warmly for hunt meets.

Mulled wine is the best drink, being hot. Heat up red wine in a big saucepan over the stove. You don't need to use a red-hot poker except for dramatic effect. The wine, as with port at a

183

shooting lunch, needn't be of superior quality, but add cloves, lemon, orange or lime rind and cinnamon to give it zest. Pouring in apple juice will make the mulled wine go further and make the taste fruitier. A drop of brandy, perhaps, might liven it up. Recipes in drinks books abound so I won't go into detail here.

Hunting people tend to be harder drinkers than shooting people because by and large in hunting you kill nobody but yourself if you're half-seas-over. Also, since hunting is so lethal a sport even when you're sober, getting drunk hardly makes any difference to your chances of surviving the day with a whole skin if you're not a superlative rider, and either way alcohol will act as an anaesthetic should you sustain a bad fall.

As for food, serve mince pies, even if it's after Christmas, hot sausages, sausage rolls. Canapés might be thought a touch effeminate by hunting people, but your fragile female guests down from London might appreciate them. If the latter group stay indoors – it would be considered bad form by any locals who caught sight of them through the drawing-room window, but there's little you can do should the Londoners insist – you can serve them champagne. However rich you are, serving champagne to the mob outside would be considered ostentatious. If you want to hobnob with the Master on a separate occasion, invite him and his wife over to drinks or dinner another day, when he is not engaged in the official performance of his mastership.

Keep all children, whether your own, your guests' or the local villagers', well away from the horses. If you have reason to suspect that saboteurs may try to spoil things either alert the police, the trouble-shooting committee of the local hunt itself or *in extremis* get in touch with one of the security firms who specialise in this sort of thing. You would be well advised to let the police know a meet is going to take place anyway, because they can then do something to marshal the cars on the open roads surrounding your property. But a competent local hunt committee or the hunt secretary or perhaps even the Master himself will probably liaise with the local police throughout the season. Do not get in some cowboy outfit of security specialists who will overreact to any 'sabs' and thereby land you in court on a charge of conspiracy to inflict actual bodily harm or criminal damage. The industry's trade association, the British Security Industry Association (BSIA), is trying to get a regulation system going for security firms. All the big boys, such as Group 4 and Securicor, already belong. A discreet chat with your local hunt committee beforehand should enable you to handle things adroitly.

SECURITY
Here might be an appropriate point at which to discuss security generally. Your rich and important guests can be relied on to provide their own security. If you suspect any of them may be bringing security personnel to a house party or even dinner party and have not warned you, do ask. It is much better to be put in the picture from the word go. You may care to know that respectable security firms submit to British Standard 7499, which covers named guarding operatings, and British Standard 5750, which covers quality and efficiency. The Inspectorate for the Security Industry (ISI) carries out inspections of security firms every so often to make sure they comply with the requisite standards. If your guests come from abroad things may be more difficult since they could be bringing unsavoury goon squads with them. All other EC countries except the Irish Republic have a regulated security firm industry, but many of your VIP guests may be flying in from Mexico, South America or Hong Kong. You should impress upon them at the earliest possible stage that what may seem unexceptional in other parts of the world, for example, wading into a crowd of students from the nearby polytechnic (or 'university' as they have quaintly been rechristened) and crushing a few skulls with baseball bats, will not look at all good in Britain, with its historic belief in the inviolability of the person of the subject.

Hawking Parties
Before hosting any entertainment connected with hawking, consult any friends of yours who practise this noble and ancient activity. If you do not know anyone who does, I can only offer a description of what we get up to in Ireland, where we annually host an entertainment for hawking friends who come from all over the country to try to kill grouse on the moorlands above the castle. The opening of the season there is 12 September, a month after grouse shooting begins in England and Scotland. The party

assembles for breakfast at the gate lodge of a castle belonging to some friends of ours. There a substantial hot meal of bacon, kidneys, eggs and grilled tomatoes is consumed, accompanied by plenty of strong liquor – Bloody Maries, whiskey – and less strong liquor – Guinness, sloe gin, cherry brandy, much as with shooting lunches, in fact. Since neither horses nor guns are going to be used it does not matter how drunk you get, providing those in charge of the cars are sober. We then drive off to the moors, parking as near to the final climb as is feasible. We trudge through conifer plantations or up tracks hewn through the woodlands by the Forestry Commission, the hawkers carrying square or rectangular wooden devices shaped like huge, crudely carved, empty picture frames, on which sit the hawks, at this preliminary stage hooded, of course. Once on the moors the hawkers stride ahead of the rest of the party with setters to flush the game. When grouse are flushed the hawkers release their birds of prey, which swoop on the grouse and kill them. We return to Ballaghmore Castle at the end of the day, have a hot bath and go over to friends for dinner. The next day everybody comes to us and we cook them an indoor barbecue over the massive grid-iron in the lesser hall of the castle. It's as simple as that. In Mongolia they hunt on horseback using golden eagles, but that's a bit highfalutin' for us in the West.

Shooting Lodges

This kind of entertaining is radically different from other sporting activity in that the lodge is almost invariably rented for a week or two weeks by the host, rather than his being the resident proprietor at his own house or hiring a shoot for a day at a time and showing his guests sport on an outing from where they live or the house they are all staying in. The host nevertheless has to act as if he were the resident landlord inasmuch as he must give orders to the staff who act as guides or gillies. Clearly he must have some concept of how weather, say, affects the prospects for fishing or stalking, not just over the next twenty-four hours but conceivably the next few days. He must be conversant with how much to tip the gillies and guides. He should be a good housekeeper himself – I mean in the sense of a good quartermaster, or someone who can supply a remote household with the wherewithal for three solid meals a day. Alternatively his wife should be good at this sort of thing, or if not her a housekeeper or major domo. Shooting lodges are often as far as thirty or forty miles from the nearest big town and even then, if in Scotland, the town may lack many of the delicacies in the food and drink line that would be thought indispensable in London.

Having organised that side of things, the host then invites a group of friends to stay, the ostensible purpose of the holiday being deer-stalking or salmon fishing. But guests need not participate in either activity. They should be reasonably active physically, however, for there is little else to do apart from long walks over rough terrain and the occasional scramble up a craggy mountain or hillside. Swimming may be possible in very warm weather, but you shouldn't count on it. Many hosts insist on their guests being out of the house for much of the day so that the staff have some opportunity to clean it, or just relax.

The decor of many lodges in Scotland is uncompromisingly tartan and you could advise any guest with even a smidgeon of Scots blood to bring a kilt and velvet doublet if a man or an evening gown in dark-coloured velvet, with plenty of lace, plus jewellery in cairngorms and other similar stones, if a woman. In fact men and women should dress rather similarly by day as well as in the evening, with the emphasis on stout tweeds and lace-up boots rising well above the ankle during the hours before changing for dinner.

The host usually settles who is going stalking the night before an operation and communicates the numbers and identities of those participating the next day to the head keeper. The gillies are now said to be much more conscious of the need to placate visitors than formerly, though they still maintain an independence of outlook which might be thought a wee bit brusque in anyone less sturdily egalitarian than a Scotsman on his native heather. Good guides will give advice at every stage of the stalk and finish off a beast if he has been badly mauled but not killed by a stalker new to the sport or one who is out of practice at shooting. The first time any of your guests kills a stag he will be smeared with blood and have to refrain from washing it off for several hours. This custom is called being blooded. The same thing happens with newcomers to fox-hunting.

Tennis Parties

Obviously you must have at least one hard court to be able to host a tennis party. Do you have a sufficient expanse of flat lawn to rig up another net and make a second court, even if it's just grass and not normally surrounded by netting? It's worth thinking about if your garden will run to it. You could always hire temporary netting to put round the stretch of lawn to prevent stray shots being lost in the shrubbery. Or you could hire local children at a sweat-shop rate of a few bags of sweets an afternoon to act as ballboys and ballgirls and chase after every ball the moment it flies off court.

A tennis party, as opposed to a series of games of tennis, is rather more than the sum of its parts. It is particularly suitable for pairing off adolescents, or at least it used to be thought of as suitable when I was young and adolescents were shyer with members of the opposite sex than perhaps they are today. A generation or two before even my long-distant youth, tennis parties were used for getting together members of the opposite sex of quite advanced ages, people in their twenties say. Nowadays it might be a method of introducing some shy old widower of moderately athletic proclivities to a woman you think he might eventually click with. At the same time a tennis party would avoid making it too obvious that you have brought them together deliberately, in the way that a dinner party would. It is undoubtedly true that with shy people a game can be excellent for breaking the ice when they have just been introduced to a stranger, however attractive they find that stranger.

You can organise a whole tennis tournament if you wish, enlisting your friends and neighbours with tennis courts of their own and arranging a shuttle service of cars to take participants backwards and forwards between the various venues. If you do this you will probably need to appoint umpires, as the sporting emotions are likely to get more wound up.

Drinks should be very light – spritzers (half white wine, half sparkling water), wine cup with plenty of dilution, weak tea, lemon tea. Food should be of the utmost lightness also, for those playing at any rate: strawberries, raspberries or white currants and redcurrants, all with sugar and cream, petits fours, wafer-thin cucumber sandwiches, ices, sorbets, fruit salad.

When you are intending to set a couple of your guests to playing tennis, or even a couple of couples, you should consider the wants of the non-combatants. The latter will probably outnumber the former by three or four to one and unless the players are of Wimbledon quality, which is unlikely, would probably appreciate being enticed away from the side of the court by other, softer distractions. Hire local music students or a professional band of wind instrumentalists or a light orchestra if possible, and get them to play Palm Court selections, just out of direct earshot of the players but within hearing range of those walking round the garden. Professional musicians earn derisory sums and the standard hourly rate set by the Musicians Union will hardly bankrupt you. Music makes all the difference to any garden entertainment, turning what might otherwise be a mere hoggish *al fresco* beano or sweaty gladiatorial display of bad temper, over-competitiveness and foul language into a true Watteau-esque *fête champêtre*.

Croquet Parties
Almost exactly the same considerations apply here as with tennis, except that croquet is a far more vicious game. Accordingly there is double the need for distraction. You might even care to have on hand some very, very mild tranquilliser for any participant who gets too worked up about being roqueted at the final hoop – something that can happen to the best players among us.

CHAPTER 11
Business

Sooner or later business entertaining is going to bulk large for nearly everybody with a prosperous and reasonably successful career. It is different from ordinary entertaining in one very crucial respect: with all other forms of social life one can pretend that one is involved in entertaining or being entertained for its own sake, even though, as I have indicated earlier, that is not necessarily the case. With business entertaining it is always in the back of the minds of both parties to the transaction that there is a deal to be struck at the end of it all. In short, you are not wining and dining someone, or being wined and dined by him, for the beauty of his or your face, the wit of your conversation or the charm of your soul.

That said, beauty of face or figure, nimbleness of wit and charm of character never did much harm to a business relationship and without them a series of meetings, whether between salesman and client or two parties to a deal of more equal status, would be a real bore – probably to both sides. In *Life at the Top*, the sequel to his more famous fifties novel about a poor northerner on the make, *Room at the Top*, John Braine depicts the wretched Joe Lampton trying to close a deal with Tiffield, the sole customer his company has for a special kind of steel it makes and with luck a future customer for another type. Lampton over-eats at lunch with Tiffield, over-drinks with him, goes to a strip club with him, over-drinks with him again and then watches him eat a four-course dinner while confining himself to orange juice and an omelette. Finally Tiffield tells him he's ready to sign the big contract, the one the company has been after all along, the next day. It is a good scene, sadly the only memorable one in the book. Anybody who feels jaded and resentful at a series of dyspepsia-inducing evenings with clients could do worse than read the passage to remind themselves of how much worse things might have been.

In another way, however, business entertaining is simply

social entertaining with a great deal more emphasis on impressing people and more concentration on efficiency by the person in charge of the entertaining. There are some hostesses in ordinary social life whose performance comes up to such high standards all the time, but most of us are too fond of relaxing when we entertain friends to meet such demands and become guilty of the odd lapse.

IMPRESSING

You want to strike the perfect balance between impressing your business guest and overawing him. Much may depend on whether your firm, which presumably reimburses you for entertainment expenses, regards it as a regular overhead or whether it will pass on the cost direct (though concealed) to the client. If your client is of a puritanical turn of mind, does he carry the attitude over into eating? Some people do, others overcompensate for being teetotal and non-smokers by gorging themselves on the solids.

If your client is old-fashioned enough to avoid the most expensive dishes at a restaurant just because they are the most expensive, you might consider telephoning ahead and asking the restaurant to supply every guest with menus on which no price is given. You yourself as host will of course have the prices printed on your menu. This tends to be the practice in clubs anyway. Of course, the very fact that the menus have no price for your guest is likely to impress him if he is reasonably sophisticated, for only pretty expensive places which are also of top quality (by no means the same thing, alas) make a practice of it. But if the food is less expensive than your client might expect, you could again try the blank price menu manoeuvre.

If you have to worry about the total bill, you might do better not to let your guests be given blank menus. There are some people who can home in on the most expensive item by intuition. Back in the sixties I was once given lunch at the Tour d'Argent in Paris by a fellow Englishman and unerringly picked out the priciest dish, *écrevisses*. It was in the days of the £50 limit for foreign currency. I'm afraid my fellow countryman felt obliged to steer me in the direction of something a good deal less damaging to Harold Wilson's balance of payments.

191

HOMEWORK

The most important bit of preparation is know your client. I use the term client in its loosest sense of the person you are trying to bring to a commercial agreement of some kind. This may be a specific one now or in the near future. Alternatively it may be that you wish to 'cosy along' your client in a general way so that he continues to do business with you or your firm, or – in the event of your going to another job elsewhere – continues to do business with you personally in preference to your current firm. If you are entertaining at a restaurant, check beforehand on how quick the service is in case your client needs to rush off somewhere afterwards. If he does, get the waiter to ring for a taxi for him just as you are both starting in on the pudding; that way it will be ready for him immediately he has finished the meal. Also check beforehand whether the restaurant does vegetarian or vegan dishes. Ask for a quiet table, preferably in an alcove, where you can talk without being overheard. Avoid restaurants with music. If you're not drinking but he is, get there first and tell the waiter that when you say you want a gin and tonic you really mean a tonic only, that when you say you want a Bloody Mary you really want a tomato juice only, that when you say you want a screwdriver you really want orange juice only.

If your client looks as if he's having difficulty with the menu don't ask him if he needs any help but say, as if *à propos* of nothing, that you're having a lot of difficulty with it. Then call the waiter over and ask him what a whole string of dishes are. Try and match your client's table manners, no matter how hoggish. He may be a devotee of 'power ordering', otherwise known as Campbell's Syndrome, which is believed to take its name from the famous occasion when the model Naomi Campbell was at a private dinner party and, apparently not liking what was put before her, sent out for a Kentucky Fried Chicken. Thus in 'power ordering' the diner orders the restaurant to prepare something not on the menu. (Actually the manoeuvre is as old as time; I was amused to see in Tony Hancock's best film, *The Rebel*, that Anthony Aloysius himself waved away a menu at a French restaurant and ordered egg and chips; when asked if he wouldn't prefer snails he amended the order to eggs, chips and snails.) If you know your guest is prone to power ordering go to Simpson's-in-the-Strand or

Le Gavroche, both of which places are on record (*Daily Telegraph*, 25 February 1994) as saying they will try to oblige, unless at Le Gavroche the order is for sausages and mash when it will be refused.

If your guest gets so drunk he starts trying to rape the waitress or throw bread at the overhead fan, make as if to go to the lavatory and then, when out of sight, call the manager and/or the police. You need not feel you should go with your client to jail if he tries to sock the police but you can and should go bail for him. Next day, or next time you meet, don't mention it if he doesn't. If he tries to apologise let it be understood that you were so boozed yourself you can't even remember the incident.

If the matter is within your control try to use entertaining as a means of generating basic goodwill rather than as a medium for detailed negotiation. If a specific point is to be raised do it just before the end of the main course. By the time the liqueur and coffee stage of the meal has been reached the business to be settled between you should have been cleared up so that you can go ahead and get drunk together properly. Always escort your guest to the door if he is leaving before you and only afterwards return and settle the bill if you have not done so already. Tell the waiter in advance that you are going to do this and leave some hostage such as your credit card, otherwise you may be chased by the restaurant staff when you make for the door.

As with social entertaining, make a note of your client's fads, his phobias, his dietary taboos, his religious practices. His fads may be personal to him, as may his phobias. His dietary taboos may be religious or cultural. His religious practices may be hereditary or acquired. Let us imagine that he is a Roman Catholic. Many Catholics who may be hugely pious in other ways no longer pay attention to the traditional prohibition on eating meat on a Friday, which in any case is no longer an official one. On the other hand they may stick to it out of sheer nostalgia. Find out which sort your client is. Similarly, find out his attitude to Lent, the forty days leading up to Easter, when traditional Catholics mortify their flesh by abstaining from wine, meat and/or perhaps tobacco as well. (And Easter falls on different days of different months from one year to the next, don't forget.) Ash Wednesday and Good Friday are still obligatory fast days, transgression against which is a sin.

But Irish people enjoy what is called an Exeat from Lent on 17 March, St Patrick's Day, which usually falls during Lent, and on that day may feast to their heart's content. In fact not to do so might be thought unpatriotic.

Even if your Catholic client is 'progressive' in outlook it may only be a superficial sort of progressiveness. Accordingly he may not like to be seen in public breaking traditional prohibitions on such matters as food and drink. Therefore you may want to entertain him at home rather than in a restaurant or your club. What sort of background do you come from? Scots Presbyterian, by any chance? If you entertain our notional Catholic at home do remember to put away the copy of *Foxe's Book of Martyrs* your Wee Free aunt bequeathed you, likewise the woodcut of John Knox and the ancient copy of *Maria Monk* you picked up in a second-hand bookshop for a few pence but admired for its 'period' quaintness and the quality of the engraved illustrations.

On the other hand he may be something of a rebel and enjoy making mildly satirical remarks about Pope John Paul II's stern attitude to contraception. Should you laugh at such remarks, or laugh nervously, or take His Holiness's side and say something like, 'You know, there's a good deal to be said for the conservative point of view . . .'? Very tricky.

High church Protestants, invariably Anglicans or Episcopalians, may take Fridays, Lent and holidays of obligation as seriously as the strictest Roman Catholic, or even more so. Low church Protestants, particularly if of the chapel-going or Methodist variety, may have a horror of alcohol. The temperance tradition is still quite strong in certain parts of the West Country and the north, also in Wales. Bear that in mind before taking any client from those parts to one of the boozier restaurants. Even if you abstain yourself the sight of other people at a neighbouring table drinking themselves under it may shock him. Christian Scientists do not drink at all, although they are so far tolerant of the failing in others that many cheerfully serve alcohol to guests in their own homes. But neither do they smoke. And since in a crowded and ill-ventilated restaurant the smoke from other people's cigarettes or cigars is bound to waft over to your table, you should either choose a smoke-free establishment in which to entertain or do so at home.

Obviously you ought not to light up yourself at any point in such circumstances.

Next time it may be a Jewish client that you take out to lunch. Is he Reform, Liberal, Orthodox or what? Besides, there's Reform and Reform, Liberal and Liberal. We all know Jewish people aren't supposed to eat pork, but several of my friends who are Jewish by birth or ancestry rather than by religious conviction take a delight in pigging out on pig to show how emancipated they are. Ditto with shellfish. Many, perhaps most, Jewish people don't drink as heavily as *goyim* (gentiles). On the other hand one or two of the heaviest drinkers I know are not only of Jewish ancestry but, frankly, are so proud of their Jewishness as to be a mite tedious on the subject.

The best approach is to phone your client beforehand and say something like 'Look, I would like to take you out to lunch/dinner. Is there anything I should know about what kind of restaurant would be suitable? Is there any food or drink you would prefer to avoid? Is there any time in the near future that would be unsuitable?' You have put the ball in his court. He need not tell you whether he is Hasidic, Orthodox, Reform or Liberal – and maybe he doesn't always know himself, there being as many shades of Jewishness as colours in a rainbow – but you have let him draw up the guidelines. Passover lasts eight days and is a particularly strict time diet-wise. The start of it is marked in all good diaries.

Muslims are forbidden alcohol at all times. It would be only polite, as well as prudent, to shun it yourself when entertaining a Muslim. Ramadan is the most important part of the year as far as your entertaining of Muslims is concerned. It lasts a month and differs in dates slightly each year, being the ninth month of the Islamic calendar – the months are lunar months so need to be calculated on an astronomical basis rather than on the Western calendar found in old-fashioned diaries. But the better, or at any rate the more multi-cultural, diaries should list the duration of Ramadan each year. (In 1994 Ramadan began on 11 February.) During it Muslims must fast from sunrise to sunset. The fast is called *Sawm* and it embraces more than just abstention from food. During Ramadan no Muslim may smoke, eat, drink liquid or have sex with his or her spouse. After sunset the rules are relaxed. Daily life during Ramadan must be slightly more tolerable in Britain than in the Middle East since in February the days are shorter here.

The first day after the end of Ramadan is called Id-ul-Fitr and is observed as a festival. Muslims express their thanks to God for having helped them keep the fast of the preceding month. They prepare special food and visit friends and relatives. Muslims are forbidden to eat not just pork but any pig product, such as sausages; also any animal that has been slaughtered without invoking the name of Allah, and the blood of any animal, so no blood puddings, for instance. They are also forbidden to eat carnivorous animals, animals which have died of natural causes or disease, animals that have been strangled to death or animals that have been devoured by wild beasts. None of these latter categories feature in British cooking, unless you count a chicken that has had its neck wrung, but even then it may be that the chicken has died of a broken neck rather than of strangulation. If in the least doubt, consult your Muslim client. Islamic law decrees that all beasts to be eaten must be killed by a sharp knife penetrating the inner part of the neck, thus allowing the blood to drain away.

Muslim codes of dress in this country are expressed in the form of guidelines rather than decrees. But among them are an insistance that men are covered between the navel and the knees and that they do not wear any garment of pure silk nor any ornament of pure gold. Women are supposed to dress modestly. That includes not just covering the body but the avoidance of tight clothes which show off the female form. Islam condemns not just blasphemy, as we are by now all aware, but back-biting, ridicule and offensive name-calling. So watch your language when entertaining Muslims.

Hindus and Sikhs don't eat beef and Sikhs don't smoke.

The Japanese are reluctant to say no, so if you doubt a Japanese guest has understood you, ask him if he would like you to repeat a question to make it more clear. If a Japanese person says yes all the time it may simply mean he has understood what you said, not necessarily that he agrees with you. If he is called Stomu Mutsu, Stomu is the first name and Mutsu the equivalent of what we would think of as his surname. Call him Mutsu-san rather than by his first name. I think this should apply even if, as with my cousin Count Ian Mutsu (a member of the Imperial family), he has a

Western first name. You should smile rather than keep a poker face even when discussing a mournful subject such as death. Your Japanese guest will certainly do so. When entertaining a Japanese person to a meal, whether at home or in a restaurant, sit up straight at the table, don't put your elbows on the table, don't lean to the side and don't sit with your legs crossed. All of these postures look too casual and may be regarded as an insult. Don't sit down four to a meal as the number is unlucky (see my remarks earlier on dinner parties and the right number to have to them).

Some Japanese people prefer not to discuss business at your first meeting. Do not be discouraged; they will get down to brass tacks eventually. Exchanging business cards with Japanese on a liberal, not to say promiscuous scale is something of an obligation. Hand your business card to your opposite number with your right hand or with both hands and facing him right way up so that it can be read immediately. If the legend is printed in both Japanese and English, one on one side of the card, the other on the reverse, hand it Japanese side up to your opposite number. If a Japanese person gives you his card do not write on it or put it in your back pocket. To do either would be considered insulting. You should study it for a few seconds before relegating it to a pocket or wallet.

With the Japanese the more senior a person the deeper the bow vouchsafed him. Non-Japanese need do no more than make a little bow, rather as with British royalty if you are a man, and a handshake. The Japanese are more punctilious than most Britons about remembering people's names and titles. Try to emulate them.

The Japanese dislike shouting, so choose a quiet restaurant in which to entertain them. They prefer polite and unobtrusive service and dislike having to ask for help. They present small but good-quality gifts to people they entertain so you should do so too. The gifts should be elaborately wrapped and presented with both hands. It is bad form in Japan to open one's gift then and there. The place of honour for Japanese people is often furthest from the door, so bear that in mind when choosing a table in a restaurant. Moreover, other guests should wait for the guest of honour to occupy the seat of honour before sitting down themselves. If the guest of honour arrives late the others should stand up to greet him. Sometimes the best seat may be left unoccupied.

If you ask a Japanese guest to 'come as you are' to a party he will probably dress smartly nevertheless. Therefore you should ask all your other guests to dress smartly when coming to any social function to which you have invited a Japanese person. The Japanese stand further apart from each other when talking than is customary in the West, and the modern habit of kissing everybody in sight on meeting is repellent to them. If you think of the Japanese as a bit like a maiden aunt you will begin to understand social life from their point of view. The Japanese appreciate good security more than most people. Cleanliness and hygiene are also important to them. They tend not to know much about wine and are happy to have tactful assistance when eating out. Buffet meals are not recommended when entertaining Japanese. They prefer still mineral water to sparkling and in any case iced water and glasses for water should always be supplied for Japanese guests. They prefer fresh food and dislike overcooked food, or food that is rich or creamy and prefer varied dishes and smaller portions to one large helping of a single kind of food. It is better to serve them vegetables on a side plate. In fact, as you may have noticed by now for yourself, many of our own eating habits have become more Japanese in recent years.

If you have any Japanese guests to your house either keep it good and warm or encourage them to put on sweaters. They may be shy of doing so for fear it implies you are too poor to heat your house properly (which with the recent VAT added to heating bills you may indeed have become).

The Japanese usually eat lunch around midday, as do many Americans, and dinner is at 6 or 6.30 p.m., again as with some Americans. If you are playing host be at the restaurant at least a quarter of an hour before the appointed time since Japanese guests are often early. Breakfast meetings are unpopular in Japan, however. Saying goodbye to one's guests is extremely important in Japan, but tipping is not much of a custom there.

When entertaining Koreans try to provide *kimchi* at every meal. This is a kind of pickled cabbage, not entirely dissimilar to sauerkraut, prepared each autumn and buried in pots out of doors. There are around ninety different varieties and in Seoul there is a whole museum devoted to it. As with the Japanese, the business card is a bit of a fetish, but the one thing you must never say to

Koreans is how like the Japanese they are. Dress formally in a suit and tie for all business. Present or receive gifts, drinks and business cards with both hands, again as with the Japanese. Open gifts in private and entertain in a Western or Japanese restaurant. Do not refuse alcohol when entertaining Koreans; it can be considered insulting. But on the other hand do not pour out your drink yourself.

APPENDIX
Precedence

Precedence concerns itself with the order in which people carry out an action or are named or listed. Most human assemblies have some kind of method of arranging their constituent members in order. It may be alphabetical, as in the telephone directory; it may be by age, as in primitive communities. It may be by physical height, as in a drill squad. In a school it may be by a pupil's achievement in last term's exams. Sometimes the order in which lists of names are printed combines an alphabetical system with official precedence, as with the reports of those attending a memorial service published in *The Times* and the *Daily Telegraph*.

Precedence in the context we will examine it here decrees the order in which people go into dinner, leave the dinner table, march in procession (though in this case people usually travel in reverse order of precedence, the least to the fore, the most important to the rear), are announced at gatherings or merely are listed in an official description of some ceremonial function. But there are various tables of precedence: social, official, political, local, ecclesiastical, legal, military. In Surtees' novel *Handley Cross* an important part of the plot is bound up with precedence. Captain Miserrimus Doleful, a half-pay militia officer who for some time has styled himself Master of Ceremonies at the watering place of Handley Cross, is trying to persuade the rich but canny London grocer Mr Jorrocks to take on the mastership of the local foxhounds. To help bring Jorrocks round the Captain writes to him to say that Mrs Jorrocks will take a high position. He pledges as follows:

> In the table of precedence among women that I have laid down for the regulation of the aristocratic visitors of Handley Cross Spa, the lady of the MFH comes on after the members of the royal family, and before all bishops' wives and daughters, peeresses, knights' dames, justices' wives, and so forth.

Well, of course Surtees is having a little joke with his readers there, because it is inconceivable that the wife of an MFH would take precedence of peeresses in a general way. But at the hunt ball given by the pack of which her husband was Master she might very well preside as hostess, receiving peeresses by the score.

Although there are numerous occasions when persons are inserted into the table of precedence in a high position out of courtesy, precedence as a general principle has the force of statute behind it. Henry VIII in 1539 pushed a law through Parliament called the House of Lords Precedence Act. It settled the relative precedence of the Great Officers of State and Lords. (By Great Officers of State is meant functionaries such as the Lord Chamberlain, Lord Great Chamberlain, Lord Chancellor and so on. Their history, duties and qualifications for office are outside the scope of a work such as this, and in practice, unless you are arranging a ceremony on something like the scale and importance of a state opening of Parliament, you are not likely to have to bother youself about their relative precedence.)

But even Henry VIII was not the first sovereign to announce a ruling on the subject of precedence, though he was the first to use Parliament to settle the matter. The late George Squibb, in his magisterial work on precedence in England, lists as the oldest pronouncement having relevance to the subject generally an instrument of 1266 – when Henry III was precariously on the throne – splendidly entitled 'The Dictum of Kenilworth'. In 1399, probably on 8 October, at the beginning of the reign of Henry IV, a regulation was drawn up entitled 'The Order of all Estates of Nobles and Gentry of England'. For Henry VI's coronation on 6 November 1429 the then Constable of England, John, Duke of Bedford, promulgated a similar decree called the 'Order of all States of Worship and Gentry of England'. A similar instrument followed in 1466–7, during Edward IV's reign, and yet another in Henry VII's reign, at some point between 1487 and 1495. The most authoritative statement on precedence before Henry VIII's 1539 Act was the order for 'the placynge of Lordes and Ladyes' called the 'Precedence of Great Estates in their owne degres' of 1520. Indeed, at the time he pushed the 1539 Act through Parliament Henry VIII declared that he was merely confirming the law of precedence which already existed. But although he used

Parliament for the purpose, he announced in the preamble (the preliminary wording to a Bill that goes 'wherefore . . . whereas' . . . and so on) that it was entirely within the royal prerogative (the monarch's personal powers, unfettered by Parliament) to 'give such honour, reputation, and placing to his Councillors and others his subjects as should be seeming to THE KING's most excellent wisdom'. Not that there could have been many people imprudent enough to object when in 1532 Henry had not only made Anne Boleyn Marchioness of Pembroke in her own right but had given her precedence above every other marchioness.

Henry VIII's son Edward VI passed a similar law in 1547, the first year of his reign. Interestingly, this Act lists the dignity of archbishop and bishop below the titles of duke and baron respectively, whereas nowadays the two archbishops and all the bishops (only Church of England ones, that is, since the C of E, and none other, is the established church) rank above dukes and barons respectively.

Actually precedence is subject not just to the monarch's personal powers, or such of them as are left, but to custom, although it is occasionally clarified by royal ordinances. For instance, the positions in the local table of precedence of the Lord-Lieutenant of the County and the High Sheriff (all of which are dealt with in greater detail later on in this appendix) are established by both custom and royal warrant. But there have been a few instances where an attempt by a sovereign to introduce modifications was resisted, for example by peers led by the Duke of Wellington when Queen Victoria tried to procure Prince Albert a higher precedence than the aristocracy thought suitable.

In James I's reign baronets were invented and a quarrel arose between barons' and viscounts' younger sons on the one hand and the new order of baronets on the other as to which lot should take precedence of the other. (Viscounts and barons are the two lowest orders of the peerage.) At one point the question was disputed by legal representatives in the presence of the King for three whole days. James I finally settled the matter in favour of the viscounts' and barons' younger sons in 1612. Unlike Henry VIII's and Edward VI's laws the ruling was issued by Letters Patent, which is usually the instrument employed for creating peerages.

Because most kinds of title are hereditary the sons and daughters, and later down the scale even the grandsons and granddaughters, of peers and baronets have their place in the tables of precedence. Rather oddly, sons and daughters of people on whom the sovereign has conferred personal titles which are not hereditary, such as knights, also are allotted places in the table of precedence. In contrast the sons or daughters of people appointed to an office come nowhere, however high up their parents. That even goes for the Archbishop of Canterbury, who ranks very high up, above even the mightiest and most noble non-royal duke in the land. In the case of children of the Archbishop of Canterbury this state of affairs only lasts till their father is made a peer, however, which usually happens when he retires. You thus end up with the odd phenomenon that the child of the highest ranking non-royal personage in the realm is nowhere, as long as his or her father is actually in office, but slips in, and at a pretty high position, once the father retires. For example, James Runcie, son of the former Archbishop of Canterbury Robert Runcie, had no standing in the table of precedence when his father was Primate of All England, but upon becoming the Honourable James Runcie when his father was made a life peer after stepping down as Primate, he entered the table of precedence above every baronet, most knights and numerous senior members of the judiciary. The same with an Archbishop of Canterbury's wife in the women's table of precedence. Thus while Rosalind Runcie was an inmate of Lambeth Palace, she was officially nowhere. But once her husband left Lambeth Palace she got an entry in the table of precedence. I put forward the modest suggestion that this state of affairs is just the tiniest bit absurd. Could it not be rectified?

One aspect of precedence which is unlikely to commend itself to modern ways of thinking is that covering people who have a place in the table by virtue of being somebody's children. Their ranking derives only from their father, not from the mother, however exalted her rank. Thus Mr Nigel Dempster's daughter, Louisa Beatrix Dempster, has no particular standing in the table of precedence although Mr Dempster's wife, Lady Camilla, *née* Osborne, is the daughter of the Eleventh Duke of Leeds, who stood seventh in the list of all the Dukes. An exception to this is when the mother is a member of that small class of women who are peeresses in their own right. The class used to be even smaller than now but the creation of a number of life peeresses over the last thirty-five years has swollen it.

Nevertheless women have their own table of precedence, derived from a time when they were segregated from men much more than at present, for instance by being under social pressure to leave the dining room before the men did and huddle over tea and coffee in the drawing room while their menfolk quaffed port. It will be interesting to see what happens in the near future as the likelihood of a female Lord Chancellor or Archbishop of Canterbury draws nearer. When Baroness Thatcher was Prime Minister as Mrs Thatcher there was the occasional press report to the effect that she counted as an honorary man for certain purposes connected with precedence.

The history of how the United Kingdom came about might seem to have little relevance to something as domestic as the order in which people go into dinner, but precedence reflects the process of national unification. The present United Kingdom came into existence gradually. In the thirteenth century England conquered Wales and by the mid-sixteenth century had incorporated the principality into its own legal and administrative system. As a result there is no separate table of precedence for Wales other than what may operate at local level, for example at a municipal function. And at a municipal function anywhere in the UK there will be a local order of precedence. In 1603 England and Scotland came under the same King, although the kingdoms remained separate, with, for instance, separate parliaments. By the Act of Union of 1707 England and Scotland became governed by a single Parliament. And by the Act of Union of 1801 Great Britain (as the union of England and Scotland had become known) and Ireland also became subject to a single Parliament. Nevertheless the sovereign remained head of state of a separate kingdom of Ireland, where he or she was represented by a Lord-Lieutenant or Viceroy.

What all this means in practical entertaining terms is that there is one table of precedence for men and one for women in England (including Wales), and one for men and again one for women in Scotland, making four in all. Before the creation of the Irish Free State in 1922 there was also a table of precedence for Ireland. And even now, nearly three-quarters of a century afterwards, there is a table of precedence for men in Northern Ireland. It used to be even more elaborate when there was a Prime Minister of Northern Ireland who governed with the help of his own cabinet ministers. But even now, when direct rule has been in place for over twenty years (since 1972), Northern Ireland recognises certain functionaries in the province as deserving a special place in its table of precedence. In fact it is much the same as that for England except that it includes various members of the Northern Ireland judiciary, Northern Irish municipal dignitaries and members of the armed forces doing a tour of duty in the province. It is also less sectarian than in mainland Britain in that it includes Catholic prelates as well as Protestant ones. If Northern Ireland gets its own Parliament back again the more elaborate former table of precedence would presumably be resurrected.

General Precedence: England and Wales
The precedence dealt with here is what is known as general or social precedence and theoretically applies at every stratum of society south of the Scottish border. As we have already seen, however, these days it is likely to be observed only on official occasions, diplomatic functions, very grand country house parties and dinners at said country houses or at grand town houses, and corporate occasions where a sufficient number of grandees are present to make a pecking order necessary.

The following table explains the relative precedence of senior members of the royal family. Unlike the general tables of precedence for England and Wales on the one hand and for Scotland on the other, it mixes the sexes.

1 **The Sovereign.** Since 1952 a Queen Regnant, as it happens, but if the Queen is present she can hardly be treated as a mere woman, even if everyboy else is male. Thus she takes precedence of all men as well as women.
2 **The Duke of Edinburgh.** A royal warrant of 15 September 1952 decreed that he should take precedence immediately after his wife and Sovereign 'except where otherwise provided by Act of Parliament'. In the Parliament Roll he is positioned as the most junior of the dukes in the peerage of

the United Kingdom inasmuch as his dukedom was only created in 1947. This reflects the provisions of Henry VIII's act of 1539.

3 **The Queen Mother.**
4 **The Prince of Wales**, or the eldest son of the Sovereign if not yet created Prince of Wales.
5 **The Princess of Wales.**
6 **The Duke of York.**
7 **The Duchess of York.**
8 **Prince Edward.**
9 **The Princess Royal.** Note that Commander Tim Laurence derives no official position in the table of precedence from his wife, any more than Captain Mark Phillips did, though in practice if he were attending a function with his wife you ought to assign him a precedence commensurate with hers.
10 **The grandsons of the Sovereign**, in order of age if born of the same two parents, and according to the laws of primogeniture generally. Hence **Prince William** would take precedence of
11 **Prince Harry.**
12 **Princess Beatrice of York.**
13 **Princess Eugenie of York.**
14 **Peter Phillips.**
15 **Zara Phillips.** Although the Phillips children are older than their York cousins, the Yorks' father, as Duke of York, is closer to the succession than is the Princess Royal. Hence Peter and Zara Phillips' seniority as grandchildren of the Sovereign, in the sense of having been a member of the category longer, does not count for precedence purposes. Incidentally, here is one of two unique exceptions to the rule that people derive no position in the table of precedence from their mother, for the Princess Royal is not a peeress and her children are plain Master Peter Phillips and Miss Zara Phillips. Should Prince Edward marry and have a son – let us call him George – and a year or two later Prince Andrew got back together with Sarah and had a son too – Frederick, say – then this younger grandson Frederick would take precedence of his older cousin George because his father, the Duke of York, is the

Sovereign's second son whereas George's father is the Sovereign's third son. But any future children of Prince Edward would slip in above the Phillips children.

16 **Princess Margaret.**
17 **The Sovereign's uncles.** Since the death of the old Duke of Gloucester there have been none living.
18 **Princess Alice, Duchess of Gloucester.** She is the widow of the late Duke of Gloucester, the Queen's uncle.
19 **Viscount Linley,** as the Sovereign's nephew. Lord Linley and his sister are the other exception to the rule that people derive no rank in the table of precedence from their mother unless she is a peeress in her own right.
20 **Viscountess Linley.**
21 **Lady Sarah Chatto.**
22 **The Duke of Gloucester.**
23 **The Duchess of Gloucester.**
24 **The Duke of Kent.** Future Dukes of Gloucester and Kent of the present creations, i.e., the present Earls of Ulster and St Andrews respectively, together with their eldest male children, if any, and their eldest male children, and so on, will have precedence above the other non-royal Dukes but beneath the two Archbishops and the Great Officers of State, in accordance with the precedent of 1439.
25 **The Duchess of Kent.**
26 **Prince Michael of Kent.** In the orders of precedence of 1479 and c. 1490 the younger sons of Dukes of the Blood Royal were placed below the eldest sons of Marquesses and above the eldest sons of Marquesses respectively.

That is pretty far down, even though such persons are entitled to the style of His Royal Highness and the title of Prince. Moreover they are grandsons in the male line of former sovereigns, even if they are not Dukes themselves. It was not really till 1840 that the problem arose, at a time when Prince George of Cambridge had attained his majority (twenty-one in those days) and was within a few years of succeeding his father Adolphus as Duke of Cambridge, the latter being George III's seventh son (all George III's other sons had either gone off to reign over Hanover, failed to produce legitimate issue or had had daughters). Accordingly

Prince George was assigned a place in the table of precedence before the Archbishop of Canterbury and after all the other members of the royal family covered by Henry VIII's act of 1539. The diarist Charles Greville, who was also Clerk of the Privy Council, described the situation as follows:

> The practice . . . does not wait upon the right, and is regulated by the universal sense and feeling of the respect and deference which is due to the Blood Royal of England. The Archbishop of Canterbury does not take a legal opinion or pore over the 31st of Henry VIII to discover whether he has a right to jostle for that precedence with the cousin, which he knows he is bound to concede to the uncle, of the Queen; but he yields it as a matter of course, and so uniform and unquestionable is the custom, that in all probability neither the Prince nor the Prelate are conscious that it is in the slightest degree at variance with the right.

Presumably all other younger sons of Dukes of the Blood Royal, such as Lord Nicholas Windsor, who is the second son of the Duke of Kent and who doesn't have the style of Royal Highness, will take precedence either before the eldest sons of Marquesses or just after. Otherwise you would have a situation in which he had precedence before his elder brother.

27 **Princess Michael of Kent.**
28 **Princess Alexandra.**

We now continue with the table of precedence for men only.

29 **Archbishop of Canterbury**, settled as taking precedence of the Archbishop of York in 1353, but in relation to lay dignitaries by the Henry VIII statute of 1539.
30 **Lord (High) Chancellor.**
31 **Archbishop of York** (the late George Squibb writes in his book on precedence that there doesn't appear to be any evidence of an official ruling as to whether the Lord Chancellor comes ahead of the Archbishop of York or after him, and in fact as late as the sixteenth century he sometimes did take precedence

of him and sometimes didn't; but with true Christian humility all Archbishops of York since Charles II's time have declined to try to elbow aside the Lord Chancellor).

32 **The Prime Minister** (by a Royal Warrant of 2 December 1905).

33 **Commonwealth Prime Ministers**, if visiting this country, in seniority of appointment.

34 **Lord High Treasurer** (Henry VIII statute); the office has been in commission since 1714.

35 **Lord President of the (Privy) Council** (Henry VIII statute).

36 **Speaker of the House of Commons** (by an Order in Council of 30 May 1919; but the present speaker is a woman, Betty Boothroyd, so features in the table of precedence for women).

37 **Lord Privy Seal** (Henry VIII statute).

38 **Ambassadors** of foreign countries and **High Commissioners of Commonwealth countries** in London according to the date of their arrival in London to take up official duties. A royal warrant of 24 December 1948 provided that if a minister of the Crown of a Commonwealth country is visiting this country he is accorded precedence just above the High Commissioner of his country. Nowadays several countries retain Commonwealth membership but have no ministers of the Crown because they are republics – India, for instance, or Zimbabwe. But courtesy would dictate that a visiting Indian cabinet minister, say, should take precedence over his country's High Commissioner resident in London. Moreover, visiting cabinet ministers of foreign countries not in the Commonwealth are accorded precedence above their country's Ambassador in the UK.

39 **Lord Great Chamberlain** if a Duke and in actual performance of his duty, or when in attendance on the person of the King or Queen for the time being or when introducing a peer into the House of Lords. (Henry VIII statute.) No Lord Great Chamberlain has been a Duke since 1779, however, after which the hereditary post descended to co-heirs. The representatives (in practice, senior descendants) of these take it in turn to perform the office in successive reigns. During the current reign of Elizabeth II the post is held by

the Marquess of Cholmondoley, who accordingly ranks at the head of the Marquesses rather than at the head of the Dukes. Moreover, he holds the post of Lord Great Chamberlain strictly speaking as a deputy, but is styled and given precedence as if he were a full Lord Great Chamberlain.

40 **Lord High Constable.** This post is only recreated for a day at a time on the occasion of a new sovereign's coronation.

41 **Earl Marshal** if a Duke (which he always has been since 1672, the post of Earl Marshal being hereditary in the Duke of Norfolk's family; but the Duke of Norfolk has precedence of all the other Dukes anyway as premier Duke of England) (Henry VIII statute).

42 **Lord High Admiral** if a Duke. The office has been in commission since 1828, when the future William IV held it while still Duke of Clarence.

43 **Lord Steward of the Household** if a Duke (Henry VIII statute). The current holder of the office is Viscount Ridley, who accordingly ranks at the head of all the Viscounts.

44 **Lord Chamberlain** if a Duke. The current holder of the office is the Earl of Airlie, who accordingly ranks ahead of all the other Earls.

45 **Master of the Horse** if a Duke (Royal Warrant of 2 December 1905). The current holder of the office is Lord Somerleyton, who as such by a royal warrant of 6 May 1907 ranks next after the Lord Chamberlain, whose own position depends on what grade of peerage he holds. Accordingly Lord Somerleyton ranks at the head of all the other Earls apart from Lord Airlie, though of course only as long as he remains Master of the Horse.

46 **Dukes in the peerage of England** ranked among themselves according to the date of creation, the earliest first, this being the general rule for all degrees of peer (Henry VIII statute). I say general rule because in a very few cases a peer or baronet has a precedence different from the date of creation of his title. Old editions of *Burke's Peerage* listed peers in full with these details. If you want to know when any titled person's dignity was created look him up in either *Burke's Peerage & Baronetage, Debrett's Peerage* or *Who's Who*. The most recent edition of *Burke's* was in 1970, however, so that

for peerages and baronetcies created since then you will have to consult another source (a new edition is planned for the mid-1990s). *Debrett's* now appears only once every five years, the last edition being 1990, so a similar problem operates there too. *Who's Who* appears annually. For any precedence relative to each other of peerages created in between one edition of *Who's Who* and another, consult the House of Lords. For any relative precedence of knighthoods conferred in between one edition of *Who's Who* and another consult the Central Chancery of Orders of Knighthood.

47 **Dukes in the peerage of Scotland** (23rd article of Act of Union 1707).
48 **Dukes in the peerage of Great Britain.**
49 **Dukes in the peerage of Ireland** created before the Union of British and Irish parliaments in 1801.
50 **Dukes in the peerages of the United Kingdom or Ireland** created since the Union of 1801.

The preceding five categories need a bit of explanation. A Duke in the peerage of England isn't necessarily an Englishman by birth as opposed to a Scot or an Irishman or whatever. Nor has he even necessarily always been British by birth as opposed to naturalisation. The same goes for all the other grades of peer: Marquess, Earl, Viscount and Baron. Perhaps the most celebrated example of what one might call an 'alien' English peerage creation is Piers de Gaveston, a Gascon created Earl of Cornwall by Edward II, an admirer of Piers's, in 1308. The Duke of Schomberg, created a Duke in the Irish peerage by William III in 1689, was born at Heidelberg of a German father and an English mother. He could have been created a Duke in the peerage of England, and indeed he was naturalised as an Englishman a few weeks before his ennoblement by William III. He was then sent over to Ireland to fight James II, who (confusingly) remained King of Ireland at that point although he was deemed to have abandoned the throne of England several months earlier (whereas the Scots waited till April 1689 before they decided to accept William and Mary as their sovereigns). What the peerage of England comprises is all peers created by sovereigns of England up to 1707. From 1603 to 1707 sovereigns of England and sovereigns of Scotland were the same

211

person, though the kingdoms themselves were still separate. The English and Scottish crowns started to be worn by the same person in 1603 because that was when James VI of Scotland ascended the English throne as James I. He had been King of Scots since his mother Mary Queen of Scots' abdication thirty-six years earlier. Between 1603 and 1707 Kings James I, Charles I, Charles II, James II (and VII of Scotland) and William III and Queens Mary II and Anne were all sovereigns of both England and Scotland. Accordingly they went on creating titles in the peerages both of England and of Scotland. The peerage of Scotland comprises all peers created by Kings or Queens of Scots up to 1707.

After the Union of English and Scottish Parliaments in 1707 there were no more creations in the English or Scottish peerages and any new creations took place in something called the peerage of Great Britain. The peerage of Great Britain continued till 1801, when upon the Union of British and Irish Parliaments taking place almost all new peerage creations were made in the peerage of the United Kingdom.

I say almost all because, again confusingly, creations in the peerage of Ireland, which had always been separate from either the English, Scottish or British peerages (that is, those of Great Britain), did continue. For example, the dukedom of Abercorn, which is a title in the Irish peerage, was created in 1866. To make matters still more confusing, titles in the peerage of Ireland had come into existence since before the sovereigns of England started calling themselves Kings (or Queens) of Ireland. In fact nobody knows exactly when the title of Lord Kingsale, which is the most ancient barony in the Irish peerage, dates from. Moreover later Irish peers were not necessarily Irish by blood, birth, culture or domicile – often quite the reverse – so much as people of relatively minor importance or with less claim on the gratitude of their sovereign or Prime Minister than 'mainstream' candidates for peerages. These people were given titles in the peerage of Ireland because among other things it didn't confer a seat in the British House of Lords. Lord Palmerston, an Irish peer, was thus able to sit in the House of Commons throughout his long and immensely successful career. The present Lord Carrington's ancestor, a Mr Smith, was, according to the nineteenth-century diarist and gossip G. W. E. Russell, made an Irish peer as Baron Carrington by Pitt the Younger as a consolation prize for not being allowed to drive through the Horse Guards, a privilege he had pleaded with Pitt to grant him.

51 **Eldest son of Dukes of the Blood Royal** if not a brother, uncle, grandson or nephew of the reigning sovereign. A Duke of the Blood Royal isn't quite the same as a Duke with royal blood. The Duke of Grafton, the Duke of Buccleuch and the Duke of Richmond and Gordon have all three of them a fair amount of royal blood, being descended from illegitimate children of Charles II, but are not considered Dukes of the Blood Royal. There are two of the latter: the Duke of Gloucester and Duke of Kent. The eldest son of the former, the Earl of Ulster, takes precedence of the eldest son of the latter, the Earl of St Andrews, because although he is twelve years younger he is nearer in line to the throne.

52 **Ministers representing foreign states as diplomats** and other very distinguished foreigners. Formerly very few countries appointed Ambassadors – usually only the great powers did so. Accordingly, most representatives of foreign countries held a lower rank of 'Ruritanian Minister'. Nowadays virtually every country, however tinpot, pampers its vanity by appointing Ambassadors.

In practice, as far as I can make out from talking the matter over with the Lord Chamberlain's office, 'other very distinguished foreigners' would tend to comprise only senior politicians visiting these shores from abroad. They would then rank among themselves according to the date of their appointment. But this book is concerned with social entertaining as much as, if not more than, the official variety. Accordingly you deserve some kind of guidance as to how to rank foreign noblemen and noblewomen at your parties. One of the old etiquette books I consulted stated unequivocally that all foreign noblemen and women should take precedence after royalty in this country but before everybody else. This is an astounding assertion, not least because bogus titles abounded even in the earlier part of this century, when there were many more monarchies abroad than now and consequently some means of checking up on people who called themselves Count This or Baron That. Now the position is worse. David Williamson, co-editor of *Debrett's*

Peerage, is of the opinion that you should rank all people with foreign titles after everybody listed in the British table of precedence, and among themselves they should rank according to the degree of their title (usually Prince, Duke – but see below – Marquis, Count, Viscount, Baron, Chevalier in that order), and when there is more than one person in the same degree of nobility according to the date of the creation of their title. But he stresses that there is no official authority for doing it this way. Moreover the title of Prince is not always higher than that of Duke, particularly among the French nobility. The most learned and lucid account of continental nobility is Philip Thomas's essay on pages cxlv to cxlix of the 1953 edition of *Burke's Peerage and Baronetage*.

You will not escape censure if, for instance, you try to rank a Napoleonic Duke above a pre-French Revolution Comte (Count). Indeed, you won't escape censure if you try to rank him above a Restoration Baron. (The Restoration in France is considered to have run from 1814, when Louis XVIII replaced Napoleon for the first time, to 1830, when Charles X was obliged to go into exile, with an intermission for Napoleon's Hundred Days in 1815.) The agony of this side of social life in France was sketched in Nancy Mitford's novel *The Blessing* and is remarked upon in Proust's *A la Recherche du Temps Perdu*.

As for foreign Sovereigns, they rank among themselves according to how long they have been on the throne, though whoever is the host Sovereign to all the others would preside at a gathering of them, just as the relatively humble mayor does at a town hall reception. Ex-Sovereigns, Constantine of Greece for example, rank (I am sorry to say) after reigning ones. Pretenders with strong claims to thrones would rank after ex-Sovereigns. The line between charlatans and genuine pretenders is not always easy to draw; once again, France is particularly difficult in this respect. Reigning Princes (Rainier of Monaco, for instance) rank with other heads of state, whether Kings and Queens or Presidents of Republics, as does the Grand Duke of Luxembourg, who is also a reigning sovereign.

53 **Marquesses in the peerage of England** (Henry VIII statute).

54 **Marquesses in the peerage of Scotland.**
55 **Marquesses in the peerage of Great Britain.**
56 **Marquesses in the peerage of Ireland** created before the Union of 1801.
57 **Marquesses in the peerages of the United Kingdom or Ireland** created since the Union.
58 **Dukes' eldest sons** according to the same internal pecking order as dukes themselves.
59 **Earls in the peerage of England** (Henry VIII statute).
60 **Earls in the peerage of Scotland.**
61 **Earls in the peerage of Great Britain.**
62 **Earls in the peerage of Ireland.**
63 **Earls in the peerages of the United Kingdom and of Ireland** created since the Union.
64 **Younger sons of Dukes of the Blood Royal.**
65 **Marquesses' eldest sons.**
66 **Dukes' younger sons.**
67 **Viscounts in the peerage of England** (Henry VIII statute).
68 **Viscounts in the peerage of Scotland.** There are only three, the Viscounts of Arbuthnott, Falkland and Oxfuird. According to Scottish practice Arbuthnott and Oxfuird are called the Viscount *of*, whereas all other Viscounts are simply Viscount Copper, Viscount Zinc or whatever, without the 'of'.
69 **Viscounts in the peerage of Great Britain.**
70 **Viscounts in the peerage of Ireland** created before the Union of 1801.
71 **Viscounts in the peerages of the United Kingdom or Ireland** created since the Union.
72 **Earls' eldest sons and the eldest sons of peeresses in their own right who are Countesses.**
73 **Marquesses' younger sons.**
74 **The Bishop of London** (Henry VIII statute).
75 **The Bishop of Durham** (Henry VIII statute).
76 **The Bishop of Winchester** (Henry VIII statute).
77 **Other Church of England Diocesan Bishops with seats in the House of Lords** in order of seniority of confirmation of election (Henry VIII statute).
78 **Church of England Diocesan Bishops without seats in the House of Lords.**

79 **Church of England Suffragan Bishops** in order of seniority of confirmation of election.

80 **Retired Church of England Bishops** in order of original date of confirmation of election (a retired Bishop is still in valid Holy Orders and remains a Bishop).

81 **Secretaries of State** if of the rank of Baron, e.g., Lord Young of Graffham in the days when he was Trade and Industry Secretary.

82 **Barons in the peerage of England** (Henry VIII statute).

83 **Lords of Parliament in the peerage of Scotland.** In Scotland the term Baron refers to a territorial dignity, roughly akin to a lordship of the manor in England, and both are alienable, that is they can be bought and sold, unlike peerages (at any rate since Lloyd George's premiership).

84 **Barons in the peerage of Great Britain.**

85 **Barons in the peerage of Ireland.**

86 **Barons in the peerages of the United Kingdom or Ireland** created since the Union of 1801. Life peers, who these days are always of baronial rank, are included here, as also are Lords of Appeal in Ordinary, who these days are made life peers too. They rank among themselves according to the date of the peerage's creation or the date of appointment as a Lord of Appeal in Ordinary.

87 **Treasurer of the Household.**

88 **Comptroller of the Household.**

89 **Master of the Horse** if not a peer.

90 **Vice-Chamberlain of the Household.**

91 **Secretaries of State** (Henry VIII statute) if not of the rank of Baron. Among themselves they rank according to the seniority of their appointment.

92 **Viscounts' eldest sons.**

93 **Earls' younger sons, and younger sons of peeresses in their own right who are Countesses.**

94 **Barons/Scottish Lords of Parliament's eldest sons and eldest sons of hereditary peeresses in their own right who hold baronies or Scottish lordships of Parliament.** Life Barons'/ Baronesses' eldest sons do not have precedence here because they cannot inherit their fathers'/mothers' peerages.

95 **Knights of the Garter.** Anyone whose name is written on an

envelope or who appears in a list of names in the form Sir Somebody Something, KG. Very few people are Knights of the Garter without already having a higher honour such as a peerage, but one of the few exceptions is also a particularly famous one, Sir Winston Churchill.

96 **Knights of the Thistle**. Anyone whose name is written on an envelope or who appears in a list of names in the form Sir Somebody Something, KT. Not to be confused with Knights Bachelors, whom one sometimes comes across misleadingly referred to as Sir Somebody Something, Kt or 'kt' or even 'KT', usually in death notices in the daily papers. As with Knights of the Garter there are very few Knights of the Thistle who do not have some higher honour as well, usually a peerage.

97 **Knights of St Patrick.** No new knights of this order have been admitted since the late Duke of Gloucester was created a KP in 1934, twelve years after the founding of the Irish Free State in 1922, but the order is still in existence.

98 **Privy Counsellors** according to the date of each one's appointment.

99 **Chancellor of the Order of the Garter** if not a peer (by decree of the chapter of the Order of the Garter, 23 April 1629). Since 1837 the chancellorship has been held with the bishopric of Oxford, however.

100 **Chancellor of the Exchequer.**

101 **Chancellor of the Duchy of Lancaster.**

102 **Lord Chief Justice.**

103 **Master of the Rolls.**

104 **President of the Family Division of the High Court of Justice** (Administration of Justice Act of 1920).

105 **Lord Justices of Appeal** ranked among themselves according to the seniority of their appointment (statute of 1851, when the Court of Appeal in Chancery was created). In practice they tend to be Privy Counsellors and often life peers as well.

106 **High Court Judges**, ranked among themselves according to the seniority of appointment. These days High Court Judges are knighted as Knights Bachelors.

107 **Viscounts' younger sons.**

108 **Barons'/Scottish Lords of Parliament's younger sons, and all**

sons of Lords of Appeal in Ordinary, all sons of life peers and all sons of life peeresses.

109   **Baronets** according to seniority of creation.

110   **Knights Grand Cross of the Order of the Bath.** Anyone whose name is written on an envelope or who appears in a list of names in the form Sir Somebody Something, GCB. Distinguished foreigners such as Presidents Ronald Reagan or George Bush of the USA do not have precedence in the UK under this qualification because their GCBs are honorary and they did not receive the accolade.

111   **Knights Grand Commanders of the Order of the Star of India** (statute of the Order of 19 April 1866). Anyone whose name appears as Sir Somebody Something, GCSI.

112   **Knights Grand Cross of the Order of St Michael and St George**. Anyone whose name appears as Sir Somebody Something, GCMG.

113   **Knights Grand Commanders of the Order of the Indian Empire** (statute of the Order of 1 June 1887). Anyone whose name appears as Sir Somebody Something, GCIE.

114   **Knights Grand Cross of the Royal Victorian Order.** Anyone whose name appears as Sir Somebody Something, GCVO.

115   **Knights Grand Cross of the Order of the British Empire.** Anyone whose name appears as Sir Somebody Something, GBE.

116   **Knights Commanders of the Order of the Bath.** Anyone whose name appears as Sir Somebody Something, KCB.

117   **Knights Commanders of the Order of the Star of India.** Anyone whose name appears as Sir Somebody Something, KCSI.

118   **Knights Commanders of the Order of St Michael and St George.** Anyone whose name appears as Sir Somebody Something, KCMG.

119   **Knights Commanders of the Order of the Indian Empire.** Anyone whose name appears as Sir Somebody Something, KCIE.

120   **Knights Commanders of the Royal Victorian Order.** Anyone whose name appears as Sir Somebody Something, KCVO.

121   **Knights Commanders of the Order of the British Empire.**

Anyone whose name appears as Sir Somebody Something, KBE.

122 **Knights Bachelors.** Anyone whose name appears as Sir Somebody Something, without any letters after it (but see the note with item 96 for misleading references in the press).

123 **Circuit Judges** in the following order:
(a) **Vice-Chancellor of the County Palatine of Lancaster;**
(b) **Circuit Judges** who just prior to 1 January 1972 were Official Referees to the Supreme Court, in order of appointment as between themselves;
(c) **The Recorder of London;**
(d) **The Recorder of Liverpool** or of **Manchester** according to whichever has seniority of appointment;
(e) **The Common Serjeant;**
(f) **Circuit Judges** who just prior to 1 January 1972 were (i) Additional Judges of the Criminal Court, or (ii) Assistant Judges of the Mayor's and City of London Court, or (iii) County Court Judges, or (iv) Full-time Chairmen or Deputy Chairmen of Courts of Quarter Sessions for Greater London, Cheshire, Durham, Kent and Lancashire, or (v) other Circuit Judges; all among themselves according to the seniority of their appointments.

124 **Companions of Order of the Bath.** Anyone whose name appears as Somebody Something, CB.

125 **Companions of the Order of the Star of India.** Anyone whose name appears as Somebody Something, CSI.

126 **Companions of the Order of St Michael and St George.** Anyone whose name appears as Somebody Something, CMG.

127 **Companions of the Order of the Indian Empire.** Anyone whose name appears as Somebody Something, CIE.

128 **Commanders of the Royal Victorian Order.** Anyone whose name appears as Somebody Something, CVO.

129 **Commanders of the Order of the British Empire.** Anyone whose name appears as Somebody Something, CBE.

130 **Companions of the Distinguished Service Order** (amended statute of Order, 12 July 1918). Anyone, usually an armed services officer, whose name appears as Major/Colonel (or

whatever the rank) Somebody Something, DSO.

131 **Lieutenants of the Royal Victorian Order.** Anyone whose name appears as Somebody Something, LVO.

132 **Officers of the Order of the British Empire.** Anyone whose name appears as Somebody Something, OBE.

133 **Companions of the Imperial Service Order.** Anyone whose name appears as Somebody Something, ISO.

134 **Eldest sons of younger sons of hereditary peers or hereditary peeresses in their own right and eldest sons of their heirs male** (usually, of course, their eldest sons) among themselves according to the precedence enjoyed by their fathers (Ordinance of the Earl Marshal's Court, 18 March 1615).

135 **Baronets' eldest sons.**

136 **Eldest sons of Knights of the Garter.**

137 **Eldest sons of Knights of the Thistle.**

138 **Eldest sons of Knights of St Patrick.** For the last few generations before new members of the Order ceased to be created every Knight of St Patrick was a peer, so any eldest son still alive would take higher precedence since he would have inherited his father's peerage.

139 **Eldest sons of Knights Grand Cross of the Order of the Bath.**

140 **Eldest sons of Knights Grand Commanders of the Star of India.**

141 **Eldest sons of Knights Grand Cross of the Order of St Michael and St George.**

142 **Eldest sons of Knights Grand Commanders of the Order of the Indian Empire.**

143 **Eldest sons of Knights Grand Cross of the Royal Victorian Order.**

144 **Eldest sons of Knights Grand Cross of the Order of the British Empire.**

145 **Eldest sons of Knights Commanders of the Order of the Bath.**

146 **Eldest sons of Knights Commanders of the Order of the Star of India.**

147 **Eldest sons of Knights Commanders of the Order of St Michael and St George.**

148 **Eldest sons of Knights Commanders of the Order of the Indian Empire.**

149 Eldest sons of Knights Commanders of the Royal Victorian Order.

150 Eldest sons of Knights Commanders of the Order of the British Empire.

151 Members of the Royal Victorian Order.

152 Members of the Order of the British Empire.

153 Baronets' younger sons.

154 Younger sons of Knights of the Garter.

155 Younger sons of Knights of the Thistle.

156 Younger sons of Knights of St Patrick.

157 Younger sons of Knights Grand Cross of the Order of the Bath.

158 Younger sons of Knights Grand Commanders of the Star of India.

159 Younger sons of Knights Grand Cross of the Order of St Michael and St George.

160 Younger sons of Knights Grand Commanders of the Order of the Indian Empire.

161 Younger sons of Knights Grand Cross of the Royal Victorian Order.

162 Younger sons of Knights Grand Cross of the Order of the British Empire.

163 Younger sons of Knights Commanders of the Order of the Bath.

164 Younger sons of Knights Commanders of the Order of the Star of India.

165 Younger sons of Knights Commanders of the Order of St Michael and St George.

166 Younger sons of Knights Commanders of the Order of the Indian Empire.

167 Younger sons of Knights Commanders of the Royal Victorian Order.

168 Younger sons of Knights Commanders of the Order of the British Empire.

Precedence in England and Wales for Ladies

Dowagers, that is to say the widows of holders of a hereditary title of honour such as a dukedom, marquessate, earldom, viscountcy, barony or baronetcy, take precedence of the wife of the present holder of the title. The more longstanding the state of widowhood the greater the precedence: if Lord Loamshire marries a woman, let us call her Gladys, then dies, and his married eldest son, whose wife is, say, Grace, dies shortly afterwards so that the title descends to the original Lord Loamshire's grandson, who happens also to be married, to a woman called Greta, and he too goes and dies, then Gladys takes precedence of Grace who in turn takes precedence of Greta.

Although, as previously noted, wives of men whose precedence derives from their official position have no precedence as a result (for example, Mrs Carey has no particular precedence just because her husband George is Archbishop of Canterbury), wherever possible they are given the precedence of their husbands.

It might seem only fair to do the same by the husbands of those women who have risen to high official position too, such as Peter, consort of Virginia Bottomley, the Secretary of State for Health, although he is an MP anyway as it happens, and indeed once held office in the government himself. But if you did that you would be obliged to give higher precedence to untitled men who had married peeresses in their own right, thus contravening the table of precedence which exists by statute law. There are a handful of Countesses, Baronesses and female holders of Lordships of Parliament in their own right, but they enjoy no greater precedence than if they were married to husbands having the same titles.

There is one respect in which females do better than males in the precedence stakes. The most authoritative early pronouncement on the subject is the 'Precedence of Great Estates in their Own Degres' of 1520. This document, among other things, says that all of a man's daughters have the same rank as their eldest brother would have among men in the lifetime of their father. That would seem to be reflected in the way all Earls' daughters take the style Lady before their first names, e.g., Lady Constance, Lord Emsworth's sister in the P. G. Wodehouse novels, though a younger brother, such as Galahad Threepwood, is a mere Honourable. Women also retain the precedence they contracted when they got married even after they are divorced, though they do not keep it on remarrying. A daughter of a peer who disclaims his title for life keeps her precedence as a peer's daughter. Thus the Hon. Melissa Benn, daughter of Tony Benn, the (briefly) *ci-devant*

Lord Stansgate, retains her precedence as a Viscount's daughter. And the celebrated television personality Lady Lucinda Lambton, now Lady Lucinda Worsthorne, has the precedence of an Earl's daughter even though her father, Lord Lambton (as he prefers to be known), has disclaimed his earldom of Durham. Yet if Lady Lucinda had married a peer of lower rank than an Earl instead of Sir Peregrine Worsthorne, a mere knight – supposing she had married her actual husband's former employer Lord Hartwell, say – she would have sunk to the rank of a baron's wife. Indeed, that is what Lord Hartwell's own late wife, Lady Pamela Berry, did when, some years after she married him, he was made a life peer, for her father was an Earl (Lord Birkenhead).

The Royal Family has been dealt with earlier. Accordingly we go straight to:

1 **Betty Boothroyd** as Speaker of the House of Commons.
2 **Duchesses** in same order as Dukes.
3 **The Countess of St Andrews** as wife of the eldest son of a Duke of the Blood Royal.
4 **Lady Davina Windsor**, as a daughter of a Duke (Gloucester) of the Blood Royal.
5 **Lady Rose Windsor** (younger daughter of the Duke of Gloucester).
6 **Lady Helen Taylor** (daughter of the Duke of Kent).
7 **Marchionesses** in same order as Marquesses.
8 **Wives of Dukes' eldest sons.**
9 **Dukes' daughters** not married to peers.
10 **Countesses** in same order as Earls.
11 **Wives of Marquesses' eldest sons.**
12 **Marquesses' daughters** not married to peers.
13 **Wives of younger sons of Dukes.**
14 **Viscountesses** in same order as Viscounts.
15 **Wives of eldest sons of Earls or of Countesses in their own right.**
16 **Earl's daughters** not married to peers.
17 **Wives of Marquesses' younger sons.**
18 **Baronesses in the peerage of England.**
19 **Wives of Lords of Parliament** or **female holders of Lordships**

of Parliament in the peerage of Scotland.

20 **Other Baronesses** in the same order as Barons. Life peeresses, who are these days always of baronial rank, are included here.

21 **Secretaries of State.**

22 **Wives of Viscounts' eldest sons.**

23 **Viscounts' daughters** not married to peers.

24 **Wives of younger sons of Earls or of Countesses in their own right.**

25 **Wives of eldest sons of Barons or of Scottish Lords of Parliament or of female holders of Scottish Lordships of Parliament.**

26 **Daughters of**
(a) **Barons;**
(b) **Baronesses in their own right;**
(c) **Lords of Parliament** in the peerage of Scotland;
(d) **Female holders of Lordships of Parliament in the peerage of Scotland;**
(e) **Lords of Appeal in Ordinary;**
(f) **Life peers;**
(g) **Life peeresses,** provided such daughters are not married to peers.

27 **Wives of Knights of the Garter.**

28 **Wives of Knights of the Thistle.**

29 **Wives of Knights of St Patrick.**

30 **Privy Counsellors.**

31 **High Court Judges.**

32 **Wives of Viscounts' younger sons.**

33 **Wives of younger sons of**
(a) **Barons;**
(b) **Baronesses in their own right;**
(c) **Lords of Parliament in the peerage of Scotland;**
(d) **Female holders of lordships of Parliament in the peerage of Scotland** and **wives of sons of** (i) **Lords of Appeal in Ordinary;** (ii) **Life peers;** (iii) **Life peeresses.**

34 **Wives of Baronets.**

35 **Dames Grand Cross of the Order of the Bath.** Anyone whose name appears on an envelope or in a list as Dame Somebody Something, GCB.

36 **Dames Grand Cross of the Order of St Michael and St George.** Anyone whose name appears on an envelope or in a list as Dame Somebody Something, GCMG.

37 **Dames Grand Cross of the Royal Victorian Order.** Anyone whose name appears on an envelope or in a list as Dame Somebody Something, GCVO.

38 **Dames Grand Cross of the Order of the British Empire.** Anyone whose name appears on an envelope or in a list as Dame Somebody Something, GBE.

39 **Wives of Knights Grand Cross of the Order of the Bath.**

40 **Wives of Knights Grand Commanders of the Order of the Star of India.**

41 **Wives of Knights Grand Cross of the Order of St Michael and St George.**

42 **Wives of Knights Grand Commanders of the Order of the Indian Empire.**

43 **Wives of Knights Grand Cross of the Royal Victorian Order.**

44 **Wives of Knights Grand Cross of the Order of the British Empire.**

45 **Dames Commanders of the Order of the Bath.** Anyone whose name appears on an envelope or in a list as Dame Somebody Something, DCB.

46 **Dames Commanders of the Order of St Michael and St George.** Anyone whose name appears on an envelope or in a list as Dame Somebody Something, DCMG.

47 **Dames Commanders of the Royal Victorian Order.** Anyone whose name appears on an envelope or in a list as Dame Somebody Something, DCVO.

48 **Dames Commanders of the Order of the British Empire.** Anyone whose name appears on an envelope or in a list as Dame Somebody Something, DBE.

49 **Wives of Knights Commanders of the Order of the Bath.**

50 **Wives of Knights Commanders of the Order of the Star of India.**

51 **Wives of Knights Commanders of the Order of St Michael and St George.**

52 **Wives of Knights Commanders of the Order of the Indian Empire.**

53 **Wives of Knights Commanders of the Royal Victorian Order.**

54 Wives of Knights Commanders of the Order of the British Empire.

55 Companions of the Order of the Bath.

56 Companions of the Order of St Michael and St George.

57 Commanders of the Royal Victorian Order.

58 Commanders of the Order of the British Empire.

59 Wives of Companions of the Order of the Bath.

60 Wives of Companions of the Order of the Star of India.

61 Wives of Companions of the Order of St Michael and St George.

62 Wives of Companions of the Order of the Indian Empire.

63 Wives of Commanders of the Royal Victorian Order.

64 Wives of Commanders of the Order of the British Empire.

65 Wives of Companions of the Distinguished Service Order.

66 Lieutenants of the Royal Victorian Order.

67 Officers of the Order of the British Empire.

68 Wives of Lieutenants of the Royal Victorian Order.

69 Wives of Officers of the Order of the British Empire.

70 Companions of the Imperial Service Order.

71 Wives of Companions of the Imperial Service Order.

72 Wives of the eldest sons of
(a) the male heirs of peers or hereditary peeresses in their own right;
(b) younger sons of peers or hereditary peeresses in their own right.

73 Daughters of
(a) the male heirs of peers or hereditary peeresses in their own right;
(b) the younger sons of peers or hereditary peeresses in their own right.

74 Wives of the eldest sons of Baronets.

75 Daughters of Baronets.

76 Wives of Knights' eldest sons.

77 Knights' Daughters.

78 Members of the Royal Victorian Order.

79 Members of the Order of the British Empire.

80 Wives of Members of the Royal Victorian Order.

81 Wives of Members of the Order of the British Empire.

82 Wives of Baronets' younger sons.

83 **Wives of Knights' younger sons.**

Generally speaking the various tables of precedence mentioned in the second paragraph of this appendix should not be mixed. That is what makes it so difficult if you have dignitaries of the Church, bar and armed services together. It is perhaps a good argument for dispensing with precedence entirely if you can get away with it. If you feel you can't, try to arrange the precedence of the various personages attending well in advance, by correspondence or phone calls to their secretaries. In assigning people to a position in the table of precedence one must consider the nature and location of the occasion. Sticking inflexibly to a given table of precedence would be socially incorrect. Those last two sentences constitute the gist of the advice heading the summary of social precedence issued by the Lord Chamberlain's Office. What does this mean in practice? I take it to mean that at a church fête, say, ecclesiastical precedence should preponderate. At a Territorial Army dance military precedence should preponderate. At a reception at one of the Inns of Court legal precedence should preponderate. At the Loamshire County Show the precedence appertaining to county dignitaries should preponderate. And so on.

LOCAL PRECEDENCE

1 At local functions generally, the **Lord-Lieutenant** of the county should take precedence of everybody else since he represents the Sovereign, unless there are also specific representatives of the Queen present, such as an equerry at a memorial service. It is possible that specific representatives of the Duke of Edinburgh and the Queen Mother might take precedence of the Lord-Lieutenant also. If you are at all in doubt, Buckingham Palace will surely give assistance. Should the Vice-Lieutenant be acting for the Lord-Lieutenant he would take his superior's precedence. Next to the Lord-Lieutenant comes:
2 **The High Sheriff** of the county in question.
3 The local **Mayor** or **Lord Mayor**. But if either of these is acting as the host at a municipal function, a reception, say, he takes precedence of everybody else.

4 **The Chairman of the County Council.**

5 **The Deputy Mayor.**

6 **The local MP.** This is by courtesy only since MPs have no precedence as such.

7 **The local Aldermen.** Among themselves they rank according to seniority of office. The only way of finding out in what order a number of dignitaries of the same degree were appointed to their office if all appear to have been appointed in the same year, or even on the same day, is to consult the *London Gazette*, which is published 'by Authority' and is the ultimate court of appeal in text form for any discrepancy you may come across between one reference book and another.

8 **The local Councillors.**

9 **Justices of the Peace.**

None of the foregoing are paid officials, though for some decades now MPs have enjoyed salaries. Next come the senior paid officials:

10 **The Clerk of the County Council.**

11 **The Town Clerk.**

12 **The Chief Constable.**

13 **The County or Borough Engineer.**

Precedence in Scotland

1 **The Queen.**

2 **The Duke of Edinburgh.**

3 **Lord High Commissioner to the General Assembly of the Church of Scotland when it is in session.**

4 **Duke of Rothesay** (title held by the Prince of Wales).

The rest of the royal family are as for precedence in England.

5 **Lords-Lieutenant** of counties during their terms of office and within the county and **Lord Provosts** of cities (who are Lords-Lieutenant of counties of cities ex-officio), subject to the same conditions as Lords-Lieutenant.

6 **Sheriffs Principal** during their terms of office and only when

within the boundaries of their counties, cities or sheriffdoms.

7 **The Lord Chancellor.**
8 **The Moderator of the General Assembly of the Church of Scotland** during his term of office.
9 **The Prime Minister.**
10 **The Secretary of State for Scotland as Keeper of the Great Seal of Scotland** if a peer.
11 **The Keeper of the Privy Seal of Scotland** if a peer.
12 **The Earl of Erroll as Hereditary High Constable of Scotland.**
13 **The Duke of Argyll as Hereditary Master of the Household** in Scotland.

The rest are as in England, till:

14 **Dukes' younger sons.**
15 **The Secretary of State for Scotland as Keeper of the Great Seal of Scotland** if not a peer.
16 **The Keeper of the Privy Seal of Scotland** if not a peer.
17 **Lord Justice-General.**
18 **Lord Clerk Register.**
19 **Lord Advocate.**
20 **Lord Justice-Clerk.**
21 **Viscounts**, as in England.

Then as in England generally, till:

22 **Privy Counsellors.**
23 **Senators of the College of Justice (Lords of Session),** including the **Chairman of the Scottish Land Court.**
24 **Viscounts' younger sons**, as in England.

Then as in England generally, till:

25 **Knights Commanders of the Order of the British Empire.**
26 **Solicitor-General for Scotland.**
27 **Lyon King of Arms.**
28 **Sheriff's Principal** other than when within their own counties.
29 **Knights Bachelors.**

30 **Sheriffs.**
31 **Companions of the Order of the Bath,** then as in England.

Precedence of Ladies in Scotland is as in England except that the current Lord High Commissioner to the General Assembly of the Church of Scotland, being currently a woman, comes after the Queen, and wives of Senators of the College of Justice, otherwise known as Lords of Session, rank with wives of Knights Bachelors. The Princess of Wales enjoys her precedence among ladies in Scotland by virtue of being Duchess of Rothesay.

Precedence in Northern Ireland
The Royal Family as in England, then:

1 **Lords-Lieutenant** of counties and **Lieutenants of Belfast and Londonderry** under the same conditions governing their counterparts in Scotland.
2 **High Sheriffs** of counties according to the same conditions as just noted.
3 **The Primates and Archbishops of Ireland,** whether Catholic or Protestant, or the **Moderator of the General Assembly of the Presbyterian Church,** ranked between themselves according to the seniority of their consecration or translation if Archbishops and the date of election if the Moderator.
4 **The Lord Mayor of Belfast** and the **Mayors of boroughs in Northern Ireland,** but as in England the Mayors take precedence next to the royal family if within their city halls' precincts.
5 **Recorders** of boroughs in Northern Ireland during civic functions in their boroughs.
6 **The High Sheriffs of Belfast and Londonderry** under the same conditions as with Recorders.

Then precedence is as with England until the most junior of the younger sons of Marquesses, who is followed by:

7 **Bishops of the Church of Ireland** and **Roman Catholic Bishops** according to seniority of consecration.

Then as with England until the most junior of the Barons, who is followed by:

8 **The Lord Chief Justice of Northern Ireland.**

Then as with England till the most junior of the Privy Counsellors, who is followed by:

9 **The Senior Naval Officer** in charge in Northern Ireland waters, the **General Office Commanding Northern Ireland** and the **Air Officer Commanding Northern Ireland**, amongst themselves according to Queen's regulations.
10 **Attorney-General.**
11 **Lords Justices of Appeal** in Northern Ireland.
12 **High Court Judges** in Northern Ireland.
13 **Recorders** of boroughs in Northern Ireland if within their cities but when they are not at civic functions.
14 **High Sheriffs of Belfast and Londonderry** if within their cities but when they are not at civic functions.

Then as with England until the most junior of the Knights Bachelors, who is followed by:

15 **The Town Clerk, City Chamberlain of Belfast** and **District Clerks** of Northern Ireland inside the bounds of their jurisdiction.
16 **County Court Judges** in Northern Ireland and **Recorders** of boroughs when outside these boroughs.

As with England until the most junior of the younger sons of Knights, who is followed by:

17 **The Head of the Northern Ireland Civil Service.**
18 **The Permanent Secretary to the Department of Finance and Personnel.**
19 **The Permanent Secretary to the Department of Education for Northern Ireland.**
20 **The Permanent Secretary to the Department of Agriculture for Northern Ireland.**

21 **The Permanent Secretary to the Department of the Environment (Northern Ireland).**

22 **The Permanent Secretary to the Department of Economic Development.**

23 **The Permanent Secretary to the Department of Health and Social Services.**

24 **The Clerk of the Northern Ireland Assembly** (who is still in office despite the Northern Ireland Assembly's dissolution).

25 **The Comptroller and Auditor General for Northern Ireland.**

26 **The Legislative Draftsman of Northern Ireland.**

27 **The Crown Solicitor for Northern Ireland.**

28 **Queen's Counsel of Northern Ireland.**

29 **The Chief Constable of the RUC.**

According to the Ministry of Foreign Affairs in Dublin, precedence in the Republic of Ireland tends to be governed by the same order as in England as regards social matters, titled people and so on. But the President of the Republic has first place, followed by the Taioseach (Prime Minister), the Tanaiste (Prime Minister's Deputy), members of the government, TDs (MPs) and Senators (members of the upper house), ranked among themselves according to the date of appointment or election. The Chief Herald of Ireland's Office is adamant that there is no place in a republic for a system of social precedence such as exists in the United Kingdom, so apart from protocol governing the relative order of precedence of those elected to office in the State, there would seem to be no grounds for observing a social order of precedence in the Republic of Ireland.

Bibliography

I do not endorse everything that appears in some of the books mentioned below, especially where they are less than entirely accurate as to facts, insensitive as to modern conditions or arbitrary as to pronouncements. They are therefore listed with the others below, all being collected in a single place for ease of reference, rather than marshalled to support my arguments. All are published in the UK unless specified otherwise.

Drusilla Beyfus, *Modern Manners – the essential guide to living in the '90s*, 1992, Hamlyn

Moyra Bremner, *Enquire Within Upon Modern Etiquette*, 1989, Century

D. H. Buss, S. P. Tan & R. W. Wenlock, *Immigrant Foods: the composition of foods used by immigrants in the UK*, 1985, HMSO Books

Lady Colin Campbell (ed.), *Etiquette of Good Society*, 1912, Cassell

Elsie Burch Donald (ed.), *Debrett's Etiquette & Modern Manners*, revised edition 1992, Headline

Barbara Gilgallon and Sue Seddon, *Modern Etiquette*, 1988, Ward Lock

Sandra Hunt, *The Food Habits of Asian Immigrants*, 1975, Queen Elizabeth College, London

Manchester Multicultural Education Resources Project, *Afro-Caribbean Food, Pakistani Food, Jewish Food, Hong Kong and China, Chinese Food*, 1984, Manchester Education Committee

Elizabeth Martyn, *Good Housekeeping Everyday Etiquette*, 1989, Ebury Press

Brian Masters, *Great Hostesses*, 1982, Constable

A Member of the Aristocracy, *Manners and Rules of Good Society*, 1926, Frederick Warne

Patrick Montague-Smith et al., *Debrett's Correct Form*, 1990, Debrett's Peerage in association with Webb & Bower

Helmut Morsbach, *Simple Etiquette in Japan*, Paul Norbury
Publications
Nigel Rees, *Best Behaviour*, 1992, Bloomsbury
Allan Sichel, *The Penguin Book of Wines*, 1965, Penguin Books
Ltd
G. D. Squibb, *Precedence in England and Wales*, 1981, Clarendon
Press
Geoffrey M(urat). Tait, *Port: from the vine to the glass*, 1936,
Harper & Co.
Philip M. Thomas, 'The Continental Nobility', essay in *Burke's
Peerage & Baronetage*, 1953
Lady Troubridge, *The Book of Etiquette*, 1926 (18th impression
1987), Kingswood Press

Index

basement 53
knives 61
  fish 65–6
  plastic 116–17
Koreans 198–9

ladies
  peeresses 203–4
  precedence 73, 203–4, 221–7, 229–30
  withdrawal from dining room 72–3, 166–7, 204
  wives 8–9
Lambton, Lady Lucinda 223
language 80
lateness, guests' 48–9
lawn meets 181–4
Lent 193–4
letter-writing 145–6
lighting 53–4, 90
livery 87–8
Llewellyn, Roddy 34
Lloyd's 9, 112
lobster extractors 66
lodges, shooting 186–7
logistics 6–9
London 7, 34, 53
lunches 94–106
  dates 104–6
  house parties 151–2
  invitations 102–4
  out of doors 99–101
  shooting 178–9
  weekends 94–5, 102, 152

Macbeth 2–3
Macmillan, Harold 175
Manners and Rules of Good Society 3–4, 233
married couples
  guests, seating arrangements 25
  guests, sleeping arrangements 150
  as hosts 8–9
matchmaking 23–4, 93
mime games 158–60

music 85, 134–5, 189
  opera 153
Muslims 195–6
Mytton, Squire 21

names 42–4
nannies 77–8, 79
neighbours
  and accommodation 134, 140–41
  and eating out of doors 100, 101
  and noise 128–9, 135
New York 17
newspapers 151
Northern Ireland: precedence 205, 230–32
numbers, unlucky 18–19
nutcrackers 66–7

obligation, social 30, 38, 128
opera performance 117–18, 153
Orso's restaurant 61
ostentation 21–2
O'Sullivan, Michael 74
out of doors, lunches 99–101
overnight accommodation 75, 133–4, 140–41, 145–6
  allotting rooms 150

paper plates 116
Paris 17, 18, 35
parties 127–38
  anniversary and birthdays 134, 138
  cost 127, 128
  see also dinner parties
pasta 61
pastry forks 66
paté 59
Peacock, Thomas Love, novels of 9, 72–3
peerage 4, 44–5, 108–9
  precedence 4, 201–5, 209–27, 229–31
  titles 44–5, 81
performance, buffets after 117, 118–19

239